EMPLOYEE BENEFIT PROGRAMS
A Total Compensation Perspective

Robert M. McCaffery

Institute of Management and Labor Relations
at Rutgers University

Kent Human Resource Management Series

Series Consulting Editor: Richard W. Beatty
Institute of Management and Labor Relations
at Rutgers University

PWS-KENT Publishing Company
Boston, Massachusetts

PWS-KENT
Publishing Company

Editor: Rolf A. Janke
Assistant Editor: Kathleen M. Tibbetts
Production Editor: Wanda K. Wilking
Interior Designer: DeNee Reiton Skipper/Leslie Baker
Cover Designer: Linda Belamarich
Manufacturing Manager: Linda Siegrist

PWS-KENT Publishing Company is a division of Wadsworth, Inc.

Printed in the United States of America

1   2   3   4   5   6   7   8   9—92   91   90   89   88

Library of Congress Cataloging-in-Publication Data

McCaffery, Robert M.
   Employee benefit programs : a total compensation perspective / by Robert M. McCaffery.
      p.   cm.—(Kent human resource management series)
   Includes index.
   ISBN 0-534-87197-6
   1. Compensation management.   2. Employee fringe benefits.
I. Title. II. Series.
HF5549.5.C67M34   1988
658.3'25—dc19   88-4038
                                            CIP

Series Preface

It is with great pleasure that we bring you the revised and expanded Kent Human Resource Management Series from PWS-KENT Publishing Company. The original four books on federal regulation, human resource costing, compensation, and performance appraisal were a great success, as evidenced by both academic and trade sales. We thank you for your support of this series.

The revised series includes strategic purposes and administrative issues in performance appraisal; and significant updating and expansion in federal regulation, human resource costing, and compensation administration. We are currently developing new series entries in executive development, recruitment, and benefits administration—issues long overdue both from an academic and practitioner perspective. We plan to add titles in areas such as international human resource management, human resource information systems, and collective begining offerings.

As organizations face the new competition created by global marketing, deregulation, and advancing technology, they are beginning to "resize." Preparing for this new competition raises concerns over the cost of human resources and clear recognition that human resources are indeed an organization's most expensive and least well-managed resource. Certainly, organizations have designed and engineered systems with specific planning and control methods; and tools for material resources, financial resources, information systems, and time management. The new competition, however, recognizes the need for better utilization of human resources. Thus, the issues raised in this series—the costs of human resources, and the function and contribution of each human resource while operating within the domestic legal framework—become more critical as organizations competitively restructure to better utilize their human resources. Ultimately, this series is designed to have an impact upon the practice of human resources in the contemporary economic environment. Implementing these approaches to solving human resource problems will be the ultimate proof of its success.

Many people have helped in the development of this important series. I would like to thank Wayne Barcomb for his faith to initiate and expand it; and Rolf Janke, Diane Miliotes, and Kathleen Tibbetts for their enthusiastic support of the revision and expansion.

Richard W. Beatty

Preface

I n most organizations the personnel/human resource (P/HR) function has the overall responsibility for employee benefit programs. Typically, benefits are aligned with pay programs and both units report to a head of compensation and benefits, who is responsible for all compensation activity.

In contrast with this organizational prototype, most employee benefit texts have been written by authorities in finance, risk management, insurance, law, taxation, accounting, or pension plan design. A representative listing of recent books and relevant periodicals may be found in Appendix B. Employee benefit practitioners and students planning to specialize in this field will find an abundance of useful technical material in these publications.

But, increasingly, employee benefit specialists need to operate within human resource and compensation organizations. They must understand the dynamics between plan selection and design and employee expectations and perceptions. They have to recognize the interdependencies between pay and benefits.

At the same time, P/HR generalists are discovering that they need to have a clear understanding of how benefit plans can influence the organization's success in recruiting and retaining staff, satisfying equity goals, and motivating employees. While the generalist doesn't need to (and can't) take time to learn how to perform detailed analysis of actuarial funding method alternatives for a defined benefit pension plan, an understanding of the choices and their implications can be critical for making informed decisions.

The aim of this book is to describe and discuss employee benefits from a total compensation management perspective. While I rely on numerous technical sources for factual information, a controlling concern throughout the book is the presentation of the subject matter in a coherent and non-technical manner. To a great extent the text is modeled after employee benefit courses I first developed and taught at New York University and now conduct at Rutgers University. Many students have entered these courses with little or no prior employee benefit involvement. The principal course objectives are to provide students with a historic and legal foundation, a survey of current practice, an introduction to and translation of seemingly arcane language, and, I hope, a heightened awareness of how employee benefits can support management objectives and meet employee needs.

Whether *Employee Benefit Programs* is read in conjunction with or independently of such a course, it has been written to enrich the human resource management student's appreciation for the unique characteristics of employee benefits and to present a broad perspective for benefit practitioners and students who plan to specialize in this field, which continues to grow in importance and complexity.

Many individuals contributed to the development of this book in a variety of ways. I especially want to acknowledge a few.

Denis Sinclair Philipps of New York University, as director of The Management Institute, approved my proposal to develop a new course in employee benefits as part of the program in personnel management and industrial relations in the mid-1960s. Dr. Philipps' early recognition of employee benefits in the context of human resource management eventually led to the introduction of similar courses by other universities and professional associations. It also encouraged me to extend my involvement in teaching and writing on the subject of employee benefits and, ultimately, to completing this text for the Kent Human Resource Management Series.

Richard Beatty, a current colleague, both at Rutgers and on the American Compensation Association faculty, was most supportive in encouraging me to write this book. As consulting editor for the Kent Human Resource Management series, he provided the needed perspective on the overall goals and objectives for the full series. He also made many constructive and helpful suggestions after reviewing each chapter of the manuscript as it evolved.

Sandra Gustavson, faculty of Risk Management and Insurance at the University of Georgia, reviewed the final manuscript, primarily from a technical viewpoint. She identified points requiring clarification or amplification, particularly with respect to laws, regulations, and special terminology.

Rolf Janke, Diane Miliotes, Kathy Tibbetts, and Wanda Wilking of PWS-KENT guided me expertly through each stage of development and were always patient whenever deadlines couldn't quite be met.

Jean McCaffery Barrett prepared the manuscript on a Tandon personal computer. This valuable assistance was critical since her author-father had previously been diagnosed by several authorities as being essentially computer-phobic.

Robert M. McCaffery

Contents

10   Communication: The Keystone   210

Appendix A: Employee Benefits Glossary   231

Appendix B: Employee Benefits, Additional Sources of Information   240

Index   243

1

From Fringes
to Flexible
Benefits

In 1943, when supplements to wages and salaries in the United States averaged less than 5 percent of pay,[1] the federal War Labor Board (WLB) chose to exclude these employee benefits from wage stabilization controls. The WLB reasoned that benefits "were on the fringe of wages," so improvements could therefore be permitted because they would not be inflationary.[2]

By 1981 those "fringes," according to the United States Department of Commerce, were averaging more than 18 percent of pay. In that year a joint task force of the American Compensation Association (ACA) and the American Society for Personnel Administration (ASPA) published a major report on base pay programs that contained this observation: "Some organizations may emphasize direct cash payments while others may minimize the relative importance of direct cash and place relatively more emphasis on employee benefits."[3]

These sharply contrasting views underscore the growth in importance, as well as costs, of employee benefits over a period of roughly four decades. Once viewed as minor enhancements to wages, by the early 1980s benefits had achieved recognition as a key element in compensation and human resources planning.

This chapter will examine the events and trends that influenced the rise in status of employee benefits from the 1940s to the present. This retrospective survey is provided at the outset to facilitate understanding of contemporary practices and viewpoints.

What Is an Employee Benefit?

One answer to this question is: "Ultimately, if employees refer to an employer consideration as a benefit, it is by definition a benefit."[4]

Without receiving any definition of the term, participants in ACA's Fundamentals of Employee Benefits course are asked at the outset to make a list of employee benefits within about two minutes. Based on responses from more than 1,500 participants, it is clear that:

1. Most individuals list health/medical coverage first.

2. Very few people mention Social Security, workers' compensation, or unemployment compensation, even though they are covered by these protective programs, which are largely paid for by their employers.

3. A considerable variety of items are considered to be benefits (but there is some disagreement among participants as to whether or not some items really are benefits).

4. Awareness of a benefit relates more to perceived utility than to how much it might cost the employer. Someone at age twenty-four, for example, may list flextime (no cost) but omit the pension plan (high cost). An older worker with high seniority in the same company would typically mention a cash or deferred arrangement plan (no direct cost) but neglect to identify a severance pay plan (expensive).[5]

These findings seem to support the position that employees *do* define the benefits. However, employers can influence employee perceptions through communication, and many companies call attention to Social Security and other mandatory coverages by mentioning them in the annual personalized benefit statements issued to their employees. Also, some firms have adopted the awareness-testing approach used in the ACA courses and use the results to help determine which benefits to include in the annual statements.

Benefits as Compensation

Employers today cannot ignore the costs of benefits; they are too important a part of total compensation. Employees, because they tend to focus primarily on the utility of benefits, often fail to recognize the magnitude of these costs. In 1984 Opinion Research Corporation conducted a national survey of employee attitudes about benefits. Almost half of the 641 respondents estimated that their employer's benefit costs were less than 10 percent of salary. Incredibly, 7 percent of this population thought the employer spent *nothing* on benefits![6]

In reality almost every employer in the United States spends more than 10 percent of wages and salaries on benefits. But how much more depends in part on what is classified as a benefit. There is no uniform standard to follow and each of the four national sources of periodic reports of costs and practices defines the term differently (see Exhibit 1.1).

The United States Department of Commerce (DOC) has published data on employee benefits in its national income statistics since 1929. Using the term "supplements to wages and salaries," the DOC includes legally required payments and expenditures for private pension and welfare plans in its reports. In 1986 these supplements averaged 19.9 percent of pay.

Starting in 1979 the Bureau of Labor Statistics (BLS) began issuing an annual report, *Employee Benefits in Medium and Large Firms*. These studies of benefit coverage in private sector firms do not include cost information, but they are widely circulated and provide another perspective on the scope of benefits for employers to consider and use as a model for cost studies. Many items not recognized in the DOC studies are covered, but legally required payments are excluded.

The BLS also compiles and publishes the quarterly *Employment Cost Index*. These reports provide a basis for measuring changes in the price of labor for both the private and public sectors. The index includes employer costs for employee benefits as well as wages and salaries. However, as displayed in Exhibit 1.1, there is considerable variation between the items classified as benefits in the index and those included in the BLS benefits report mentioned earlier.

Since 1947 the U.S. Chamber of Commerce (USCC) has conducted benefit cost surveys in a national cross section of private sector firms. Summary reports of these surveys have been published annually since 1978, and in 1981 the USCC issued a detailed comparative study for the period 1951 to

Exhibit 1.1   Definitions of Employee Benefits

Compensation Element (Employer Cost)	Classified as an Employee Benefit?			
	DOC	BLS	ECI	USCC
1. Legally Required Payments (e.g., Social Security, unemployment compensation, worker's compensation)	yes	no	yes	yes
2. Private Pension and Welfare Plans (e.g., retirement income, health insurance, life insurance, disability and profit sharing and savings plans)	yes	yes	yes	yes
3. Pay for Time Not Worked	no	yes	yes	yes
A. While not at work (e.g., vacations, holidays, sick leave, and personal absence pay)				
B. While at work (e.g., rest and lunch periods, coffee breaks, wash-up time)	no	yes	no	yes
4. Premium Pay (e.g., overtime, holiday and weekend premiums, shift differentials)	no	no	yes	no
5. Miscellaneous Benefits (e.g., employee services and discounts, education assistance, child care)	no	no	no[a]	yes

[a]Except for merchandise discounts in department stores

Sources: DOC: United States Department of Commerce annual reports of supplements to wages and salaries; BLS: Bureau of Labor Statistics annual report, *Employee Benefits in Medium and Large Firms;* ECI: Employment Cost Indexes compiled and issued quarterly by the Bureau of Labor Statistics; USCC: U.S. Chamber of Commerce annual surveys of employee benefits.

1979.[7] For 1986 the USCC reported that employee benefit payments among 833 survey participants ranged from less than 18 percent to more than 65 percent of payroll. The average payment for this group of companies was 39.3 percent of payroll.

The definition of benefits used in the USCC surveys is generally considered by compensation practitioners to be the most appropriate and useful of the four alternatives described here. Influencing this view is the fact that it is fully compatible with the American Compensation Association's concept of total compensation (see Exhibit 1.2). The ACA is the leading professional organization in the field of employee compensation. Its more than 10,000 members represent the practice of compensation within organizations of all sizes in both the private and public sectors.

The term *indirect compensation*, as delineated in the ACA model, shown below is almost identical to the USCC survey definition of employee benefits.[8] The balance of financial rewards results from *direct compensation*, which includes base wages and salaries, premium payments, and other forms of immediate cash compensation.

Benefits as Nonfinancial Rewards

Not all employee benefits involve employer expenditures, and some that don't are much appreciated by employees. Benefits of this type are classified as nonfinancial extrinsic rewards in the ACA model of total compensation.

Exhibit 1.2   The Concept of Total Compensation

Source: Courtesy of American Compensation Association, Scottsdale, Ariz.

Flextime, or flexible work hours, is an example of a totally cost-free benefit. Employers allow their employees a limited amount of flexibility to tailor work hours to accommodate personal needs, but this has no effect on payroll costs. A company can also gain employee satisfaction and appreciation by publicizing the activities of a credit union. By law, however, a credit union must be financially and operationally independent from the employer(s) of its members.

Company-operated or -facilitated van pools can benefit employees by offering them low-cost commuter transportation. But usually the fares paid by employees cover the employer's capital investment and operating costs, and the program runs on a break-even basis.

Another class of benefits that does not cost the employer anything out of pocket is known as voluntary or employee-pay-all insurance. Through arrangements made by an employer with an insurance company, employees are able to obtain substantial discounts on such coverages as supplementary life and disability insurance, dependent life insurance, and automobile insurance. Insurers are able to offer reduced rates because their sales and administrative expenses are lower for group plans and premium collection problems are minimized by payroll deductions.

Reasons for Growth of Benefits

A comparison of the U.S. Chamber of Commerce surveys for 1951 and 1986 shows that the average employer cost for benefits rose from $644 to $10,283, or 1,497 percent. Perhaps even more impressively, average benefits costs as a percent of payroll increased from 18.7 percent to 39.3 percent during a period when wages and salaries were also rising steadily.

Why did this extraordinary increase in emphasis on employee benefits occur during this period? Seven principal factors were influential.

1. Wage stabilization (1950–1953)
2. Expansion of Social Security
3. Federal tax policy
4. Federal social legislation
5. Labor union efforts
6. Employer initiatives
7. Influence of insurance, financial, and benefit plan consultants

Wage Stabilization (1950–1953)

Continuing to view benefits as "fringes," the federal government again decided to exempt them from pay controls when they invoked wage stabilization during the Korean conflict. Once more this prompted employers to revise their compensation strategies by concentrating on benefit improvements, thus effectively deemphasizing the relative importance of wages.

Expansion of Social Security

When the Social Security program was enacted in 1935, it was primarily a retirement income system; it covered about 60 percent of all working persons. Subsequently, both the scope of benefits and the percentage of eligible workers increased substantially. Today, Social Security provides survivor, disability, and health benefits in addition to retirement payments. By extending coverage to the self-employed, agricultural workers, and most government employees, the program now applies to about 95 percent of all workers in the United States.

The following comparison highlights the huge impact of this expansion on employer costs during this particular period:

Year	Maximum Employer Tax for an Employee
1951	$ 54.00
1986	$ 3,003.00

Federal Tax Policy

From the 1920s until 1986, group pension and welfare plans were greatly favored by tax legislation and regulations. Subject to specified conditions and limits, employers were allowed current-year tax deductions for plan expenditures, and employees received the benefits on a tax-free or tax-deferred basis. During a period that saw individual income tax rates rise significantly, these characteristics made employee benefits an increasingly attractive alternative to direct compensation for most employees. Currently there is much speculation about the future effects of federal tax policy on employee benefits. The Tax Reform Act of 1986 retained many tax advantages for benefits, but it also imposed numerous new restrictions and conditions on employer-sponsored plans. Since this law also lowered individual income tax rates, the tax advantages of benefits in the future may become less attractive for employers and employees when balanced against other considerations.

Federal Social Legislation

A key rationale for the favorable tax treatment of employee benefits has been the belief that they contribute positively to the attainment of national social goals. However, in exchange for their preferred tax status, employer-sponsored benefit plans must comply with myriad legislative and executive branch regulations and guidelines. The following major social legislation has significantly influenced employee benefits:

1. The Age Discrimination in Employment Act (ADEA) of 1967. The 1978 and 1986 amendments to this legislation effectively prohibited mandatory retirement based on age for most employees and established benefit protections and minimum coverage standards for older workers.
2. The Health Maintenance Organization (HMO) Act of 1973. This act set requirements for employers to offer their employees this alternative form of group health coverage under certain conditions. HMO coverage is a prepaid arrangement that stresses preventive health care.
3. The Employee Retirement Income Security Act (ERISA) of 1974. This landmark legislation specified a massive number of employee protections and minimum standards for group benefit plans.
4. The Retirement Equity Act (REA) of 1984. This act strengthened ERISA protections for employees and made coverage less exclusive.

Cumulatively, these laws, reinforced by numerous administrative agency regulations and court decisions, had a dual effect on employee benefits growth. First, many specific provisions required employers to expand plan coverage and eligibility. In turn, the changes raised the awareness of employees and caused them to become much more demanding consumers of and advocates for comprehensive benefits.

Labor Union Efforts

Bolstered by the National Labor Relations Act of 1935 and by subsequent National Labor Relations Board rulings, labor unions achieved much success in securing benefits for millions of members. Under an evolving body of labor law, it had become clear by the late 1940s that practically all benefits are mandatory bargaining items. On the basis of this principle, an employer is required to bargain in good faith on union proposals to add or improve benefits that are submitted as part of contract negotiations.

Union contract settlements also gave impetus to the growth of benefits in nonunion firms. A prime example of this was the widespread implementation of dental plans in the mid-1970s following patterns set in negotiations by the United Auto Workers, the United Steelworkers, and the Communications Workers unions.

Employer Initiatives

From the introduction of a profit-sharing plan at Albert Gallatin's glassworks in 1794 until the implementation of a cash balance pension plan by Bank of America in 1985, private enterprise has been in the vanguard of benefit plan invention and development. Some of the initiatives, such as major medical insurance, long-term disability plans, and child-care allowances, reflect a genuine concern for employee needs. Other provisions, including employee stock ownership plans, suggestion award systems, and educational assistance benefits, seem to have been inspired more by employer objectives to improve productivity and employee skills.

Whatever their motives, employers have long recognized the value of employee benefits and have played a leadership role in expanding the variety of benefit plans.

The Influence of Insurance, Financial, and Benefit Plan Consultants

While employers have been largely responsible for the adoption of new forms of benefits, they have usually relied on outside professional and technical assistance. Initially, most of the expertise needed for the development and design of plans resided in insurance companies and financial institutions. Those resources continue to be important, but a significant employee benefits consultant industry now exists, often in combination with actuarial, systems, and communications services. Aggressive marketing of these services through personal contacts and print media promotion, particularly since the early 1980s, has unquestionably had a sizable impact on the growth of flexible benefit arrangements and other types of innovative plans.

Current Views: Employees and Employers

Although employees may fail to accurately recognize how much their employers spend for benefits, most now seem to understand the importance of benefits. A study reported in 1985 by Hewitt Associates strongly supports the latter view.[9] Hewitt analyzed paper-and-pencil surveys and focus-group interview responses from over 12,000 employees and found that:

1. Twenty-eight percent of respondents rated benefits as more important than pay.
2. Fifty-six percent said that benefits and pay were of equal importance.
3. Only 16 percent rated benefits as less important than pay.

Equally significant in this study was the consistency of responses at different annual income levels. At each of seven levels (ranging from under $12,000 to more than $45,000), over half of the employees considered benefits and pay to be equally important. The combined ratings of benefits as "more important" or "equally important" ranged from 80 percent to 88 percent. These findings tend to deflate the conventional view that connects benefit plan attractiveness with higher-paid employees because of tax advantages. Coupled with this belief has been the traditional assumption that lower-paid workers are predominantly concerned with cash in the pocket. Comments made during the focus-group meetings indicated that rank-and-file employees fully comprehend the safety net role of benefits. The concept of "living on the paycheck" and relying on benefits for protection was clearly expressed by a number of participants.

The importance of benefits to employees is also acknowledged by the authors of *The 100 Best Companies to Work for in America* (1984).[10] This compendium of "superlative employers" used benefits as a standard rating criterion (along with pay, advancement opportunity, job security, and ambience) in evaluating candidates for the top 100. Characteristically, the leading companies tended to focus on profit-sharing plans, savings incentives, and employee stock ownership arrangements. This suggests that employers offering these piece-of-the-action types of extra benefits gain a distinct advantage in the employment marketplace. Scanning the display-type employment advertisements in most Sunday newspapers should confirm that assertion. Typically, companies offering these extra or unique employee benefits highlight them in the advertising copy.

Employer awareness of the importance of employee benefits began to increase markedly during the late 1970s. At the beginning of that decade it was clear that benefits had advanced beyond the fringe, and the USCC survey for 1969 revealed that employers were spending 27.9 percent of pay on benefits. But the great wave of government regulation had not yet begun, and costs for health care and retirement income plans still seemed manageable. Conversely, employers were much more concerned with direct compensation issues such as cost of living adjustments (COLAs), negotiated wage increases, and tandem salary adjustments. According to the USCC, however, by 1979 the cost of benefits had risen to 36.6 percent of payroll. Flexible benefit plans had been implemented by Educational Testing Service, TRW, and American Can Company (now Primerica). ERISA and ADEA had been enacted. Benefit management had become much more complex. At this point the benefit function in most large organizations ceased to be an isolated, technically oriented unit. Benefits had become important to the *total* organization, and in particular to the head of human resources activity. In 1982 a group of 309 senior Personnel/Human Resource (P/HR) executives were surveyed concerning the most critical issues they expected to deal with in the following year. In a list of twenty-four issues, "controlling the costs of employee benefits" received the second highest average ranking in the survey ("productivity improvement programs" ranked first).[11]

Summary

The USCC annual surveys since 1979 show a leveling off of benefits as a percent of pay at 37 to 39 percent. This seems to be attributable largely to stronger management control, employer cost-containment efforts, and benefit tradeoffs rather than net additions. It is unlikely that benefit costs will ever equal or exceed direct compensation in the United States (as they do in some other countries). But this should in no way diminish the importance of employee benefits to employees, employers, and our society. They continue to represent a significant part of total compensation; they are a major source of employee security and protection; and they involve an intricate integration of public and private social programs.

During the past few years, the following twelve statements relating to employee benefits have evolved from an extensive literature review and from numerous discussions with practitioners, educators, and students. They are provided here as a foundation for closer inspection of particular program aspects in succeeding chapters.

1. An employee's base pay income tends to create his or her standard of living; benefits protect it.

2. Because of current tax policies and group purchasing power, employers can obtain most employee benefit coverage more cheaply than can individual employees.

3. Benefit programs that require or permit some employee contributions can offer broader coverage and tend to gain a higher level of employee awareness and understanding.

4. The overall responsibility for employee benefit management is best placed in personnel/human resources. Although a variety of supporting resources is needed (for example, tax, investment, insurance, actuarial, legal, accounting, and data processing expertise), the logical focal point for centralized responsibility is the function most broadly concerned with employee needs and concerns.

5. To optimally manage the total compensation dollar, employee benefits and direct compensation should be closely coordinated, ideally on a peer level with a common supervisor.

6. Each organization should articulate its own set of objectives and priorities for employee benefits. These statements need to be consonant with other organizational and employee relations objectives; they can therefore be expected to vary from company to company.

7. The foundation for any firm's employee benefit program is the group of applicable federal and state mandatory benefits, such as Social Security, workers' compensation, and unemployment insurance. No private plan adoptions or revisions should be undertaken without a clear understanding of current requirements and projected changes in these public programs.

8. To be effective, benefit plans must be responsive to the analytically identified and/or expressed needs of employees. This is ideally achieved through the cafeteria or flexible plan approach.

9. Benefit cost control is essential, but it must be performed openly and with employee understanding and involvement. Otherwise, employee perceptions of the value of benefit plans may be overshadowed by suspicion and distrust.

10. Since many benefits are part of a hidden payroll, their value must be regularly and clearly communicated to employees through all available media to gain a desirable level of awareness.

11. Employees must have easy access to prompt and knowledgeable answers to questions about benefits. Meeting ERISA reporting and disclosure requirements is not enough. Provisions for effective two-way communication are essential.

12. At least annually, an organization should measure its performance against stated benefit objectives. This should include a review of the objectives themselves, results of efforts to reach short-term goals, individual plan performance, and some assessment of employee views.

Notes

[1]U.S. Chamber of Commerce, *Employee Benefits 1985* (Washington, D.C.: U.S. Chamber of Commerce, 1986), p. 31.

[2]Donna Allen, *Fringe Benefits: Wages or Social Obligation?* (Ithaca, N.Y.: New York State School of Industrial and Labor Relations, Cornell University, 1964), p. 25.

[3]The American Society for Personnel Administration and the American Compensation Association, *Elements of Sound Base Pay Administration* (Berea, Ohio: ASPA; ACA, 1981), p. 1.

[4]Robert M. McCaffery, *Managing the Employee Benefits Program* (New York: AMACOM, 1983), p. 4.

[5]Information gathered by the author as course coordinator and leader for ACA (1978–1986).

[6]See *Employee Benefit Plan Review*, October 1984, pp. 46–47.

[7]U.S. Chamber of Commerce, *Employee Benefits Historical Data: 1951–1979* (Washington, D.C.: U.S. Chamber of Commerce, 1981).

[8]A minor difference is that perquisites, benefits limited to incumbents in high-level positions, are not included in the USCC studies. In general the Chamber of Commerce surveys exclude employees who are exempt from the Fair Labor Standards Act.

[9]Hewitt Associates, *On Employee Benefits* (Company newsletter.), (November/December 1985): 1–2.

[10]Robert Levering, Milton Moskowitz, and Michael Katz, *The 100 Best Companies to Work for in America* (Reading, Mass.: Addison-Wesley, 1984).

[11]Jack Herring, "Human Resource Managers Rank Their Pressure Points," *Personnel Administrator* 28, no. 6 (June 1983): 115.

2

Planning
a Total
Program

For many years academicians ridiculed the term "benefits planning," considering it an oxymoron. That view now seems to have been justified when the pre-1980s employee benefit programs of most organizations are examined. Characteristically they consisted of a patchwork of overlapping, inadequate, or excessive forms of coverage. The absence of rational planning prompted Peter Drucker to observe in 1971 that "we spend fabulous amounts of money on benefits which have little meaning for large groups of employees and leave unsatisfied the genuine needs of other, equally substantial groups."[1] The impression lingers that benefits were at one time more a result of inspiration and imitation than a product of planning.

In the late 1970s, when employers started to realize that rising healthcare costs were causing financial problems, benefit plan managers were called on for solutions. At first their remedies were reactive and often inappropriate. By abruptly increasing the employees' share of group insurance plan costs, some companies incurred serious labor relations problems. After a while, though, the complexity and diversity of the health cost issue led some benefit managers to develop a comprehensive strategy. Typically this involved assessing internal and external factors, setting and prioritizing goals, establishing timetables, and integrating their planning with that of other organizational units. Some of the reported results were outstanding. Through effective execution of a strategic approach, for example, Chrysler cut its health-care costs for 1984 by $5.8 million, a savings of more than $300 for each employee and retiree.[2]

As they gained familiarity with this type of formalized approach to planning in the health benefits area and saw that it *worked*, benefit plan managers began to use it throughout their function. Lately strategic planning has proved to be particularly useful in organizations that have shifted from a traditional benefit program to a flexible design, that have changed a uniform approach to a decentralized program, or that have greatly enhanced their benefit communications.

This chapter describes benefit planning as it is now commonly practiced in larger companies. While smaller organizations may have practical limitations for considering such a formal approach, the conceptual framework presented here is equally applicable to them.

The Planning Environment

The planning environment for employee benefits is uniquely multifaceted. Exhibit 2.1 depicts ten principal factors that can, in continually varying degrees, influence planning assumptions and analyses. To plan effectively, a company's benefit manager must have a sound grasp of all of these factors and their implications for employee benefits in that particular organization. The first five of these factors involve *internal* considerations.

1. Human Resource Management (HRM) Philosophy

This is the most stable of the ten factors. Whether it is formally communicated or simply implied, it represents fundamental beliefs about employees and the employer-employee relationship in an organization. The basic philosophy tends to be fairly permanent, although it is vulnerable to ownership or top leadership change. The benefit manager needs to understand the underlying basis of the philosophy and the extent of commitment that it is *currently* receiving from senior management. That knowledge will facilitate consistent selection and design of benefit plans and programs that reflect the company's HRM philosophy. Exemplifying this compatibility are firms with profit-sharing

Exhibit 2.1 Employee Benefits Planning Environment

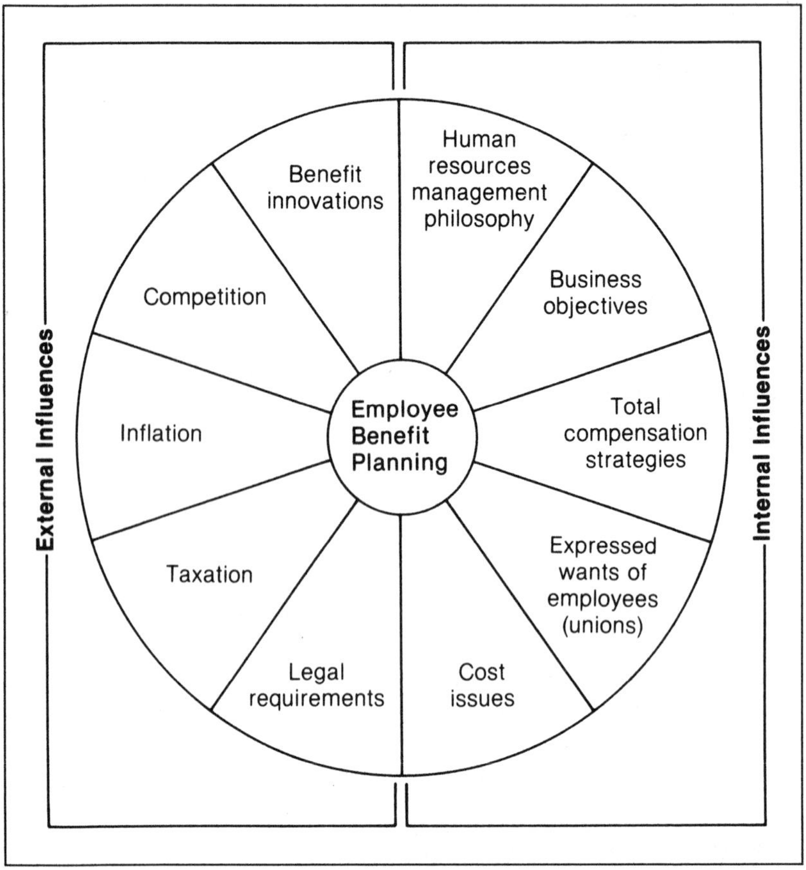

or stock ownership plans, which reflect a belief in giving employees a sense of commitment to business success and a stake in the future. Also, some organizations demonstrate a philosophy of egalitarianism, or equal treatment, by insisting that the same set of benefit plans apply across the board, from custodians to the president. In contrast, other companies embrace a "rank has its privilege" (RHIP) culture and therefore want to offer many supplements and special benefits to upper-level employees exclusively.

In a study of large nonunion companies, Fred K. Foulkes identified benefits as one of the key policy areas that reflects top management's belief in individual worth and equity.[3] Among the twenty-six nonunion companies studied, Foulkes found a prevalence of profit-sharing, stock purchase, and savings plans. In general these companies also favored noncontributory plans, although several participants said they believed in employee contributions as a way to build understanding of benefit plans — and to offset company costs.

Another example of human resource philosophy affecting benefit planning is the attitude of highly paternalistic employers towards flexible benefit plans. Because the element of choice in these plans creates more risks for employees, this type of employer usually rejects the flexible approach. Alternatively, a paternalistic organization typically offers a standard package of "security blankets" to its employees on a noncontributory basis.

2. Business Objectives

This factor relates to the key short-term (e.g., one year) and longer-term (e.g., three to five years) objectives in an organization's overall business plan. To develop sensible and timely plans for the benefit function, the manager must be aware of the basic directions in which the organization is heading.

Some examples of business objectives and possible responses from the benefits area are:

Business Objective	*Benefits Objective*
1. Convert company acquired last year from an independent subsidiary to integrated division status by the end of next year.	Perform "pro-con" analysis of immediate vs. gradual transfer of subsidiary employees into corporate benefit plans. Make recommendation by first quarter of next year.
2. Decentralize product distribution activity; open six new branches in third plan year.	Review employee relocation assistance policy this year; propose any needed changes by middle of next year.
3. Double the size of the sales staff during the second half of next year.	Study feasibility of including part of incentive compensation in base for group life insurance and pension benefit purposes; submit proposal by year end.
4. Close remote production satellite at year end; notify 500 affected employees at end of third quarter.	Calculate costs for various termination subsidies, such as severance pay, outplacement assistance, and early retirement incentives; complete analysis for review with HRM by end of first quarter.

Unless an employee benefit manager is included in the organization's business planning process, access to this kind of information may be on a haphazard basis. When that occurs, the benefit manager's effectiveness is severely hampered and the organization loses valuable input.

3. Total Compensation Strategies

Benefit managers and their counterparts in direct compensation operate in essentially the same planning environment and usually have common functional objectives. However, prior to the early 1980s, strategic planning linkage between the two functions was rare. Even where they had been joined organizationally they tended to operate quite independently. This practice, coupled with what might be called a "market fascination" (keeping up with competition), produced many inconsistent, inefficient, and inappropriate compensation and reward systems. In recent years there has been a significant movement to merge direct compensation and benefits *operationally* and to tie them more closely together in the strategic planning process. Compensation authorities Robert J. Greene and Russell G. Roberts have stressed the importance of this integration:

> Implementation of strategic management . . . requires that direct pay and benefits programs be integrated, balanced, and structured to meet the reward package requirements of the caliber of people needed. . . . The strategic management approach dictates that actual levels of compensation should not be strictly a matter of what is being paid in the marketplace. Instead, compensation levels derive from an assessment of what must be paid to attract and retain the right people, what the organization can afford, and what will be required to meet the strategic goals of the organization.[4]

Furthermore, costs for many benefits roll up automatically as wages and salaries increase. Projected increases in direct compensation also influence pension funding assumptions. Because of these realities, a benefit manager who plans independently, apart from the total compensation environment, may become a disenfranchised dependent of the direct compensation function.

4. Expressed Wants of Employees (Unions)

Employers provide the benefits and employees are the consumers. Initially most employers affected a "father knows best" attitude about this relationship and assumed that they knew what was the most appropriate coverage for their employees. However, during the 1960s, inspired by a national rise in consumer activism, employees began to express their dissatisfaction with employer dogmatism in a variety of ways. In some instances this led to union affiliation for the purpose of gaining bargaining power. It seems obvious today that the enactment of ERISA and subsequent benefit laws and regulations in the 1970s was largely attributable to employer unwillingness to listen to employee concerns.

Today's employee benefit managers recognize the importance of paying attention to the *vox populi* as part of the planning process. In small firms they can accomplish this through informal queries and observations. But in larger organizations, particularly those in which the work force is very heterogeneous, more formal methods are needed to ensure that a balanced cross section of employee views is collected. For this purpose benefit managers have found techniques associated with consumer research to be quite useful. Specific applications of these will be discussed later in this chapter.

When a union represents employees in bargaining for benefits, the planning role of the manager is changed in two significant ways. First, expressed employee wants are filtered through the collective bargaining process, which limits the amount and quality of employee opinion data available to the benefit manager. Second, benefit plan priorities may be overlooked in negotiations or sacrificed to the politics of that process. The benefit manager also needs to understand that realistically both the employer and the union need to concentrate on *current* contract issues in negotiations. Neither party can bargain openly or effectively about future plans that reach beyond a two- or three-year horizon. As a result, the planning period may be quite compressed, and consideration of longer-term issues may be suspended until the next contract negotiations.

5. Cost Issues

"Get the estimated price of a series of improvements in your benefit plans. Then, after carefully analyzing the effect on your P & L [profit and loss statement], pick the price that seems to fit best with your projected earnings for the year. Only then should you look at the improvements in benefits. This process can be simplified if the improvements are identified only by a code number."[5]

This tongue-in-cheek recommendation is from an article entitled "How Not to Plan Employee Benefits" that appeared in a financial journal in 1973. Some employee benefit plan authorities mistook it for an accurate representation of recommended planning practice and, like most spoofs, it had some basis in fact.

Although benefit planners have an inescapable responsibility to deal with cost issues they need to keep it in proper perspective. Ideally, the more intricate analyses of costs should *follow* explorations of needs and opportunities, and then it is generally considered wise to enlist the cooperation of the finance function within the organization. Not only is financial expertise essential for determining the effect of any proposed benefit changes on cash contributions and expense charges, but it can often help in developing funding and financing alternatives.

The advantages of cooperation in planning between the benefits and finance functions at IBM were described by R. N. Beck, director of benefit and personnel services, in a 1980 published interview:

> When we feel there is a need for a new employee benefit, we will take our case to senior management. The financial people will discuss how this benefit will be paid for. In a sense we are charged with developing appropriate programs which have a price tag — and the financial people are charged with assessing the company's ability to fund the program in the long and short run. . . . This means that there will have to be considerable give and take. In the end, we may compromise on a design feature that will cost less to fund but will yield approximately the same in [benefits] to the employee[6]

The following factors are *external* to the organization.

6. Legal Requirements

Legislation concerning employee benefits in the United States has taken two basic directions. The first includes the federal Social Security program and the state unemployment, workers' compensation, and temporary disability insurance laws. These are government-operated programs that effectively form the foundation for many plans developed by employers. Benefit plan managers must be constantly alert to pending and potential changes in the mandatory coverages in order to plan for possible adjustments in related company plans.

The second form of legislation is regulatory in nature. It controls the essential provisions of private benefit plans. Included in this category are ERISA, the Health Maintenance Organization (HMO) Act, the Retirement Equity Act (REA), and the various state laws regulating group insurance provisions. This type of legislation has increased progressively since the mid-1970s, and that trend is expected to continue indefinitely. Because of the uncertainties about the content and timing of pending legislation, strategic planning for employee benefits demands many contingency provisions.

While benefit managers groan under the burden of increasing legal requirements, they should find some solace in the knowledge that there is still less government involvement in benefits here than in most developed countries throughout the world.

7. Taxation

As mentioned in Chapter 1, employee benefits overall have received rather favorable treatment under federal tax law. Yet in recent years benefit planners have been confounded by shifts and reversals in tax policy, which seem to proliferate in response to rising revenue requirements and calls for tax simplification.

Educational assistance benefits are an example of tax policy oscillation. In 1978 Congress passed a law that specified that for the next five years all employer payments for an employee's educational assistance would be excludable from the employee's gross income. That exclusion expired at the end of 1983. Late in 1984 it was restored, but with a $5,000 annual limit on tax-free payments and with an expiration date of December 31, 1985. At that point educational benefits again became subject to tax withholding requirements until they were granted another "reprieve" for 1986 and 1987 (subject to a $5,250 cap) in the Tax Reform Act of 1986. The uncertainties about the tax treatment of educational assistance payments continue to be an irritating impediment to effective benefit planning.

Another illustration of tax policy reversals causing benefit managers to alter planning strategies is the following sequence of events involving individual retirement accounts (IRAs). IRAs were created by ERISA and became available in 1975 to workers who did not have employer-sponsored pension coverage. Eligible participants were permitted to set aside the lesser of 15 percent or $1,500 of their annual income on a tax-deferred basis for use in retirement. Later Congress decided that IRAs should be available to all workers. Starting in 1982 any individual with earned income became eligible to contribute the lesser of 100 percent of income or $2,000 to an IRA on a tax-deferred basis. Some companies then established employer-sponsored plans as a convenience to employees. But effective in 1987 the tax rules were changed again, this time eliminating or limiting the deductibility of IRA contributions for active participants in qualified pension plans based on their income level.

These descriptions are not presented as a lamentation, but rather as a reminder of the importance of monitoring tax bills being considered by Congress and proposed regulations coming from the Internal Revenue Service and other regulatory agencies. Sometimes this will lead to a planned lobbying effort by the employer. In all cases it will help to facilitate the development of alternative strategies in anticipation of change.

8. Inflation

The concept of real wages, wage earnings deflated by a price index, is well understood by compensation managers. They recognize the importance of projecting inflation factors in the planning process and providing for countervailing pay and pay structure adjustments to keep employees "whole." When this is done, the real value of such wage replacement benefits as sick pay, paid vacations and holidays, and paid personal absence is also protected.

But employee benefit managers must face additional concerns about inflation in their planning deliberations. They need to anticipate the impact of inflation on medical plan expenses, service awards, food service, educational assistance, and other benefits that are not tied directly to base pay. And what about pension payments to retired employees? The image of double-digit inflation eroding the purchasing power of pensions from 1979 to 1981 is still fresh in the minds of many retirees and employees now nearing their retirement. Even though the rate of inflation has been much lower since the early 1980s, the cumulative effect of inflation on the real value of pension income needs to be tracked and postretirement adjustments considered when needed and appropriate.

9. Competition

Reference to employee benefit packages in recruitment advertisements are frequently preceded by the adjective "competitive." Clearly this is intended to be persuasive. But a discriminating prospect could easily ask, "Competitive with whom?" or "How do you determine competitiveness?" Benefit managers are expected to address these questions as part of their planning responsibilities.

In the first instance they are expected to compare the organization's benefit plans with those offered by the principal competitors in the job marketplace. This requires a familiarity with current employment forecasts and sourcing plans to identify the most appropriate organizations for benefit comparisons. If the firm has a philosophy of uniform benefits for all employees, a single panel of employers can be surveyed to determine competitiveness. However, the panel should be representative of *all* of the markets in which the firm competes for employees. On the other hand, if there is a policy of tailoring benefits to major groups (e.g., managerial, technical, clerical, hourly, etc.), separate panels should be surveyed.

The how-to part of assessing benefit competitiveness is more difficult. Traditionally, simple cost comparisons have been used, but these can be misleading. A company might determine, for example, that its benefit costs are 5 percent above the average of its principal competitors. But this apparent "advantage" might be largely due to unusually high insurance company retention charges and accelerated funding of pension plan liabilities. Since neither of these expenditures has any direct bearing on benefits *values*, there can be no assurance that the program is competitive. Plan-by-plan feature comparisons are an alternative form of measurement. These are entirely appropriate when the company is considering a particular coverage. They are not suitable for obtaining quantifiable comparisons of total benefit packages.

The most broadly useful methodology for incorporating competitive data in a benefit planning process is actuarial value analysis. This approach, developed and marketed by a number of the major benefit consulting firms, is based on an analysis of actuarially calculated benefit values and/or levels for an employer's plan compared with those in competitors' plans. One consulting firm's methodology is shown in Exhibit 2.6 and discussed later in this chapter.

10. Benefit Innovations

Several years ago two large Texas banks merged and quickly agreed that their benefit plans, although different in many ways, should be unified. Executive management also wanted a program that would reflect the aggressive and entrepreneurial character of the new organization. A benefit task force was formed to develop a strategy. Rather than attempting to blend elements from the plans of each bank, the task force conceived a totally new program, which was given the name "The Edge." In introducing the innovative package, emphasis was placed on the *edge* that employees were gaining through new options and the ability to tailor benefits to their individual needs. Employee reactions to the new program were assessed by a postimplementation survey and found to be very positive. In this case a creative adaptation of some new approaches to flexible benefits enabled an organization to achieve some key objectives.[7]

A benefit manager's success in planning can be greatly enhanced by an awareness of what's new in the field and, more importantly, how it might relate to organizational objectives. One way of ensuring currency about benefit developments is to selectively review presentations by consultants and firms offering specific services. It is *essential* to read at least two or three current benefit periodicals. A benefit manager should also join one or more of the national professional associations and participate in as many meetings and seminars as time and funds permit. Listings of these various resources are included in Appendix B.

Maintaining a keen sense of awareness about the relevant environmental factors is a continuous challenge for benefit professionals. But operating within the prescribed format and timetable of an organization's planning system introduces the discipline of periodic assessments and reports. Although practices and terminology vary, a benefit manager typically needs to be concerned with three levels of planning:

1. *Policy Planning* — the fundamental purpose and guiding principles for all benefit plans. Once established, policies tend to be relatively permanent, but they still require periodic reviews.

2. *Strategic Planning* — significant revisions and advances in the present program. Efforts to achieve these objectives usually require at least three years.

3. *Operational Planning* — setting annual goals for introducing change or achieving a specified level of improvement in the performance of a plan or plans.

Policy Planning

Organizational statements of benefit policy range from expressions of philosophy to specific guidelines and standards for plan management. Benefit managers differ in their preferences but they are virtually unanimous in recognizing that operating a program without policies is like trying to sail a ship without a rudder.

Key internal and external considerations for developing an overall policy statement are:

1. The degree of income protection and replacement to be provided for employees, for dependents, and for retirees.

2. The provisions (if any) to be made for income supplementation benefits.

3. The relation of benefits to job level.
4. Recognition for seniority.
5. Recognition for performance or productivity.
6. The employer's responsibility for the costs of employee benefits, dependent benefits, and retiree benefits.
7. The basis and use of external comparisons.
8. The effect of union settlements on benefits for nonrepresented employees.
9. The application of plans to employees of acquired companies.
10. Coverage for part-time employees.
11. Employee choice and plan flexibility.
12. Responsibility for planning and managing the program.

Exhibit 2.2 is an example of a benefit policy statement for a company that has addressed these issues after making a thorough environmental assessment. This type of document normally would be grouped in a manual with statements covering such subjects as equal employment opportunity, employee development, health and safety, and pay administration. In addition to distributing the complete policy to managers, many organizations also provide an abbreviated version to all employees. Since policies are identified with commitment, they should never be altered capriciously. However, given the dynamism of the planning environment, a benefit manager needs to recognize circumstances that may render some policies unlawful, counterproductive, or inappropriate, or that create a need for new policies. At times it may be necessary to make policy changes on an ad hoc basis, but actions should preferably be integrated with the strategic and operational planning cycle.

In Exhibit 2.2, for example, the policy provision for temporary and part-time employees (A-11) is not especially inviting. Presumably it is related to cost concerns, the existence of a favorable employer's market for these types of workers, or both. But suppose that through the company's strategic planning process (covering the next three years), the benefit manager learned that a much greater utilization of part-time telecommuters was projected and a shortage of candidates anticipated. This suggests that the policy might need to be revised within the next three years and an operational goal for the following year could be to "survey competitive benefit provisions for part-time employees."

Exhibit 2.2   Policy Statement for Employee Benefits

The benefit program, and all individual plans, will be responsive to employee needs and competitive considerations. All plans will fully comply with governmental requirements and the program will be guided by the specific internal and external considerations contained in this policy. The vice president for human resources is responsible for implementation and accountable for results.

A. *The following are* internal *considerations:*

1. The company will provide sound and meaningful welfare and security benefits as part of compensation for competent and continuing service. These aids are intended to complement, not replace, the efforts of individual employees.
2. Employee benefits shall be established and maintained on the basis of the employees' relative need for income protection, income supplementation, survivor benefits, retirement income, and paid leisure time.
3. The company will review all benefits as part of an annual audit of total compensation. Costs of proposed new or improved benefits will be evaluated in relation to costs of projected wage and salary increases.
4. The total benefits program shall be evaluated on the basis of contributions to both morale and productivity. Criteria to be considered in this evaluation will include open positions, turnover, attendance, grievances, and responses to surveys of attitudes.
5. To the greatest extent possible, basic benefits for employees will be provided through company contributions. Employees will be expected to pay at least part of the costs of *dependent* coverage.
6. Since employees help create profits, they will, in years when earnings permit, be awarded a fair share of company profits before taxes on the basis of a published formula that takes into account years of service and annual earnings.
7. All new and changed benefits will be discussed in detail with supervision before general communication to employees.
8. Each employee will receive an annual statement itemizing the personal value of earned benefits, the related costs of company contributions, and any plan changes.
9. Benefits for retired employees will be reviewed biennially for adequacy and adjusted accordingly.

Exhibit 2.2 *Continued*

10. Benefits for employees in acquired companies will be assimilated into plans of the parent company only when operational integration takes place, or there are opportunities for cost reduction without loss of benefit values.
11. Except as legally required temporary and part-time employees will generally not be covered by company benefit plans.

B. The following are external considerations:

1. The employee benefits of the company will be compared each year with the programs of twenty leading companies in our industry and geographic area. Based on an actuarial benefits value analysis our objective is to maintain an index value 5 to 10 percent above the twenty-company average.
2. Through the industry association, management views on legislation and administration of legally required benefits and controls on private plans will be communicated to appropriate government officials.
3. All company benefits will be coordinated with related statutory plans that provide benefits to employees.
4. All trustees and carriers administering employee benefits plans will submit detailed annual reports to management for review, analysis, and communication to employees.
5. Benefits negotiated for unionized employees will be simultaneously extended to nonrepresented employees at the same location(s). These benefits usually will be identical, but if this approach is impractical they may be extended in a different form representing the same level of company expenditures.
6. Personnel forecasts and reports of employment requirements will be reviewed annually to ascertain the need for changes in benefits to support recruitment.

Strategic Planning

A typical strategic plan for employee benefits is shown in Exhibit 2.3. It covers a three-year period in a large multidivisional organization and consists of a set of environmental assumptions, an analysis of the current situation, and seven strategic objectives. The last-mentioned represent high priority

Exhibit 2.3   Three-Year Strategic Plan for Employee Benefits

Environmental Assumptions

1. A continuing increase in benefit costs will result from:
   - salary increases projected at a 20 percent compounded rate;
   - increased utilization of health and disability benefits;
   - an increase in average age and length of service of employees due to low turnover and minimal hiring;
   - implementation of new benefits such as prescription drug plan, vision care insurance, child-care benefits, etc., and improvements in holidays, vacations, medical and retirement plans, required by competitive pressures;
   - legislative and regulatory requirements;
   - labor unions' continuing to press for more job security and income protection benefits.
2. Requirements for consistency among divisions will increase pressure on the corporation toward greater commonality of benefits among divisions, particularly for exempt employees.
3. Increasing utilization of part-time and temporary employees.
4. The corporation will continue to grow through acquisition and merger, requiring in some cases assimilation of employees of other organizations into company benefits plans, and in other cases the maintenance of separate plans for business units that will not be operationally integrated.

Current Situation Analysis

1. Benefits programs throughout the corporation are, in total, equal to or above average competitive levels.
2. Although most benefits program levels are consistent throughout the corporation, there are some significant plan feature differences among divisions. This impedes interdivisional transfers and is a source of significant employee dissatisfaction.

Strategic Objectives

1. Review and recommend changes in major benefits programs, where needed, to support overall human resources goals, especially in areas of employment and employee relations.
2. Keep informed of competitive practices in each geographic area to ensure consistent application of the corporate policy pertaining to benefits plan levels.

Exhibit 2.3   *Continued*

---

3. Adapt benefits plans as required to meet new regulatory requirements at minimal cost.
4. Working with the risk management department, study improved, more economical ways to fund and administer benefits plans; e.g., self-insurance of long-term disability plan and health plan; consolidation of insurance with a single carrier.
5. Improve communication with employees to increase awareness and understanding of benefits plan values.
6. Resist, to the extent possible, pressures for more holidays and other time off with pay.
7. Become more actively involved in earlier stages of acquisitions and merger discussions to ensure thorough and accurate assessment of benefits issues.

---

areas for special attention during the years covered by the plan. Each objective has implications for organizational productivity and profitability. While not subjected to the rigorous challenges of an annual budget, any objective proposing additional staff or significant funding would typically require some preliminary cost projections. Strategic plans need to be updated annually and revised to reflect changing concerns and new opportunities.

Operational Planning

Even among organizations that have not yet fully adopted a comprehensive approach to benefit planning, the use of an operational, or annual, plan is quite common. In most cases it is part of the regular budget process, and frequently it is the basis for management by objectives (MBO) performance measurement. The benefit manager and his or her supervisor establish a manageable number of objectives that are significant, measurable, and capable of completion within the plan period.

In a comprehensive planning system an operational goal may be part of a strategic objective. In Exhibit 2.3, for example, the fifth strategic objective refers to improving benefit communications. A parallel operational goal for the first plan year might be:

Goal Statement	• Develop and issue new summary plan descriptions (SPDs) for all benefit plans
Major Action Steps (with completion dates)	• Select advertising agency; develop design concept (February)
	• Revise copy to include most recent plan changes and to improve readability (March)
	• Finalize graphics and printed material (April)
	• Review finished booklets with HR staff and key line managers (June)
	• Distribute SPDs to all participants in small group meetings (July)

Funds to implement this goal would need to be provided in the benefit manager's annual budget. The linkage between the strategic plan and the operating plan would be a positive consideration in securing the necessary budget approvals.

Planning Aids and Techniques

Successful benefit program planners have adapted a number of aids and techniques originating in other fields to their particular needs. Approaches used in consumer and market research have been especially helpful in collecting and analyzing employee views about benefits in an organized way. And adaptations of actuarial analysis have been very useful in determining the relative value of a designated group of benefit programs.

All of the methods described in this section have been implemented successfully in benefit planning, and they appear to have potential for much greater usage. It should also be noted that in most cases adaptation has required the aid of outside consultants or specialists from other parts of the organization.

Structured Questionnaires

To some extent, data about employee opinions of their benefits derived from a general organizational attitude survey can be quite useful to the benefit manager. But to obtain more precise information about employee satisfaction, understanding, and preferences, a separate audit should be performed. Questions must be phrased very carefully to ensure clarity, and response alternatives should be realistic and discrete. Exhibit 2.4 is an example of a structured questionnaire used by a benefit manager for planning purposes.

Exhibit 2.4   Illustrative Employee Benefits Survey Questionnaire

---

Employee Benefits Questionnaire

1. In the space provided in front of the benefits listed below indicate how important each benefit is to you and your family. Indicate this by placing a "1" for the most important, and "2" for the next most important, etc. Therefore, if Life Insurance is the most important benefit to you and your family, place a "1" in front of it.

Importance		*Improvement*
(5) _____	Dental insurance.........	(18) _____
(6) _____	Disability (pay while sick)	(19) _____
(7) _____	Educational assistance....	(20) _____
(8) _____	Holidays	(21) _____
(9) _____	Life insurance	(22) _____
(10) _____	Medical insurance	(23) _____
(11) _____	Retirement annuity plan	(24) _____
(12) _____	Savings plan............	(25) _____
(13) _____	Vacations	(26) _____
(14–15) _____	_____	(27–28) _____
(16–17) _____	_____	(29–30) _____

   Now, go back and in the space provided after each benefit, indicate the priority for improvement. For example, if the Savings Plan is the benefit you would most like to see improved, give it a "1", the next a priority "2", etc. Use the blank lines to add any benefits not listed.

2. Would you be willing to contribute a portion of your earnings for new or improved benefits beyond the level already provided by the Company?   (31) ☐ Yes   ☐ No

   If yes, please indicate below in which area(s):

   (32) ☐ Dental insurance   (35) ☐ Medical insurance

   (33) ☐ Disability benefits   (36) ☐ Retirement annuity plan

   (34) ☐ Life insurance   (37) ☐ Savings plan

---

continued

Exhibit 2.4 *Continued*

---

3. As you know, in the past the Company has made certain employee benefit improvements each year, in addition to wage and salary adjustments. Which of the following statements reflects your view:

(38)   ☐   a. Place more emphasis on improving wages and salaries and less on employee benefits.

☐   b. The current mix of benefit improvements and wage and salary adjustments is about right.

☐   b. Place more emphasis on improving employee benefits and less on wages and salaries.

Source: Courtesy of Pfizer Inc.

Advocates of this technique stress the elements of privacy and confidentiality that it affords respondents. Also, costs can be minimized by limiting the number of questions and using significant sample groups rather than the entire employee population. A concern that must be confronted is the expectation for follow-up action that can develop among employees. The purposes for conducting the survey should be openly revealed at the outset and a target date for reporting results established ahead of time. When done effectively, this prevents false expectations yet lets employees know that their voices will be heard.

Trade-off Analysis

This is a simplified version of conjoint measurement, a technique used in consumer research that is based on the notion that the importance of various objects in an individual's environment can be determined relative to the value of other objects. It has been applied in employee benefit planning by involving representative groups of employees in exercises where they individually judge the relative value of benefits.[8] Administratively it is handled in ways similar to applications of the paired comparison system of job evaluation.[9] Each participant is given a set of trade-off grids. The rows and columns of each grid represent alternative levels of two different attributes (e.g., pay or paid time off, child care or life insurance, etc.). The number of grids involved is a function of the number of attributes since each attribute must be compared, pair-wise, with every other attribute. Exhibit 2.5 illustrates a trade-off grid and the responses of one employee. The respondent put a 1 in the cell that represented her most desired combination of the two attributes and a 9 in the least acceptable combination. These selections are totally predictable, but choice behavior at other levels varies. This person's second choice is to trade two additional vacation days to secure the maximum pay increase. But the next choice would mean trading 3 percent in salary increase dollars to obtain five more vacation days. Through aggregate statistical analysis, quantitative values can be derived for each attribute level for the total sample.

Utility/Cost Analysis

This approach combines measures of employee utilities (preferences) for benefit change alternatives with related cost data. It produces ratios of benefit cost effectiveness that can be used as guides in benefit planning.

A specific application of this methodology was reported in 1983 by the Seattle First National Bank, an employer of 4,000 people that devotes significant resources to employee benefit planning.[10] Using a form of trade-off analysis, the bank obtained quantitative measures of employee preferences for possible improvements in fifteen generic benefits. This "utility" analysis disclosed that paid sick leave ranked first and medical/dental/vision insurance second as desired categories for improvement. When the actual "utility scores" were divided by the required costs, however, it became evident that an

Exhibit 2.5 Trade-off Grid

I would like my salary to:

Remain the same	Increase 3%	Increase 6%	I would like my vacation to:
9	6	5	Remain the same
8	4	2	Increase by 3 days
7	3	1	Increase by 5 days

improvement in the latter category made much more sense for the bank. They could get more than double the employee satisfaction per dollar spent by increasing medical coverage as opposed to liberalizing the sick plan.

Cost effectiveness measures developed from similar evaluation procedures were effectively utilized with 250 salaried employees at a division of a large international corporation in the early 1980s.[11] In this instance the information gathered allowed the organization's management to directly compare a variety of alternative plans, including a cafeteria plan, with the current plan at constant cost levels.

Benefits Choice Simulations

This technique, now used frequently as a pretest for flexible benefit installations, was originally developed as a planning aid for traditional benefit programs. In the mid 1960s, General Electric's Behavioral Research Service Group designed a model in which a representative sample group of employees was invited to participate in an exercise involving defined choices for improvements in pay and benefit coverages subject to a dollar limitation. The participants' choices were then matched with demographic and personal characteristic information they provided confidentially. From this data general inferences were ascribed to the total employee population for purposes of benefit planning.[12]

Focus Group Research

Focus group meetings with employees to discuss benefit issues and concepts have been compared to advertising agency meetings with groups of potential customers to test new product ideas. The technique is an organized way of "testing the water" before plunging ahead with a full-scale implementation or requesting financial approval to proceed.

Continental Cablevision, Incorporated (CCI), a Boston-based employer of 2,800 people, made good use of focus groups prior to implementing a comprehensive retirement income program in 1985. Founded in 1963, CCI initially attracted younger, upwardly-motivated applicants through competitive pay, challenging work, and excellent advancement opportunities. But by the 1980s, when the company and the employees had matured, the absence of longer-term security plans began to be a problem. A special retirement planning committee was appointed and that group identified the basic objectives for a retirement income program. But before proceeding further, it scheduled four focus group meetings to assess employee reactions and concerns. The invited participants were randomly selected within general parameters to ensure broad cross sectional input. Sessions were conducted at an outside location by a benefit consultant to minimize distractions and to maximize candor. On July 1, 1985, CCI introduced a defined benefit pension plan and a capital accumulation plan with a pretax employee contribution feature and employer matching. Both plans were reported to "have attributes that were formulated based on the messages delivered by participants in the focus group meetings."[13]

Proponents of focus groups maintain that the approach brings forth instructive information for planners and at the same time builds employee trust and respect for management.

Relative Value Analysis

Once an employer identifies the principal marketplace competitors with respect to employee benefits, relative value analysis is an objective and consistent, albeit somewhat complex, way of measuring the competitiveness of the benefit program. Because the methodology involves actuarial assumptions and the collection of confidential information from competitors, it is normally obtained on a service basis from a benefit consulting firm.

The Relative Value Indices prepared by Hewitt Associates typify the analysis offered by consultants. Exhibit 2.6 illustrates comparisons of one company's benefit program to a base of fifteen identified competitors' programs. To facilitate comparisons, one common employee population base was used in factoring benefit values. In general, the value of a benefit was determined in one of two ways:

1. For each individual, the probability of an event such as disability or death was multiplied by the lump-sum value of all amounts to be paid arising from that event.

2. A value was calculated as a percentage of pay for the year (e.g., holidays).

The benefits measured (using realistic actuarial and participation assumptions) included pensions; capital accumulation plans; death, disability, and medical benefits; and time off with pay. In the chart in Exhibit 2.6, the index base point of 100.0 was set at the average of the values of the fifteen base companies. The client company's Relative Value Index (RVI) for the total benefit program was 103.4, or 3.4 percent above average. When the

Exhibit 2.6   Sample Relative Value Comparisons

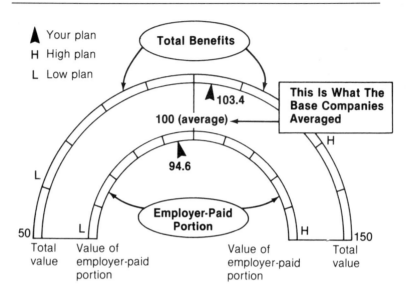

Ranking Among Plans in Study	Employer-paid Index	Total Value Index
First	147.2	139.3
Fifth	107.6	110.7
Tenth	88.3	91.6
Fifteenth	52.1	62.0

Your position relative to the base companies:

	Employer-paid Value	Total Value
Index	94.6	103.4
Ranking	6th/7th	5th/6th

Source: Copyright 1987 Hewitt Associates.

employer-paid portion was measured separately, however, the RVI was 94.6, or 5.4 percent below the competitive average.

Summary

Serious planning for employee benefit programs is a relatively recent phenomenon. Even when employers became concerned about escalating costs for health insurance in the late 1970s, benefit management was characteristically reactive — at least at first.

But today, mostly in large organizations, the benefit function has become an integral part of systemwide planning. This means that a benefit manager, to be effective, must know much more than plan technology alone. He or she must recognize and understand numerous internal and external environmental factors or run the risk of basing planning on invalid assumptions and misleading the organization.

Every organization has its particular time frames, formats, and style for a planning system or process. But benefits managers must typically develop basic policy statements, strategic plans of three years or longer, and annual operating plans. All three must be purposefully integrated. Collectively, they provide both a cohesive sense of direction for benefit management and a basis for evaluation of the program.

The collection and analysis of information about employee wants and preferences concerning benefits has been facilitated by the adaptation of methodologies used in the fields of consumer research, market research, and advertising. Also, more meaningful comparisons of program values are now being made with the aid of actuarial valuation techniques. To utilize these newer approaches for benefit planning, however, it is usually necessary to employ outside resources or obtain assistance from internal specialists.

Notes

[1]Peter F. Drucker, "What We Can Learn from Japanese Management," *Harvard Business Review* 49 (March-April 1971): 115.

[2]For details, see "Chrysler Reports Success with Benefit Cost Control," *Employee Benefit Plan Review* 40 (October 1985): 114–120. This article contains excerpts from a speech given by Joseph A. Califano, Jr., a director for Chrysler Corporation and the chairman of its committee on health care.

³Fred K. Foulkes, *Personnel Policies in Large Nonunion Companies* (Englewood Cliffs, N.J.: Prentice-Hall, 1980), pp. 209–229.

⁴Robert J. Greene and Russell G. Roberts, "Strategic Integration of Compensation and Benefits," *Personnel Administrator* 28, no. 5 (May 1983): 82.

⁵"How Not to Plan Employee Benefits," *Financial Executive* (October 1973).

⁶Ronald Derven, "IBM Computes Competitive Employee Benefit Plan," *Pension World* (April 1980): 11.

⁷See "Flex as a Merger Tool," *Benefits News Analysis* 6, no. 6 (June 1984): 12–20.

⁸For a more complete discussion of this technique, see Lawrence B. Chonko and Ricky W. Griffin, "Trade-off Analysis Finds the Best Reward Combinations," *Personnel Administrator* 28, no. 5 (May 1983): 45 ff.

⁹See Marc J. Wallace, Jr., and Charles H. Fay, *Compensation Theory and Practice* (Boston: Kent, 1983) pp. 152–153.

¹⁰Philip Kienast, Douglas MacLachlan, Leigh McAlister, and David Sampson, "The Modern Way to Redesign Compensation Packages," *Personnel Administrator* 28, no. 6 (June 1983): 127–133.

¹¹Randall B. Dunham and Roger A. Formisano, "Designing and Evaluating Employee Benefit Systems," *Personnel Administrator* 27, no. 4 (April 1982): 29–35.

¹²"New Tool Predicts Most Desired Benefits," *Employee Relations Bulletin*, Special Report, March 21, 1972.

¹³"When a Start-up Company Matures," *Benefits News Analysis* 7, no. 10 (November/December 1985): 22.

3

Mandatory Programs: Laws and Regulations

To perform effectively, the employee benefit manager must fully comprehend the diverse ways in which government involvement affects company programs. At both the federal and state levels, there are essentially three major roles that government performs in relation to private benefit plans: plan designer and administrator, controller, and facilitator.

Social Security exemplifies the first role. The federal government designs and operates the program, which covers virtually all private sector workers and many in public employment. The challenge for benefit managers is to select and design supplementary private coverages for health care, pensions, and disability and survivor benefits that are efficiently integrated with Social Security. State-operated unemployment compensation programs also require the attention of a benefit manager with respect to both claims control and coordination of benefits with supplementary employer payments.

ERISA (1974) represents the Magna Charta of government control of private benefit plans. It still ranks as the most comprehensive employee benefit legislation ever enacted in the United States. Since its passage, a steady stream of modifying laws and regulations has been enacted, causing frequent and substantial changes in private plans. At the state level, insurance

39

commissioners regulate minimum standards and requirements for group in-surance plans.

Many employee benefit authorities now view the Economic Recovery Tax Act of 1981 (ERTA) as a high-water mark in the facilitation of private benefit plans by the federal government. In addition to extending the avail-ability of individual retirement accounts (IRAs) to all employed persons, this legislation provided employer tax credits for payroll-based employee stock ownership plans; made dependent care benefits from a qualified plan non-taxable; and increased employer tax deduction limits for employee recognition award expenses.

After ERTA, the federal government began to grow increasingly con-cerned with the cost of facilitating benefits through favorable tax treatment. For example, the Treasury Department estimated that tax expenditures for IRAs and Keogh pension plans for the self-employed in the 1985 budget were three times the size of the 1984 estimates.[1] As a result, the Tax Reform Act of 1986 contained numerous provisions that diminished the tax-favored status of benefit plans.

Trying to cope with the ebb and flow between government control and facilitation, while coordinating company plans with mandatory coverages, can lead the benefits practitioner into a state of bewilderment. The purpose of this chapter is to focus on the challenges and suggest response options from a benefit management perspective. A more comprehensive discussion of federal (and state) regulation of personnel and human resource manage-ment may be found in James Ledvinka's book on this subject in the Kent Human Resource Management Series.[2]

Social Security

Many employers spend more in Federal Insurance Contribution Act (FICA) payments for Social Security coverage than for any other employee benefit. The 1986 Employee Benefits survey of the U.S. Chamber of Commerce reveals that to be particularly evident among manufacturing firms, and in some nonmanufacturing industries, that report relatively low expenditures for employer-sponsored benefits.[3]

In 1988, employers match employee FICA taxes at a rate of 7.51 percent of earnings up to $45,000. In return, the organization's employees and their dependents are protected by a comprehensive program of retirement, survivor, disability, and health benefits. Although business leaders often denounce their tax burden, their relative lack of influence on the program, and the uncertain future of the system, it is clear that without Social Security *benefits* employees would expect employers to provide comparable protections. An employee benefit manager is not required to be completely authoritative on all aspects of Social Security provisions. It is important, however, to maintain a current familiarity with the program's key features. This is critical in carrying out four basic managerial functions:

1. Selecting and designing private plans
2. Administering private plans
3. Dealing with the Social Security Administration
4. Communicating with employees

Plan Selection and Design

A common technique used by benefit managers for analyzing the content and needs of a complete benefit program is known as the "functional approach." As defined by Rosenbloom and Hallman, this is "a consistent and organized method for analyzing the risks and needs of an organization's employees and their dependents, as well as for planning how those risks and needs can and should be met through an employee benefit plan."[4] Once the needs and risks have been identified, the next step is usually to determine how they are being met by existing mandatory coverages, especially Social Security. Exhibit 3.1 illustrates one benefit manager's functional analysis and how Social Security applies to four basic needs of her company's work force. By isolating the degree to which Social Security (and subsequently other mandatory coverages) meet benefit program objectives, the adequacy of existing elective or negotiated plans can be measured. This type of analysis is useful in highlighting gaps in coverage and in preventing or correcting costly duplication of benefits.

Assume, for example, that the company represented in Exhibit 3.1 had a retirement income objective of replacing 60 percent of an employee's final pay at age sixty-five after thirty years of service. Suppose that Social Security was currently satisfying about half of that objective, but the company pension plan had been designed with an assumption that Social Security would cover two-thirds of the objective. In this case the company plan would be deficient and consideration would have to be given to improving the private plan.

The same company's income replacement goal for employees with extended disabilities might be 60 percent of pay (a typical level in 1987). The benefit manager might then conclude that no supplementary coverage was

Exhibit 3.1   Functional Needs Analysis—Social Security Benefits (1988)

Need/Risk	Eligibility Requirements	Provisions/Effects
A. Retirement income	—Age 65 (full benefits) or —Age 62–64 (benefits reduced up to 20%)	Monthly payments for life beginning at retirement. Maximum individual benefit approximately $838/month at age 65; $687 at age 62. Provisions for additional payments to spouse. Estimate that Social Security benefits replace about 30% of final year earnings for average employee retiring at age 65 in this company.
B. Disability income	—Totally and continuously disabled for 5 full calendar months	Monthly payments comparable to retirement benefit levels as long as totally disabled. Provisions for payments to dependents.
	—Disablement must last or be expected to last at least 12 months or result in death	Integrated with workers' compensation and other public programs so that combined payments cannot exceed 80% of prior average current earnings. Average income replacement rate from these sources for our disabled group is 62%.
C. Health care expense	—age 65 or —receiving Social Security disability payments for 24 months	Medicare Part A covers hospital, skilled nursing home, and home health agency expenses subject to a $540 deductible amount. Part B covers medical expenses and

Exhibit 3.1 *Continued*

Need/Risk	Eligibility Requirements	Provisions/Effects
		charges participants a $24.80 monthly premium. Active employees age 65 and over must be allowed to maintain the employee health plan as their primary source of coverage. However, the group plan can become the secondary payer for retirees eligible for Medicare.
D. Survivor benefits	The deceased employee's:	
	—widow, widower, or divorced spouse 60 or over, or 50–59 and disabled —widow, divorced parent of deceased worker's child, or widower, any age, caring for a child under age 16 —child or grandchild under 18 (or to 19 if in elementary or high school) —dependent parent, age 62 or over	Monthly payments related to amount of the deceased worker's primary retirement benefit. Maximum family benefit of up to 188% of that amount. Lump sum death benefit of $255.

needed since the analysis shows current claimants are receiving an average benefit of 65 percent of pay from Social Security and other public programs.

In the case of health-care expense, the principal selection and design issue relates to retirees and their spouses who are sixty-five or older. If the employer has a health plan that includes such persons, it can be designed as a supplementary plan with Medicare serving as the primary coverage. This is an important cost consideration since it limits the employer plan's exposure to expenses not covered by Medicare. However, in firms with twenty or more employees, the employer plan must be offered to active workers and their spouses who are sixty-five and above, *without* any offsets for Medicare. Eligibility of claimants for Social Security survivor benefits is based on such factors as age, marital status, and relationship to the deceased. The considerations are quite different from most group life insurance policies that pay benefits to any designated beneficiary. One form of group coverage that is conceptually similar to the Social Security design, however, is survivor income benefit insurance (SIBI). SIBI plans (to be described more fully in Chapter 4) are patterned upon Social Security in that they specify income benefits rather than lump-sum proceeds and they are normally only payable to surviving spouses and minor children. In designing an SIBI plan, Social Security benefits need to be recognized either as an offset against plan payments or as a "floor" of protection to be supplemented.

Plan Administration

Most private pension plans for salaried employees are formally integrated with Social Security retirement benefits. This places an important responsibility on benefit departments to produce uniform and accurate calculations of Social Security offsets in determining the amount to be paid to participants in a company plan. Another consideration of Social Security in pension plan administration is the need to track and project changes in the taxable wage base and benefit formulae for use in actuarial valuations of pension funds.

Systems and procedures need to be established to apply Social Security offsets against company long-term disability plan payments. Unless benefits from the two sources are synchronized, employees may be underpaid or temporarily overpaid. Also, once an employee has been continuously disabled for six months, all FICA taxes related to benefit payments (insured and noninsured) must cease.

In the area of health care, the principal administrative concern is the proper coordination of benefits when Medicare coverage is a factor. Specifically, for retirees and spouses who are sixty-five and older, claims should only be accepted *after* Medicare benefits have been applied.

Dealing With the Social Security Administration

Effective liaison with local Social Security officials can produce many valuable services for employers. Small quantities of explanatory literature for distribution to employees can be obtained without charge, and larger quantities can be purchased at costs well below the rates for privately published Social Security information. Social Security officials are an excellent resource for speakers in company preretirement planning programs. In addition to making group presentations, the government representatives will often agree to set up displays and booths in employee cafeterias and lounge areas and be present during nonworking hours to answer individual questions about Social Security benefits and eligibilities.

Most benefit managers have learned that in dealing with the Social Security Administration it is advantageous to take a proactive approach. Local offices tend to be extremely busy dealing with individual claimants, but once an employer takes the initiative and makes an effective contact, it usually evokes a highly positive response. The government officials gain an opportunity to reach a larger audience through employer communication channels. This permits the dissemination of authoritative information about the program to potential claimants, who have undoubtedly been subjected to many negative views about Social Security in newspapers and popular magazines. Also, once some ongoing liaison is established, company benefit plan managers become more knowledgeable about Social Security and better equipped to guide employees on basic benefits and filing procedures. This in turn provides some relief for local Social Security offices.

As in the case of a successful trade between two professional sports teams, cooperation between employee benefit managers and Social Security administrators benefits both parties.

Communicating With Employees

As mentioned in Chapter 1, employees normally fail to perceive Social Security as an employee benefit unless they are told it is a benefit by their employers. Furthermore, when some portion of Social Security benefits is used as an offset in calculating benefits from company plans, employees often view the process as a "take-away." To counter employee apathy and negativism, benefit managers need to communicate about Social Security in a positive manner. Employees should be reminded that the program protects younger people against major economic risks resulting from disability and death as well as providing pension and health benefits for older workers. It is also useful to report the magnitude of employer contributions and to point out that the concept of plan integration means that company plans are *supplementing*, not *reducing*, individual Social Security entitlements.

Social Security information can be communicated in summary plan descriptions of related company plans, annual personalized benefit statements, articles in employee periodicals, and employee meetings. Some companies promote employee awareness by distributing earnings statement request cards (see Exhibit 3.2). The Social Security Administration will often furnish these cards at little or no cost so that employees can verify the earnings reported and used as the basis for benefit calculations. The Social Security Admin-

Exhibit 3.2 Specimen Copy of "Request for Statement of Earnings"

		FOR SSA USE ONLY		
REQUEST FOR STATEMENT OF EARNINGS (PLEASE PRINT IN INK OR USE TYPEWRITER)		**AX**		●
		SP		●

I REQUEST A SUMMARY STATEMENT OF EARNINGS FROM MY SOCIAL SECURITY RECORD

NH — Full name you use in work or business

First	Middle Initial	Last		

SN — Social Security number shown on your card

DB Your date of birth — Month | Day | Year — **A**

MA — Other Social Security number(s) you have used

SX Your Sex — ☐ Male ☐ Female

AK — Other name(s) you have used (Include your maiden name)

FOLD HERE

PRIVACY STATEMENT

The Social Security Administration (SSA) is authorized to collect information asked on this form under section 205 of the Social Security Act. It is needed so SSA can quickly identify your record and prepare the earnings statement you requested. While you are not required to furnish the information, failure to do so may prevent your request from being processed. The information will be used primarily for issuing your earnings statement.

I am the individual to whom the record pertains. I understand that if I knowingly and willingly request or receive a record about an individual under false pretenses I would be guilty of a Federal crime and could be fined up to $5000.

Sign your name here: (Do not print) | TELEPHONE NO. (Area Code) | DATE

SEND THE STATEMENT TO: (to be completed in ALL cases.)

PN — Name

AD — Address (Number and Street, Apt. No., P.O. Box, or Rural Route)

City and state | **ZP** Zip Code

Form **SSA-7004-PC-OP1** (9/85)

Source: Social Security Administration.

istration encourages workers to submit these requests every three years to ensure timely corrections of any errors in the data base. Benefit departments can also help employees in their preretirement planning by preparing projections of Social Security benefits coupled with retirement plan estimates to produce a total income perspective.

Unemployment Compensation

The Social Security Act of 1935 laid the groundwork for unemployment compensation insurance (UCI) in the United States. The federal government, however, does not directly manage UCI as it does Social Security benefits. The dominant role in UCI is delegated to the states, each of which administers its own program and decides what benefits will be paid and under what conditions. There is a federal unemployment tax (FUTA) imposed on employers, but this is largely offset by a credit for employer taxes paid into state unemployment funds. As a result, the net FUTA rate for employers is currently only 0.8 percent of an employee's wages up to $7,000 a year. The proceeds from this tax are used to finance the administration of the state programs, maintain local offices, and fund extended benefits to workers during periods of extremely high unemployment.

The federal government originally set broad guidelines for the state programs, and these must be followed to qualify for the FUTA tax credit. Some of these principles and benefits that human resource administrators should be aware of are:

1. A worker must establish wage credits through earning a certain amount of pay or working a certain amount of time to be eligible for benefits.

2. Claimants must register for work at a public employment office and prove their availability for work.

3. An unemployed worker is expected to accept suitable offers of employment but must have the right to refuse any job that is unsuitable for his or her skills and standards.

4. A claimant has the right to an impartial hearing if benefits are initially denied.

Despite periodic congressional consideration of more precise standards, the states continue to maintain a high degree of autonomy in designing and administering their UCI programs.

Within the states, benefits to the unemployed are financed almost entirely through taxes levied on employers, although four jurisdictions (Alabama, Alaska, New Jersey, and Pennsylvania) have mandated small contributions from employees. The employers are taxed according to their degree of employment stability and the volume of UCI payment to their former employees. Each employer's tax rate is set annually based on the company's own account balance, or reserve ratio, which reflects taxes paid in and benefits paid out. This concept of experience, or merit, rating serves as an incentive for employers to avoid layoffs and to police the system for improper payment and inappropriate determinations.

In about half the states, an employer may elect to obtain a reduced tax rate by making a voluntary contribution to its account at the beginning of the tax year. This requires only a simple calculation to see if the projected savings from having a lower tax rate over the next twelve months would be greater than the one-time contribution expense needed to secure the rate reduction.

State UCI taxes for individual employers vary greatly according to state laws and turnover experience. In some states, for example, a company with very high turnover could be assigned an annual rate of 10 percent of employee wages (typically on a wage base of $7,000 to $10,000), while a competitor with stable employment could be exempt from any tax for that year. Individual benefit formulas also vary substantially among the states, but conceptually they are all constructed to replace a targeted portion (usually about one-half to two-thirds) of a worker's earnings up to a maximum, which represents a similar proportion of the statewide average wage. The duration of benefits is a function of how long the employee had been working prior to termination, but the standard maximum period for payments is twenty-six weeks.

For employee benefit managers, the principal implication of UCI is the integration of the available benefits with an overall package that protects employees in the event of unemployment. Functional analyses of the risks and needs associated with group layoffs and individual terminations should routinely recognize the significant income replacement capacities of the state plans. Functional analysis, however, should also highlight the fact that UCI benefits become progressively less meaningful at higher income levels because of relatively low benefit ceilings. Assume, for example, that in 1987 two long-service employees laid off by a Michigan firm applied for state UCI benefits. The weekly average after-tax earnings had been $327 for employee A and $1,000 for employee B. Both individuals would have been eligible for the maximum weekly benefit of $229. For employee A, this would have represented the standard replacement of 70 percent of after-tax earnings, but employee B would only realize about a 23 percent replacement level.

Not only do higher-paid employees receive smaller percentages of income replacement from UCI plans, but in many instances the twenty-six-week limit on payments is too short to cover the time they need to find another job. For these reasons, a well-designed unemployment assistance package (to be discussed in Chapter 6) requires more generous employer supplements for management-level and other exempt positions.

The primary responsibility for administrative control of UCI benefits is normally assigned to a personnel operations office. This facilitates access to termination records and prompt responses to requests for information from state offices. If an employee is ruled eligible for benefits by the state agency, and company records show a "voluntary quit without good cause attributable to the work," it is generally advisable for the employer to appeal the decision. This will lead to a hearing, a thorough review of the circumstances, and in many cases a reversal of the initial finding.

Some organizations with very high turnover rates contract with outside firms that specialize in claims-control systems. By auditing claims and account charges, these firms assert that the fees paid to them by employers can be recovered by credits received from errors they identify. Other companies maintain their own unemployment cost control systems (see Exhibit 3.3). In addition to serving as a check on excessive charges, an internal system can be coordinated with recruitment of open positions. In some cases, individuals receiving benefits will be eligible for recall or reemployment. If they refuse an offer to return to work, UCI benefits will usually be suspended.

Workers' Compensation

Unlike unemployment compensation insurance, workers' compensation (WC) programs have been initiated and are administered at the state level with no direct federal involvement or mandatory standards. Employers are fully responsible for benefit costs, and they may not require any employee contributions.

The first laws for handling occupational disabilities and death were enacted in 1911, and they have existed in all states since 1948. Although specific benefit provisions vary widely, all of the programs are committed to six basic objectives:[5]

1. Provide sure, prompt, and reasonable income and medical benefits to work-accident victims, or income benefits to their dependents, regardless of fault.

Exhibit 3.3 Cost Control Card — Unemployment Compensation
Payments

NAME: _____ SS#: _____

LAST DAY WORKED: _____ DATE OF CLAIM: _____ / ____ / _____

BASE YEAR: ___ / ___ ___ / ___

REASON FOR SEPARATION: _____

_____

SEPARATION IS: PERMANENT: ___ TEMPORARY: ___ DATE OF RECALL: _____

SEPARATION PAYMENTS: AMOUNT $_____ PAID THROUGH ___ / ___
[TYPE: LIEU OF NOTICE, VACATION/HOLIDAY (for temp. lay-off), PENSION]

WEEKLY BENEFIT RATE: _____ % CHARGEABLE TO OUR ACCOUNT: _____

WEEKLY AMOUNT CHARGEABLE TO OUR ACCOUNT: _____

MAXIMUM BENEFITS CHARGEABLE: _____ (50% BASE YEAR WAGES): _____

BENEFIT YEAR: ___ / ___ to ___ / ___

DATE OF APPEAL: _____ FORM: _____ DECISION: _____

_____ FORM: _____ DECISION: _____

DISQUALIFIED FROM: ___ / ___ THROUGH ___ / ___

U.C. BENEFITS PAID

Week Ending	Amount	Week Ending	Amount	Week Ending	Amount

Total Benefits: _____

Source: Courtesy of Employers Association of New Jersey.

2. Provide a single remedy and reduce court delays, costs, and workloads arising out of personal-injury litigation.

3. Relieve public and private charities of financial drains resulting from uncompensated industrial accidents.

4. Eliminate payment of fees to lawyers and witnesses as well as time-consuming trials and appeals.

5. Encourage maximum employer interest in safety and rehabilitation through an appropriate experience-rating mechanism.

6. Promote frank study of causes of accidents (rather than attempting to conceal fault) and thereby reduce preventable accidents and human suffering.

In 1972, a national commission on state workmen's compensation laws proposed nineteen essential improvements in the state programs. If these were not promptly instituted, the commission urged federalization of WC. Since that report was released, most states have made substantial movement towards adopting the recommendations, but to date no state has fully implemented all nineteen changes. And so far, efforts to establish federal standards have generated little enthusiasm in Congress.

To facilitate the consideration of claims, most states have established separate WC commissions or boards. A few states rely on their basic court system. Except for six states that maintain monopolistic insurance funds (Nevada, North Dakota, Ohio, Washington, West Virginia, and Wyoming), employers are free to select their own carriers to insure the risk, investigate claims, and process payments. Also, all states except North Dakota, Texas, and Wyoming permit self-insurance for workers' compensation.

In planning and designing company benefit plans, it is important for a manager to recognize the diversity of WC benefits. In making a functional needs analysis, managers should consider that these programs protect employees, dependents, and survivors against:

1. Income loss resulting from total disability

2. Income loss due to impairment

3. Income loss resulting from death

4. Medical expenses

5. Rehabilitation expenses

Although specific terms and levels of coverage vary by state, characteristics common to all states address the following major risks and needs.

Total Disability Benefits

Weekly income replacement benefits are payable after a brief waiting period, usually three to seven days. If the disability continues for two to four weeks, benefits are typically paid retroactive to the date of injury. The national commission report in 1972 recommended a weekly cash benefit of at least 66⅔ percent of the worker's weekly wage, with a maximum equal to the state's average weekly wage. Most states now meet or exceed this standard. As Exhibit 3.1 indicates, combined payments from WC and Social Security may not exceed 80 percent of an employee's average current earnings prior to the disability.

Impairment (Permanent Partial Disability) Benefits

When an occupational injury causes loss or loss of the use of specific body members, WC laws presume that some income will be lost due to the impairment. An award is made based on a schedule of permanent partial disabilities. The amount is related to the degree of impairment and the worker's wage level. For example in Illinois, as of 1987, the maximum award for the loss of an eye was $81,600. The scheduled limit for loss of the fourth finger was $10,880. In most states, these payments are in addition to any total disability benefits.

Survivor Benefits

In the event of death, all states provide for a burial allowance (typically in the range of $1,000–$2,000) and income benefits for surviving spouses and children. Income benefits are a proportion of the deceased worker's pay (usually up to 66⅔ percent, depending on the number of eligible survivors). They normally continue to be paid to a spouse until remarriage and to dependent children up to a specified age. These benefits are not integrated with Social Security survivor payments.

Medical Expense Benefits

Benefit administrators need to recognize that unlimited coverage of medical expenses is required under the state WC laws. This differs from group health plans that cover nonoccupational medical expenses, in which employees ordinarily are responsible for deductible amounts, copayments, and expenses beyond stated limits. It is important that both employees and claims processors grasp these distinctions. Controls need to be established to prevent duplicative payments to employees or providers from these two sources of medical expense coverage.

Another issue of concern to employee benefit managers, as well as medical directors and employee relations managers, is the choice of physician under workers' compensation laws. The states are about evenly divided between those that give the decision to the employer and those that give it to the employee. In the latter case, however, the employer normally has the right to have his own physician conduct an examination. In the interest of assuring prompt and expert care to rehabilitate and reemploy disabled workers, most employers and insurers try to exercise as much control in this area as state laws allow.

Rehabilitation Expense Benefits

To help seriously injured and impaired workers return to gainful employment, rehabilitation benefits are provided in all of the state WC laws. In addition to coverage of physical rehabilitation programs, provisions may include tuition, meals, lodging, travel expenses, and a maintenance allowance associated with vocational training. Although some of these items may appear costly, success in rehabilitating claimants can be measured in lower medical costs, less time away from work, and reduced effects from a residual disability.

In a study of some 7,500 closed workers' compensation cases, one private insurance rehabilitation firm calculated the average dollar savings per file at $13,876, or $10.33 per dollar invested. Its study of almost 43,000 cases showed an average charge per file, over 10 years, of $1,343.[6]

Historically, workers' compensation developed as a mechanism for dealing with injuries caused by occupational accidents. Today, state laws place an additional responsibility on employers for covering the effects of diseases arising out of and in the course of employment. Recently growing concern about the latent effects of exposure to radiation and toxic substances has raised some challenging questions concerning workers' compensation benefits. Economist Peter S. Barth has observed:

> It is hardly possible to justify differential benefits for victims of industrial injuries and diseases, either in terms of compensation or medical-health treatment. It is also difficult to justify benefit payments for workers or survivors that are based on earnings levels at the time of (last) exposure, when the disease develops one or two decades later. The combination of inflation and productivity gains renders such historically based benefit levels hardly worthy of the extended and costly controversy that can follow the filing of a claim.[7]

The probable reform of state workers' compensation laws to better deal with occupational disease is one more external consideration in the employee benefit manager's planning model.

Temporary Disability Laws

In 1942 Rhode Island enacted a temporary disability insurance law to protect employees against income loss during absences due to non-job-related illnesses and accidents. Since that time only four other states (California, Hawaii, New Jersey, and New York) and the Commonwealth of Puerto Rico have mandated similar programs. There are no federal requirements for these benefits.

Despite this limited government involvement, the patterns set by the five state programs have had a strong influence on the growth of employer-initiated and -negotiated short-term disability plans in the United States. In 1986 94 percent of the 21 million employees represented in the Bureau of Labor Statistics' annual benefit survey had some form of this protection.[8]

The state laws are all designed to replace a portion of pay, the provisions ranging from 50 to 75 percent subject to a statutory maximum. In general the plans are quite similar, but it is important for multistate employers to be aware of areas of difference. Some of the common features (and exceptions) are:

1. Benefits begin on the eighth consecutive day of disability with some provisions for retroactive first-day coverage in instances of extended absence.

2. Benefits are payable for up to twenty-six weeks (fifty-two weeks in California). This dovetails with Social Security disability benefits, which may be payable after five full calendar months of total disablement.

3. There can be no duplication of benefits with respect to workers' compensation and unemployment compensation payments.

4. Employers may substitute a private plan (insured or self-insured) for the state plan under certain conditions, except in Rhode Island.

5. There are provisions for both employer and employee contributions to fund the plans in all cases. In California and Rhode Island, however, employers are not required to make payments; rather, they have the option of paying all or part of the amount specified for employee contributions.

A benefit administration issue that requires a clearly communicated and consistently applied policy is the coordination of sick pay allowances with temporary disability benefits. Many employers continue a disabled worker's full pay under the former pending availability of the latter. To prevent duplication of benefits, some states permit the disability plan to reimburse the company directly for the advance payments. Frequently, though, the burden is on the employer to recover the equivalent amount from an employee who has already received an overpayment.

ERISA

The Employee Retirement Income Security Act of 1974 (ERISA) was signed in that year by President Ford on Labor Day. It was hailed as significant social legislation by most leaders of organized labor and employee rights advocates, but the acronym was converted into "Everything Ridiculous Invented Since Adam" by some benefit practitioners. The main reason for the hostility was the multiplicity of costly changes that had to be made in the design and operation of benefit plans within a short period. Prior to ERISA, there had been relatively little federal control over the management of private plans. The Internal Revenue Service (IRS) required certain participation standards and limits on deductibility of benefit expenditures, and the Pension Plans Disclosure Act of 1958 (amended 1962) had given the secretary of labor limited investigatory and regulatory authority over benefit plans. Beyond that, the employee benefit community had been allowed great latitude in creating and administering group plans. That state of freedom ended with ERISA. The consequences of noncompliance included the loss of the unique tax advantages offered employers who had qualified plans.

In retrospect, it seems clear that design deficiencies and mismanagement of private benefit plans were largely responsible for the enactment of ERISA. A president's commission report in 1965 had highlighted many weaknesses in plan funding, design, reporting, and disclosure. During the next nine years, while Congress considered remedial legislation and employee distrust and public indignation grew, employers did little to remedy the identified problems.

The ultimate product of the prolonged legislative process was a law that, although it did not totally satisfy anyone, eliminated many faults in the system. In 1984, on the tenth anniversary of the passage of ERISA, Senator Lloyd Bentsen of Texas, one of the authors of the bill, wrote this important law has strengthened and improved our private pension system by ensuring that earned pension benefits become a reality, not a broken promise. ERISA eliminated some glaring pension abuses that cost senior citizens hard-earned pension benefits: [these abuses included] unreasonable vesting and service requirements and inadequate funding.[9]

ERISA is subtitled "an act to provide for pension reform" and it applies most broadly to private pension plans of the defined benefit type, which specify a predetermined retirement benefit based on plan service and, sometimes, earnings (see Exhibit 3.4). However, it also covers employee savings and thrift plans, deferred profit-sharing plans, employee stock ownership plans, and money purchase plans, all of which are classified as defined contribution plans. These plans have the common characteristics of a predetermined level of employer contribution to individual employee accounts to be invested for retirement and other longer-term purposes. Since defined contribution plans do not guarantee participants any fixed level of benefit payments, they are not subject to the ERISA funding rules or plan termination insurance requirements. As shown in Exhibit 3.4, defined benefit pension plans are covered by *all* of the ERISA provisions.

Employee welfare plans, which provide benefits in the case of sickness, accident, disability, death, or unemployment, also fall under the scope of ERISA. These plans are only subject to provisions dealing with reporting, disclosure, claims procedure, and fiduciary requirements. However, the Tax

Exhibit 3.4   Applicability of ERISA Provisions

	Private Plans			
	Defined Benefit Pension Plans	Defined Contribution Pension Plans	Welfare Plans	**Plans for Government Employees**
ERISA Provisions				
1. Reporting and disclosure	yes	yes	yes	no
2. Fiduciary standards	yes	yes	yes	no
3. Plan participation rules	yes	yes	no	no
4. Vesting standards	yes	yes	no	no
5. Funding rules	yes	no	no	no
6. Plan termination insurance	yes	no	no	no

Reform Act of 1986 extended many ERISA concepts of making tax-qualified pension plans nondiscriminatory to the category of welfare plans. A complex set of nondiscrimination rules contained in Section 89 in the Internal Revenue Code is scheduled to take effect in 1989 subject to the issuance of implementing regulations.

Although there have been numerous attempts to extend ERISA, or parallel legislation, to the public sector since 1974, benefit plans for government employees continue to remain exempt from this type of law. The following summary of ERISA requirements is current as of early 1988 and the summary incorporates enacted revisions scheduled to take effect at a specified future date.

Reporting and Disclosure

Employees and beneficiaries must be informed of their entitlements and rights under covered plans. Regular reports must also be filed with the Department of Labor, Internal Revenue Service, and the Pension Benefit Guaranty Corporation. These ERISA requirements will be discussed further in Chapters 9 and 10.

Fiduciary Standards

These standards protect employee pension and welfare plans from financial losses caused by mismanagement and misuse of assets. Any person who exercises discretionary authority over benefit plan management, assets, or administration is considered a fiduciary. Outside investment advisers who are paid for their services are also fiduciaries. Inside fiduciaries who are full-time employees may not receive any compensation directly attributable to this responsibility.

ERISA specifies bonding requirements and certain "prohibited transactions" for fiduciaries. There are also four general duties:[10]

"A fiduciary must:

1. discharge his or her duties solely in the interest of plan participants and beneficiaries and for the exclusive purpose of providing plan benefits to them and defraying the reasonable expenses of administering the plan.

2. act with the care, skill, prudence, and diligence under the circumstances then prevailing that a 'prudent man' acting in like capacity and familiar with such matters would use in the conduct of an enterprise of a like character and with like aims.

3. diversify plan investment to minimize the risk of large losses unless it is clearly prudent not to do so.

4. operate in accordance with plan documents and instruments."

Any fiduciary who breaches an ERISA duty or rule can be held personally liable for any plan losses attributable to the breach and required to restore to the plan any personal gains realized through improper use of plan assets.

Plan Participation Rules

The basic standard applicable to most pension plans is that a plan cannot deny eligibility for participation beyond the time an employee reaches age twenty-one and completes one year of service. Once those requirements are satisfied, an employee must be permitted to participate within the next six months.

Generally, a year of service means 1,000 hours or more of service during a twelve-month period. Once an employee begins to participate in a plan, vesting rights and benefit accruals depend heavily on additional year-of-service credits. A plan is not required to credit any year in which a participant does not have at least 1,000 hours of service. A year in which the participant does not have more than 500 hours of service can be considered a break in service. During absences resulting from pregnancy, childbirth, and adoption, however, at least 501 hours of service must be credited to the employee. This applies to paternity as well as maternity leaves. If a participant incurs five consecutive one-year breaks, all previously credited years of service and benefits can be forfeited unless the person had vested rights to benefits.

Vesting

Vesting is a pension plan provision guaranteeing that a participant, after meeting certain requirements, will retain a right to benefits he or she has accrued, or some portion of them, even if employment with the plan sponsor terminates prior to retirement. In the congressional hearings preliminary to ERISA, there was much discussion of restrictive vesting provisions in company pension plans. Examples were given of plans requiring attainment of a specified age (forty-five or fifty) and long service (fifteen to twenty years) in order to acquire a nonforfeitable right to benefits. The ERISA standards that became effective in 1976 prohibited such severe requirements and enabled many more plan participants to secure at least some of their pension accruals. Initially there were three alternative standards:

1. *Cliff Vesting:* full (100 percent) vesting after ten years of service (with no vesting required prior to that time)
2. *Graded Vesting:* 25 percent vesting after five years of service, plus 5 percent for each additional year of service up to ten years (50 percent after ten years), plus an additional 10 percent each year thereafter (100 percent vesting after fifteen years of service)
3. *Rule of Forty-five:* 50 percent vesting for an employee with at least five years of service when his or her age and service add up to forty-five, plus 10 percent for each year thereafter

Under any of the options, an employee must be at least 50 percent vested after ten years of service and 100 percent after fifteen years, regardless of age.

ERISA also specified a special vesting requirement for certain defined contribution plans. "Class-year" plans in which each year's contributions are treated separately for vesting purposes had to provide for 100 percent vesting not later than the end of the fifth plan year following the plan year for which the contributions were made.

Since 1984 special vesting rules have applied to "top-heavy" pension plans. These are plans in which the accrued benefits for a statutorily-defined category of "key" employees exceed 60 percent of the accrued benefits for all participants. In these plans, which are more common in smaller organizations, participants must vest at least as rapidly as

1. 100 percent after three years of service, or
2. 20 percent after two years of service and 20 percent for each year thereafter (100 percent vesting after six years of service).

In the early years of ERISA compliance, most employers limited changes in pension plan vesting to those that were necessary to meet the minimum standards. The usual reason for this was cost containment. But in the early 1980s other factors caused some organizations to rethink their positions. Pressures to attract new employees, curb turnover in the early years of employment, and ease the trauma of large-scale layoffs were among the factors that led to some liberalization of vesting requirements, particularly in defined contribution plans. However, most defined benefit plans continued to follow the ten-year cliff vesting standard. In 1981, a president's commission report[11] noted that this requirement was preventing large numbers of employees from receiving pension income that had been represented to them as part of their total compensation. In response to this report and some effective lobbying by such groups as the American Association of Retired Persons, the ERISA vesting standards were amended as part of the Tax Reform Act of 1986. The new minimum standards, which generally become effective in 1989, are that a participant's employer-provided benefit must vest at least as rapidly as:

1. full vesting after five years of service, or

2. 20 percent after three years of service and 20 percent for each year thereafter (100 percent vesting after seven years of service).

Class year vesting is no longer permitted. Multiemployer plans are permitted to require ten years of service for full vesting, and collectively bargained plans are given until January 1, 1991, to comply with the new standards.

Funding Rules

Before ERISA the Internal Revenue Service had already issued regulations requiring pension plan administrators to fund on an annual basis the future benefits earned in the current year by participants. This is known as the "normal cost." But there was no effective requirement to fund the "past service costs" for future benefits based on preplan service. As a result, some plans remained perpetually underfunded. This was the case when Studebaker closed its South Bend, Indiana, auto plant in 1963 and terminated its pension plan. Because of severe underfunding, a typical worker of age forty with twenty years' service only received a lump sum payment of $350 in lieu of a pension.[12]

For most employers the key feature of ERISA funding rules, which is applicable to defined benefit plans only, is the requirement that past service liabilities and plan improvements be amortized over a period not to exceed thirty years. In addition, funding must be monitored by enrolled actuaries and adjusted at least every three years to assure the plan's financial soundness. And starting in 1989, under-funded plans will be required to amortize existing liabilities over eighteen years.

Plan Termination Insurance

The Internal Revenue Code provides for full and immediate vesting of all accrued benefits, *to the extent then funded,* upon the termination of a qualified pension plan. In combination with the ERISA funding rules, this gives plan participants considerable protection, but it does not address what happens if a plan terminates *before* it is fully funded. To cover this possibility, ERISA created a system of pension plan termination insurance and set in motion the establishment of a separate government agency, the Pension Benefit Guaranty Corporation (PBGC).

The PBGC administers an insurance program for private defined benefit pension plans, and if a plan terminates guarantees the payment of basic retirement benefits to participants. Employers pay premiums to the PBGC for this coverage. The rates change from time to time and are subject to congressional approval. When the program became effective in 1975, the annual rate for single employer plans was $1.00 per participant. Currently the basic rate is $16.00 and sponsors of under-funded plans are required to pay additional risk-based premiums that could raise their total annual cost per participant to $50.

When a pension plan terminates and the assets are insufficient to meet vested benefit requirements, the PBGC becomes the trustee for the plan, assuming responsibility for benefit payments up to a statutory maximum that is adjusted periodically. For 1988 the maximum was approximately $1,900 per month. Initially the PBGC would receive all assets from a terminated plan and the plan sponsor would become liable to the PBGC for up to 30 percent of the business's net worth. The latter provision was intended to deter companies from terminating pension plans. However, insolvent businesses calculated that the 30 percent liability was less than the cost of unfunded plan liabilities and, as a financial strategy, terminated their pension plans. In effect, these companies were taking advantage of other employers' PBGC premium dollars to fulfill their pension obligations, and they were indirectly contributing to rate increases. The conditions for voluntary plan terminations were made much more stringent as part of the Consolidated Omnibus Budget Reconciliation Bill of 1985 (COBRA) and in 1988 budget deficit reduction legislation. Two types of terminations are now specified:

1. *Standard termination* is the termination of a defined benefit pension plan whose assets equal or exceed all benefit commitments.

2. *Distress termination* is the termination of a plan pursuant to a petition in bankruptcy for certain business necessity reasons.

To qualify for the PBGC bailout assistance, an employer must be able to qualify for a distress termination. If this cannot be done, the sponsor of an underfunded plan is required to contribute assets to the plan's trust to make the plan sufficient for benefit commitments and qualify for a standard termination.

If the plan qualifies for a distress termination and has insufficient assets to cover obligations, the plan sponsor becomes liable to the PBGC for

1. immediate payment of the total amount of all unfunded vested benefits, up to 30 percent of the employer's net worth, plus

2. payment, over time, of any excess of unfunded vested benefits beyond 30 percent of the net worth of the sponsor, plus

3. interest payments calculated from the termination date.

Individual Retirement Accounts (IRAs)

As mentioned in Chapter 2, ERISA fathered the tax-deductible IRA, which has been the object of both liberalization and curtailment since its birth in 1975. Under current law, an employee who is not an active participant in an employer-sponsored pension plan during any part of a year may take a deductible contribution of up to $2,000 to an IRA, with an additional $250 allowed for a spousal account if a joint tax return is filed. Active plan participants are also permitted to make the same level of deductible contributions as long as their adjusted gross income (AGI) does not exceed $25,000 (single filing status) or $40,000 (joint return). Proportional deductions for IRA contributions are allowed for pension plan participants whose AGI is between $25,000 and $35,000 (single filing status) or between $40,000 and $50,000 (joint return).

Post-ERISA Legislation

All of the major tax laws enacted since 1974 have materially affected employee benefit plans. In many instances, exemptions or rules specified in one law have been eliminated or revised by subsequent legislation; therefore, a full chronology would have minimal utility for a current or prospective benefit practitioner. The most recent law, the Tax Reform Act of 1986, is however presently viewed as the most dramatic change in the U.S. tax laws since 1913. Its pervasive effect on benefit plans will be further discussed in later chapters.

Other federal legislation in the post-ERISA period has included a law dealing discretely with benefit issues (the Retirement Equity Act of 1984) and a catchall law with major new requirements for group health insurance plans (COBRA — 1985). This contrast underscores the need for vigilance on the part of benefit planners in tracking and anticipating a wide variety of pending legislation.

Exhibit 3.5 summarizes the major federal laws after ERISA that have affected employee benefit plans.

The Courts

Benefit laws and their administrative interpretation are continually subjected to judicial review, and on occasion this leads to a U.S. Supreme Court decision. For example, in 1978 the high court ruled that employers were prohibited under the Civil Rights Act from requiring women to make larger pension plan contributions to obtain the same benefits as men.[13] In 1983 the Supreme Court extended this concept and made it clear that retirement benefits based on plan contributions must be calculated without regard to sex.[14] These two decisions led to many changes in pension plan design and administration.

Notably, one U.S. Supreme Court decision affecting employee benefit plans was negated rather swiftly through the legislative process. On December 7, 1976, the Court ruled that employers did not have to include pregnancy benefits in a disability income plan.[15] This provoked strong opposition from the National Organization of Women and other worker equity groups. Within a few months, bills to amend Title VII of the Civil Rights Act by specifically prohibiting sex discrimination on the basis of pregnancy had been introduced in both houses of Congress. In October, 1978, the Pregnancy Discrimination Act was signed into law. This law requires that pregnancy, childbirth, and related conditions be treated in the same manner as any other illness or disability for all employment-related purposes. In a 1983 decision the U.S. Supreme Court clearly affirmed that these employee protections also applied to wives of male employees.[16]

Obviously, it is not necessary for all benefit plan disputes to be heard by the U.S. Supreme Court. Many individual complaints can be taken care of by administrative agencies such as the Department of Labor or the Equal Employment Opportunity Commission (EEOC). Within the judicial structure most matters are resolved at a district court level. But when a fundamental issue is involved, such as retiree health benefit rights, litigation can be expected to escalate until a definitive Supreme Court ruling is obtained.

Exhibit 3.5   Chronology: Principal Federal Laws After ERISA Affecting Employee Benefit Plans

1978	*Revenue Act* added Section 125 covering cafeteria plans and Section 401(k) covering cash or deferred income arrangements to the Internal Revenue Code.
	Age Discrimination in Employment Act Amendments extended benefit protections for most employees from age 65 to age 70.
	Pregnancy Amendments to the Civil Rights Act required employers to treat disabilities caused by pregnancy the same as other disabilities covered under group benefit programs.
1980	*Miscellaneous Revenue Act* made it possible for employees to be given a choice among benefits, cash, and deferred income as part of a Section 125 cafeteria plan.
1981	*Economic Recovery Tax Act (ERTA)* created payroll-based tax credit employee stock ownership plans (ESOPs), extended eligibility for individual retirement accounts to all wage earners, and made employer-provided child care programs non-taxable for employees.
1982	*Tax Equity and Fiscal Responsibility Act (TEFRA)* imposed tax withholding requirements on pension plan payments and placed numerous limitations on tax qualified plans including lowered maximum benefit accruals and employer contribution levels.
1984	*Retirement Equity Act (REA)* extended employee benefit rights and protections by amending ERISA pension plan provisions regarding plan participation, vesting, survivor provisions, and break-in-service rules.
	Deficit Reduction Act (DEFRA) included a variety of restrictions on benefit plans as part of a comprehensive effort to lower a large budget deficit.
1986	*Consolidated Omnibus Budget Reconciliation Act of 1985 (COBRA)* required employers to offer extended group health plan participation for up to thirty-six months to employees and dependents whose coverage would otherwise end due to certain qualifying events, such as termination of employment.
	Tax Reform Act of 1986 contained the most sweeping legislative changes affecting benefit plans since ERISA. Major themes were: (1) more uniform provisions for controlling discrimination in favor of

Exhibit 3.5 *Continued*

highly paid employees under different types of plans; (2) firmer guidelines to make tax-advantaged plans more equitable; and (3) tighter pension plan standards and tax penalties to ensure use of deferred income for retirement purposes.

Age Discrimination in Employment Act amendments established that effective January 1, 1987, mandatory retirement based on age would no longer be permitted for most employees.

Omnibus Budget Reconciliation Act of 1986 (OBRA) required, starting in 1988, pension accruals and pension participation beyond a plan's normal retirement age [usually 65] for employees in company pension plans.

State Involvement

ERISA preempts state laws in virtually all respects concerning benefit plans except for state control of insurance coverage. The states continue to exert much influence over group welfare benefit plans through laws and standards issued by insurance regulators. Typically state requirements relate to minimum benefit levels, employee rights, and services that must be included in insured health plans. There is considerable variation in the state specifications, and the National Association of Insurance Commissioners actively promotes greater uniformity through the development and issuance of model laws. State laws also affect holiday observances and some time-off-with-pay practices.

Summary

Today it would be sensible and appropriate for employee benefit managers to accept government as a major partner in the business of managing company plans. This association is the result of mandatory programs, such as Social Security, serving as a foundation for employer-sponsored benefit plans, and the latter becoming increasingly subject to federal and state laws and regulations.

An effective benefit executive recognizes that there are opportunities to influence all of the laws affecting company benefit plans. In large organizations it is often possible to shape features while laws are in the early stages of development through direct contacts with sponsoring legislators and key staff members. For benefit program managers in smaller firms, groups such as the U.S. Chamber of Commerce can serve as a channel for transmitting employer views to lawmakers.

For benefit planning purposes it is important to monitor pending legislation and, once laws are passed, to audit company plans for compliance requirements and cost implications.

Although employees tend to overlook the many protections they receive from mandatory programs, employers should refer to the coverages in their benefit communication efforts. For example, annual benefit report statements should remind employees of their Social Security, workers' compensation and unemployment compensation protections and summarize the extent of employer contributions to these programs.

In 1974 ERISA caused a shock wave in the employee benefit community when it introduced massive regulation of private sector pension and welfare plans. Benefit plan managers gradually adjusted to the requirements of that near-revolutionary legislation, and then began to cope with more frequent enactment of federal laws affecting their company plans. To date the most comprehensive of the post-ERISA laws is the Tax Reform Act of 1986. Many provisions of this law have taken effect already but some significant requirements will not occur until after 1988.

Except for insurance laws, state regulation of employee benefit plans was largely preempted by ERISA. Nonetheless, benefit managers, especially in large companies with employees in many states, must be familiar with state mandatory coverages, such as workers' compensation, and insurance commissioner standards.

Notes

[1]Employee Benefit Research Institute, *Why Tax Employee Benefits?* (Washington, D.C.: EBRI, 1984), p. xii.

[2]James Ledvinka, *Federal Regulation of Personnel and Human Resource Management* (Boston: Kent, 1982), particularly Chapters 1, 7, 10, and 11 and pages 244–249.

[3]U.S. Chamber of Commerce, *Employee Benefits 1986* (Washington, D.C.: U.S. Chamber of Commerce, 1987), p. 13.

⁴Jerry S. Rosenbloom and G. Victor Hallman, *Employee Benefit Planning* (Englewood Cliffs, N.J.: Prentice-Hall, 1986), p. 8.

⁵U.S. Chamber of Commerce, *Analysis of Workers' Compensation Laws*, 1986 ed. (Washington, D.C.: U.S. Chamber of Commerce, 1986), p. vii.

⁶*Insurance Decisions, What Ails Workers' Compensation?* (Philadelphia: CIGNA Corporation, n.d., circa 1981).

⁷Peter S. Barth, "On Efforts to Reform Workers' Compensation for Occupational Diseases," in *Current Issues in Workers' Compensation*, ed. James Chelius (Kalamazoo, Mich.: W. E. Upjohn Institute for Employment Research, 1986), p. 333.

⁸U.S. Department of Labor, Bureau of Labor Statistics, *Employee Benefits in Medium and Large Firms, 1986* (Washington, D.C.: U.S. Government Printing Office, 1987), p. 12.

⁹"ERISA Remembered," *Employee Benefit Plan Review* 39, no. 2 (August 1984): 11.

¹⁰U.S. Department of Labor, Office of Pension and Welfare Benefit Programs, *What You Should Know About the Pension Law* (Washington, D.C.: U.S. Government Printing Office, 1986), pp. 36–37.

¹¹President's Commission on Pension Policy, *Coming of Age: Toward a National Retirement Income Policy* (Washington, D.C.: U.S. Government Printing Office, 1981), p. 45.

¹²Ledvinka, *Federal Regulation*, p. 206.

¹³Los Angeles v. Manhart, 435 U.S. 702 (1978).

¹⁴Arizona Governing Committee v. Norris, 103 U.S. 3492 (1983).

¹⁵General Electric v. Gilbert, 429 U.S. 125 (1976).

¹⁶Newport News Shipbuilding and Dry Dock Co. v. EEOC, 103 S. Ct. 2622 (1983).

4

Employee Welfare
Benefit Plans

Employee welfare benefit plans form the core of a package of benefits provided by an employer. These are the plans that protect employees and their dependents against the major economic risks associated with (1) health care, (2) disability, and (3) death. Except those who work in very small businesses, employees today can expect to receive some form of group coverage against each of these risks. And satisfying employee expectations in a cost-effective way is a continuous high-priority challenge for managers of benefit programs.

While some type of coverage has become nearly universal, there are many variations in group plans that address the three basic areas of need. Compared with pension plans, employee welfare benefit plans have, until recently, been subject to relatively limited government regulation. This relative freedom allowed employers to tailor plans to their own particular requirements, and in some instances this meant discriminating in favor of highly paid executives. As a result, recent federal legislation, notably the Deficit Reduction Act of 1984 (DEFRA) and the Tax Reform Act of 1986, has contained provisions that remove tax preferences for "discriminatory" welfare plans.

Although the steady encroachment of federal and state legislation and regulation has eroded some management flexibility, employers continue to retain considerable latitude in the selection, design, and overall management of employee welfare plans.

Health Care

In the context of "core" benefits, health care is the usual term applied to coverage for hospital, surgical, and medical expenses. Although the total benefit package might also include dental care, vision care, and prescription drug plans, these are usually offered separately as "noncore" coverages.

Alternative Sources

Health-care benefits can be financed and provided to employees in a variety of ways, but there are five typical alternatives:

1. Insurance companies
2. Blue Cross/Blue Shield associations
3. Self-funding arrangements
4. Health maintenance organizations
5. Preferred provider organizations (PPOs)

Insurance Companies These are the most widely used source for financing group medical benefits. In recent years, however, many large and medium employers have self-funded at least some portion of their total risk exposure, buying insurance only for protection against a very high level of claims. Proponents of the insurance alternative usually cite these advantages over other arrangements:

> Insurance carriers offer a broad range of products and design options from which each sponsor can select coverages to best fit the unique needs of the group in a single integrated package. For example, one carrier might insure all of the employee welfare plans — health, disability, and death benefits.

> As a third party in the claims administration process, an insurance company can minimize employer-employee conflicts and also reconcile problems between patients and health-care providers.

Insurance companies have the administrative systems and experience to perform certification reviews, claims audits, coordination of benefits, and other cost containment services. Insurance companies offer a variety of risk financing arrangements and rating techniques that allow employers considerable risk management flexibility.

Blue Cross/Blue Shield (BC/BS) Associations   These are nonprofit organizations that operate within defined geographic boundaries. Blue Cross plans cover hospital expenses and Blue Shield plans provide medical benefits. Typically, a Blue Cross association negotiates arrangements with its member hospitals to reimburse the hospital at a discounted rate when a subscriber incurs charges. For employees and dependents, this means that whenever they are treated in a participating hospital, full benefits are provided directly as a service. Blue Shield plans have been developed by state and local medical associations whose members agree to accept a fixed rate for medical and surgical services to subscribers. In most plans that rate represents full payment for the service and there is no additional charge to the employee.

In many areas of the United States, the two organizations have merged into a single association to gain staffing and administrative economies. Whether or not they are joined, each plan is governed by a local board in accordance with broad standards set by a national Blue Cross and Blue Shield association. To display the familiar "Blues" logotypes, the local plans must comply with the national standards.

Some of the advantages of using this source for providing group health benefits are:

The recognition factor: employees tend to view Blue Cross/Blue Shield as generic terms and have a high degree of confidence that hospitals and doctors will readily accept them upon presentation of a plan participation card.

The hospital discount is a competitive advantage for Blue Cross in rate setting compared with insured plans.

As nonprofit institutions, BC/BS associations are exempt from state income and insurance premium taxes giving them tax advantages over insurance companies.

The provision of benefits on the basis of direct service to the patient with BC/BS reimbursing the provider simplifies the process for employees and streamlines plan administration.

Self-funding Arrangements   Interest in this alternative has grown substantially in recent years as employers have sought ways to control health plan costs and gain relief from state insurance regulations. One national survey revealed that among twenty-six large companies the use of self-insured features rose from 19 percent in 1980 to 60 percent in 1984.[1] By eliminating or reducing insurance protection the employer saves on a carrier's retention charges, that portion of the premium that is not utilized to pay for claims. This includes the insurer's state premium taxes, administrative costs, risk and contingency expenses, and reserve requirements. Also, since only insured welfare benefit plans are exempt from the ERISA preemption of state laws, a self-funded plan only needs to satisfy federal requirements, which to date have been less comprehensive than most state regulations.

There are several different approaches to self-funding. One involves the creation of a voluntary employee beneficiary association (VEBA) by the employer. Under provisions of Internal Revenue Code Section 501 (c) (9), a tax-exempt trust can be established for the payment of medical expenses (and certain other) benefits for employees and dependents. The trust's investment income is tax exempt as long as it is used to provide benefits to members of the association. Although VEBAs continue to represent an attractive alternative for financing benefit coverage, their advantages have been diminished somewhat by funding limitations included in the Deficit Reduction Act of 1984 (DEFRA) and subsequent regulations.

Another common arrangement is stop-loss insurance, in which the employer assumes the primary risk but buys insurance coverage for protection against large losses. For example, the stop-loss coverage could apply to individual claims that exceed a specified amount, say $10,000, or aggregate claims once they surpass a targeted level, perhaps $1,000,000. A company can also remain within the traditional insurance framework and structure a similar arrangement called a minimum premium plan. The employer pays only a portion of its premium (typically about 10 percent) to the carrier to cover administrative and risk charges. The carrier processes the claims, which are paid from an employer fund or bank account up to an agreed-upon level. If that level is exceeded, the carrier assumes the risk and retrospectively charges the employer for the excess coverage.

When employers self-fund group health benefits, they may enter an administrative services only (ASO) agreement with an insurance company, or utilize a third party administrator (TPA) to handle claims management. Recent practice suggests that the latter alternative is favored by most benefits managers in the belief that TPAs are more responsive to the unique needs of individual plans and more intensely involved in cost containment efforts than insurers. An employee relations factor to consider in making the choice, however, is the credibility of a nationally recognized insurance company compared with that of a local claims processing group.

Health Maintenance Organizations (HMOs)   A comprehensive prepaid group health plan for employees and their families was established in 1938 by the industrialist Henry J. Kaiser. The Kaiser-Permanente Medical Program later served as a model in the development of the Health Maintenance Organization (HMO) Act of 1973. By 1987, largely because of the dual-choice alternative mandated in that law, there were approximately 25 million HMO participants in the United States.[2] The law specifies that companies with at least twenty-five employees living in an HMO service area must offer membership in that organization to employees as an alternative to regular group health coverage as long as the HMO meets federal qualification requirements and makes timely application. However, within any particular service area, an employer need offer the opportunity to only one of each of the two basic types of HMO.

1. Group practice ("closed panel"). Physicians are employed by the plan or are under contract, and most medical services are provided at a central location.

2. Individual practice association (IPA) ("open panel"). Physicians continue to practice medicine individually but are paid by the IPA on a fee-for-service basis according to agreed-upon fee schedules. Services to members are provided from a variety of locations.

For employees who elect HMO membership, the employer is required to make only the same level of payment as it is making to the conventional plan. If the HMO cost is higher, the added amount is normally paid by the employee. Although some employers have viewed HMOs as a government-imposed burden, many immediate and potential advantages are becoming apparent:

An emphasis on preventive medicine increases the likelihood of early diagnosis and treatment, thus reducing the incidence and costs of more serious illness.

There is a direct incentive for the HMO to keep members well to eliminate unnecessary hospitalization and to keep costs down.

Members receive comprehensive health care, often in an integrated facility.

The element of choice itself is consistent with the increasing desire among employees for flexible benefits plans.

Once an employee elects the HMO alternative, the HMO becomes the exclusive source of benefits from his or her employer's group health program for the next twelve months. Federal regulations require, however, that employers provide for a group enrollment period of at least ten working days each calendar year. During that time employees may transfer between alternative health plans without penalties or limitations based on their health status.

Preferred Provider Organizations (PPOs)   PPOs represent a relatively new alternative for health-care delivery, one that has developed rapidly in the 1980s, largely because of its cost containment potential. By late 1986 it was estimated that 21 to 25 million employees had a PPO option available to them.[3]

As illustrated in Exhibit 4.1, employers contract directly (or indirectly through an insurance company) with a provider organization, which secures agreements from physicians, hospitals, and/or laboratories to deliver services to group health plan participants on a discounted fee basis. The main incentives for the providers to accept lower fees are an expected increase in patient volume and expedited claims payment. In addition to offering employers a preferred pricing arrangement for health services, the PP organization also collects data necessary to evaluate provider performance, review utilization, and perform quality assurance checks.

PPOs are relatively unregulated with respect to rate-setting and requirements for employers. This allows a great deal of flexibility among the parties involved in structuring an agreement. Unlike the HMO dual-choice election, employees need not use PPO providers exclusively to obtain group health benefits. Instead there are incentives for not using other sources. For example, a plan might specify full coverage of allowable charges when a patient goes to a PPO hospital, but the standard 80 percent reimbursement of allowable expenses in excess of a $150 deductible allowance would apply if that person were admitted to a nonparticipating facility.

One potential obstacle to further growth of PPOs is their uncertain antitrust status. In 1982 the U.S. Supreme Court ruled that two medical societies in Maricopa County, Arizona, had engaged in price fixing by setting standards for physician's fees.[4] This case does not establish a broad precedent for PPOs, however, since the number of physicians involved was large enough

Exhibit 4.1 A Simple Preferred Provider Organization

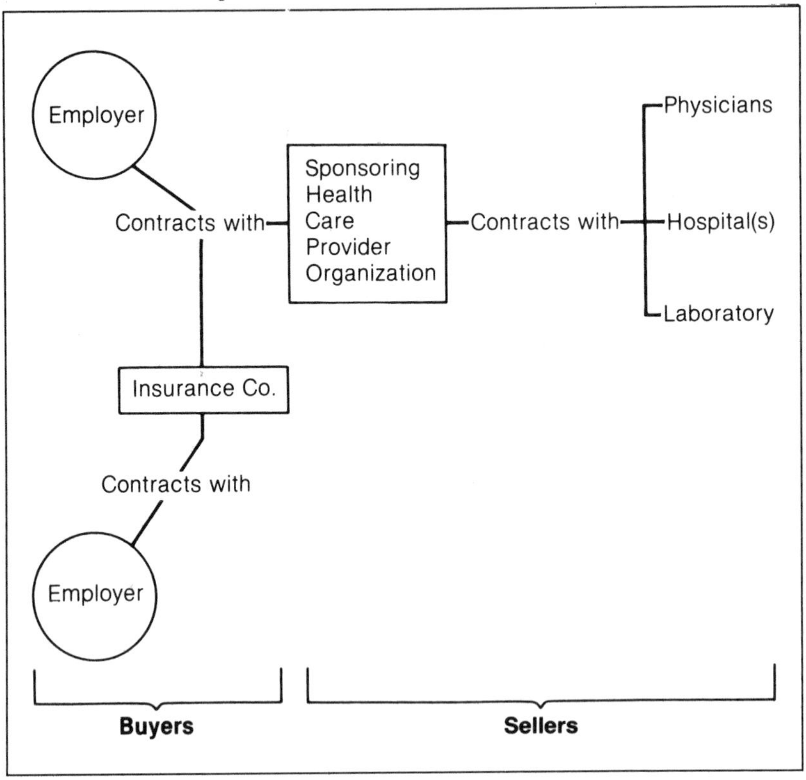

Source: Reproduced with permission of A. S. Hansen, Inc. Copyright 1984 by A. S. Hansen, Inc. All rights reserved.

to constitute a monopoly in the area. That status does not apply to most PPOs.

In "The Future of Health Care Delivery in America," a research report issued by Sanford C. Bernstein and Company in 1986, Kenneth S. Abromowitz predicted that by 1990 PPOs and HMOs would dominate the health-care delivery system in the United States.[5] At this time most corporate benefit managers seem unwilling to fully accept this prophecy but they are heartened by the prospect of greater competition among the various available sources of group health coverage.

Coverage and Plan Design

Early group health-care plans consisted of coverage for hospitalization expenses and physician fees for surgery performed in a hospital. These plans protected employees and their dependents against large expenses but also encouraged some inappropriate and excessive use of hospitals for medical care. Obviously, whenever a choice was available an employee would opt for treatment in a hospital rather than on an outpatient basis in order to receive plan benefits, even though hospitalization would tend to be more expensive, time-consuming, and inconvenient.

When major medical plans began to be introduced in the 1950s, the range of covered expenses in group plans was expanded to include a variety of outpatient treatments and procedures. In many arrangements, the basic hospital/surgical benefits would be provided by Blue Cross/Blue Shield and the major medical supplement was insured with a commercial carrier.

This plan design model is still widely used, although it has experienced many variations over the years. A typical contemporary arrangement is shown in Exhibit 4.2. The basic plan covers the full cost of hospital charges, surgical fees (based on reasonable and customary charges), and certain medical expenses, such as physician fees for hospital visits. The major medical plan supplements the coverage after a deductible amount (normally $100 per person) has been excluded each year. After that the plan pays for 80 percent of allowable charges, including a broad range of medical expenses, such as doctor office visits, prescription medicines, laboratory fees, and X rays. The employee is responsible for the remaining 20 percent of charges, and this form of coinsurance continues until the employee's share reaches a "stop-loss" point (typically $1,000). After that the plan pays 100 percent of the allowable charges.

Because hospital expenses are exempt from the annual deductible provision, plans that consist of basic plus the major medical supplement also tend to encourage overutilization of hospitals for health care. To counter this, and as part of a total cost containment strategy, most benefit plan authorities now recommend the comprehensive model (Exhibit 4.2) with a "front end" deductible applied to all expense categories.

According to one national survey of 250 major employers, only 14 percent were using a comprehensive design in 1979, but by 1984 52 percent of the same companies had adopted some form of that model.[6] Today, virtually all newly designed health plans contain the initial deductible feature. A covered employee or dependent must annually incur a stated level of expenses before *any* plan benefits are applied. The most common deductible is still

Exhibit 4.2   Alternative Medical Plan Designs

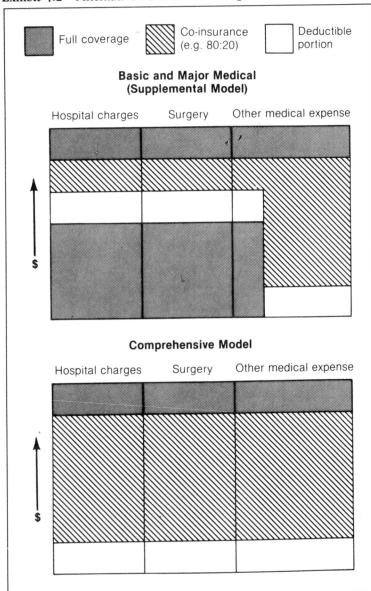

$100, but there is a clear trend towards increasing this amount to $150 or $200, and some plans base the deductible on a percentage of salary. The co-insurance and stop-loss provisions operate in the same way as in the alternative model. To neutralize the potential for employee dissatisfaction with the "front end" deductible, benefit plan designers have developed a variety of enhancements to accompany the introduction of a comprehensive medical plan. They have included a more favorable coinsurance provision (for example, 90:10 percent); waived deductibles when preferred providers are used; covered additional services; and offered greater flexibility in choice of optional plans.

Coordination of Benefits

An important consideration in managing group health plans is fixing responsibility for paying benefits when an individual is covered by more than one plan. This has become more of an issue with the steady increase of two-income families in the work force. Since 1971 the model guidelines issued by the National Association of Insurance Commissioners (NAIC) have governed the coordination of benefits (COB) among most plans in the United States. While NAIC standards are not mandatory, most states either incorporate the provisions into their insurance laws or informally adopt the same guidelines.

The basic objective of NAIC guidelines is to prevent duplicate payment for the same health-care service. It is essential that one plan be designated the primary source of benefits. In that way benefits paid from a secondary plan can be controlled so that the total benefits available do not exceed 100 percent of allowable expenses. The fundamental NAIC rule is that a plan covering expenses for an employee is primary and the duplicate coverage (as from a spouse's plan) is secondary. Another standard applies to paying benefits for dependent children when both parents are covered by a group plan. The original NAIC rule specified that the father's plan was always primary, but starting in 1987 the primary plan became that of the parent whose birthday (month and day) falls earlier in the year.

Another important change in NAIC standards that became effective in 1987 was the issuance of two alternate forms of coordination, which can reduce the financial consequences for a secondary plan. Under the basic rule, a secondary plan's payments are limited to the difference between primary plan benefits and 100 percent of allowable expenses. Now, alternatively, a plan may adopt one of the two new COB standards that permits a secondary plan to ensure that either

1. total reimbursement from both sources is not less than 80 percent of allowable expenses, or
2. total benefits are at least equal to what that plan would have paid if it were primary, and at least 75 percent above any deductible amount.

Cost Containment Strategies

From 1976 to 1981 health-care expenditures in the United States grew by an average of 13.9 percent a year.[7] As pointed out in Chapter 2, once organizations began to understand the enormity and complexity of the health costs issue, a multipronged strategic benefit management approach started to evolve. This occurred only after some firms suffered unpleasant side effects from attempting quick remedies, such as simply increasing employee contributions. Although not all of the following strategies can produce immediately measurable results for every employer, they each offer a range of options for which many impressive savings have been reported:

1. Data analysis
2. Alternative funding arrangements
3. Plan redesign
4. Claims administration efficiencies
5. Wellness programs
6. Employee communications
7. Health systems intervention
8. Individual case management

Data Analysis   Benefit managers become acutely aware of health-care costs whenever they receive a notification of an increase in plan premium rates. To challenge such adjustments and to evaluate compensating actions regarding funding, design, or administration, it is critical to have access to accurate, detailed information. By analyzing such factors as plan utilization patterns, relative costs for treating different medical conditions, variations in provider changes, and the ratio of administrative expense to claims payments, a benefit manager can formulate a selective cost management approach. Although small firms may lack the capacity to develop their own data banks for this purpose, local employer coalitions now make the service feasible for members on an information- and cost-sharing basis.

Alternative Funding Arrangements Since the advent of HMOs and PPOs, employers have the advantage of being able to shop for funding sources in a highly competitive marketplace. These newer types of delivery systems not only compete among themselves, but they represent a major challenge to the indemnity plans and service benefits offered (respectively) by insurance carriers and "the Blues." This situation, coupled with the feasibility of self-funding for most plans, has created a predominantly buyer-dominated market. Benefit plan managers need to be well informed about the characteristics of the many potential resources for funding the plans, and they need to be skillful in negotiating agreements.

Plan Redesign Projects of this type offer benefit managers excellent opportunities to analytically determine optimum ways to contain costs. By using a series of "what if?" postulations in combination with known cost data and experience-based utilization assumptions, the effect of various design changes on plan costs can be projected. As shown in Exhibit 4.3, a wide range of possibilities can be measured, after which the employer can decide on the best mix for achieving cost containment and other goals.

Another approach that combines the concepts of flexible benefits with cost containment is the multiple option design. This involves giving employees a choice of two or more plans with different levels of benefits and cost-sharing. The company makes the same contribution to each plan, but the employee contribution varies according to the actual cost of the option selected. To illustrate:

Single employee	*Plan A* (low option)	*Plan B* (standard option)	*Plan C* (high option)
Deductible	$500	$300	$100
Coinsurance ratio	80/20	85/15	90/10
Annual stop-loss	$2,000	$1,500	$1,000
Monthly contribution	$3.00	$9.00	$15.00

In adopting this type of model an employer effectively assumes primary responsibility for minimum coverage and requires employees to share in paying

Exhibit 4.3   Plan Redesign Assumptions

Benefit Change	% Change in Cost Compared with Standard Plan
• Add hospital precertification and concurrent utilization review penalty for noncompliance — $400 deductible	−3.0
• Add 100%/no deductible benefit for preadmission testing	+0.125
• Add 100%/no deductible benefit for second surgical opinion	+0.125
• Raise lifetime benefit maximum from $250,000 to $500,000	+0.5
• Add provision to cover hospice facility and birthing center as any other hospital	0
• Remove deductible and coinsurance carry-forward provisions	−0.5
• Remove waiver of deductible for accidents	−0.5
• Add $25 per occurrence deductible for *outpatient* emergency room treatment	−0.5
• Change calendar year deductible from $100/300 to $200/400	−2.0
• Change coinsurance percentage from 85/15 to 80/20	−3.0
• Change coinsurance stop loss from $500/1,000 to $1,500/3,000	−12.0
• Add per-hospital confinement deductible of $200	−2.0
Net Change	−22.75

the costs for more expensive options. Generally employees have found these arrangements to be very satisfactory since they gain the advantages of choice and have an opportunity every year to switch to another plan — in many instances, to an HMO.

Claims Administration Efficiencies   Whether a firm handles its own claims administration or uses an insurance company or TPA, it should be alert to opportunities for cost savings in this aspect of health benefit management. Because of the inherent monotony of the claims payment process, with or without computerization, an error rate of 5 percent is considered acceptable by many plan administrators. Some of the more frequent causes for costly errors are:

inadequate checking on eligibility
failure to apply coordination-of-benefits adjustments
incorrect application of deductibles and copayments
failure to observe plan maximum limits
failure to detect provider overcharges

Since employees are more likely to challenge an underpayment than to report receiving excessive amounts, the net effect of claims errors is additional cost for the employer.

The conventional remedies for lowering the error rate in claims handling are audits and special training for processors. Some companies have enlisted employees as auxiliary auditors. For example, in 1983, GenRad of Waltham, Massachusetts, introduced a hospital audit program that offered employees 50 percent of money saved (up to $1000) from corrected errors they discovered on their hospital bills. Employees are responsible for finding the errors and following up with the hospital to be sure that a correction is made.[8]

Wellness Programs   Also known as health promotion strategies, these programs are designed to identify employee's risks through assessment tools (history and examination) and then educate and motivate the individual to reduce those risks through participation in appropriate preventive or remedial programs. These may include smoking cessation, nutrition, exercise, stress management, and other positive health activities. Some large firms, such as IBM, Control Data, and Johnson and Johnson, and at least one major union (the International Ladies Garment Workers Union), sponsor comprehensive wellness programs. Thousands of other employers now offer a limited number of options to employees, often in conjunction with local chapters of a Y, the American Heart Association, the American Cancer Society, or some other health-related agency. In some instances, a wellness intervention can be in the form of an incentive reward. In an effort to discourage smoking, one company put a color TV in the nonsmokers' section of the employee lunchroom — paid for by revenues from the cigarette machine in the smokers' section.[9]

It is difficult to quantify savings from a wellness program because of the inability of attributing a health result to a discrete wellness intervention and the length of time needed to meaningfully measure the effects of change. However an ever-increasing number of employers seem willing to accept intuitively that improvements in employee health and fitness will result in lower group health plan costs — as well as improved attendance, morale, and productivity.

Employee Communications   Unless employees are convinced that cost containment programs are necessary and are willing to cooperate with employer initiatives, efforts to achieve objectives will be frustrated. Acceptance and positive involvement are essential, and they require a credible and candid communications approach. Benefit consultant Peter D. Abarbanel has identified five critical guides for developing an internal communications program on health-cost containment:[10]

1. Explain why cost containment is necessary.

2. Explain your program's goals.

3. Show employees how they can benefit.

4. Make imaginative use of communications media.

5. Keep employees informed and educated.

The introductory message from a company brochure entitled "Working Together Toward Benefits That Balance" (Exhibit 4.4) exemplifies an effective synthesis of these key points.

Health Systems Intervention   For many years employers were content to pay the bills for employee health-care plans while allowing provider practices to remain inviolate. Once business executives started to get more involved in health delivery systems as board members for HMOs, hospitals, Blue Cross/Blue Shield associations, and health system agencies, they learned that certain provider practices and behaviors were contributing to rising group health plan costs. This heightened awareness was a major factor in rapid development of health-care coalitions aimed at controlling costs in the 1980s. Prior to 1979 there were fewer than ten such organizations in the country. By 1986 there were more than 150.

A health care coalition has been defined as "a group of concerned leaders assuming greater responsibility and coming together in response to a need to develop local solutions to local health care problems, primarily high and rising health care costs."[11] A typical coalition's activities include member education, data base services, employee communications materials, facilitation of alternative delivery systems, utilization review management, and prototype benefit designs. Although business interests have been the moving force in the formation of most coalitions, many groups have a broad-based membership. The principal advocate for this concept is the Dunlop Group of Six, which encourages and assists coalition formation that

Exhibit 4.4   Benefits That Balance

November 1985

Recently, you received a letter from Dr. Vagelos announcing upcoming changes to Merck's benefit program for employees not covered by a collective bargaining agreement. This brochure — and the meeting you'll be invited to soon — will explain the significant new features and changes which will go into effect during 1986.

With these benefit changes, the Merck benefits program continues to be one of the strongest in our industry. "Benefits That Balance" describes our objective for the 1986 changes: balance within the program, which is necessary for Merck's business success and for your continued comprehensive coverage and protection under the benefit program.

♦ **Within the total benefit program,** we must allocate dollars to help employees meet their needs for both day-to-day protection and long-term security.

♦ **Within our business,** we must balance the need to manage benefit costs with the need to offer benefits that are responsive to the needs of a high caliber workforce.

In each case, we are balancing dollars and needs.

♦ **On the benefit side,** we are putting more emphasis on how we can work together to slow runaway health care costs so Merck can continue to provide substantial, Company-paid medical protection for you and your family. At the same time, we are extending the limits and adding new coverages under the medical plan, and improving the life insurance, survivor income benefits, disability income, retirement benefits, and the savings plan.

♦ **On the business side,** we will actually spend **more** on the total program, but we will achieve a program that provides **better control of medical costs.**

Please review this brochure carefully and share the information with your family so you are prepared to ask questions and learn as much as possible when you attend the upcoming benefits meeting we are arranging.

We are glad to move forward into the coming years with a total Merck benefits program that offers protection for you and your family and at the same time makes wise use of Company dollars. The new benefit program has been designed to control unnecessary health care expenditures and use the dollars saved — plus additional Company dollars — to enhance other benefit areas. Simply put, a program of **Benefits That Balance.**

Sincerely,

Walter R. Trosin

Walter R. Trosin
Vice President, Human Resources

Source: Courtesy of Merck & Company, Inc.

brings together groups with different perspectives to address health-care use and expenditure management. The six organizations in this group are the AFL-CIO, the American Hospital Association, the American Medical Association, the Business Roundtable, and the Health Insurance Association of America.

Individual Case Management   Until recently employers avoided any direct involvement in health-care delivery to employees, considering it to be an intrusion. But when some reports indicated that 80 percent of their rising health plan costs were being spent on only 20 percent of their employees,[12] that approach began to change. Today, many companies sponsor individual case management programs for claims with high costs potential. These are usually administered by outside professionals and aimed at ensuring that employees receive high-quality health services that are cost-effective. These programs vary in design, but they typically include elements of preauthorization of treatment and hospital admission, ongoing review of provider care, extensive communication with patients and providers, health promotion, and rehabilitation initiatives.

Continuation and Conversion of Coverage

After group health care had become a near-universal benefit during active employment, employees began to express concerns about events that could cause plan coverage for themselves or their dependents to cease. Some of these events were termination of employment, divorce or legal separation, death, and a dependent child becoming ineligible because of age or other factors.

To address these needs, most group plans permit conversion to individual coverage whenever protection under the employer-sponsored program ends. However, the benefits and provisions of these individual coverages are usually less comprehensive and more expensive than the group plans. Many state insurance laws set minimum standards for conversion coverage, and some have required limited periods of continuation of group coverage.

In 1986 group health-care continuation coverage became a federal requirement. The Consolidated Omnibus Budget Reconciliation Act of 1985 (COBRA) specifies that all group health plans (except for federal government and church plans) must offer this opportunity, as summarized in Exhibit 4.5. Employers are permitted to charge individuals the regular group rate plus a 2 percent administrative fee for this continuation coverage and to require coverage elections and premium payments within prescribed time periods. The coverage ends when a person becomes entitled to benefits under another group plan or, if it is later, when the maximum period of protection shown in Exhibit 4.5 expires. In cases where the latter applies, conversion options become available.

Exhibit 4.5 COBRA Group Health Care Continuation Requirements

Protected Individuals	Qualifying Events	Maximum Length of Coverage
1. Covered employee	• Termination of employment for reasons other than "gross misconduct" • Reduction in hours of employment, including layoffs and leaves of absence	18 months
2. Covered spouses and dependent children	• Death of employee • Divorce or legal separation of employee and spouse • Enrollment of employee in Medicare program	36 months
3. Covered dependent children	• No longer considered a covered dependent under the group plan based on age, marital or student status, etc.	36 months

Retiree Coverage

Another event that frequently precipitates a change in health-care benefits is retirement. When Medicare began operating in 1966, many benefit plan managers expected this federal program of health insurance for older Americans to become the prime source for satisfying the health-care needs of their retirees. Managers in companies that were already providing retiree coverages saw significant cost savings opportunities through coordination with Medicare; those in firms that had not adopted a group plan could consider relying on Medicare as a substitute form of coverage. Neither of these optimistic expectations was ever realized, for several reasons:

1. Unlike Social Security retirement benefits, which can begin at age sixty-two, Medicare coverage does not become available until age sixty-five (except for long-term disabled persons).

2. Since 1966 there has been an ever-increasing number of retirements prior to age sixty-five. One recent survey by Charles D. Spencer and Associates showed that in 105 companies, 80 percent of retirements occurred before age sixty-five, and a Conference Board study of 400 companies revealed an average retirement age of sixty-two or less in a majority of the firms. [13]

3. Since its inception, Medicare has progressively shifted cost responsibility back to its subscribers by raising deductibles, copayments, and the Part B (medical expenses) premium. In turn, claimants who have supplementary coverage through group retiree plans submit these ever-larger expenses to their employers' plans for reimbursement. The following comparisons illustrate the effect of progressive cost shifting on group plans:

	1966	1988
Inpatient hospital deductible	$40	$540
Individual copayment (61st–90th day of hospitalization)	10	135
Annual premium (Part B)	3	24.80

Medicare is definitely a factor in the design of health benefit plans for retirees, but managers must deal with this issue on a much larger scale. From a strategic perspective, it is essential to recognize that there are legal, accounting, and financial constraints as well as human resources concerns.

From a legal standpoint, there is the issue of the employer's right to terminate or reduce benefits for those already retired. Several U.S. district courts ruled in the early 1980s that this could not be done, but in 1986 the U.S. Court of Appeals for the Sixth Circuit reversed a lower court position in one case.[14] Until the matter is fully clarified most employers have concentrated on avoiding promises of specific levels of benefits for future retirees.

Because employers' liabilities for postretirement health benefits have been estimated to be in the trillions of dollars, the Financial Accounting Standards Board (FASB) now requires disclosure of these liabilities by corporations. And within the next few years FASB is expected to specify that these liabilities be included in corporate balance sheets. In the meantime, recent tax laws have imposed major disincentives for prefunding the obligation through tax-qualified trusts and insurance arrangements.

In spite of the various impediments, retiree health benefits are important to the success of many organizational strategies. They represent a significant part of the reward package that employees earn in return for long service with a company. Conversely, a failure to provide adequate coverage could adversely affect attitudes among active workers — particularly those nearing retirement. Also, organizations that want to stimulate early retirements as a key element in reducing staff size have discovered that the assurance of continuing health coverage is a critical factor in an individual's decision to elect retirement.

Disability Income Benefits

It is a near-certainty that everyone during his or her lifetime will miss at least one day of work due to illness or injury. Furthermore, the probability of an extended absence (i.e., ninety days or more) because of disability is four times greater than the probability of death during active employment years.[15]

These realities concern most employees and cause them to seek guarantees from their employers for income protection during periods of disability. Employers need to consider programs that provide adequate and equitable benefits but at the same time do not create disincentives to work. For a benefit plan manager the quest for the optimum balance between these diverse objectives can seem like searching for the Holy Grail.

Mandatory Coverages

As indicated in Chapter 3, several mandatory coverages offer income replacement benefits for disabled employees. Before analyzing an organization's need for disability income benefit plans, it makes sense to inventory the mandatory coverages that already protect employees and in most instances require employer payments. The Social Security program and state workers' compensation laws cover virtually all workers, and there are statutory requirements for nonoccupational temporary disability benefits in five states. In public employment, too, full income replacement during short periods of illness is normally a mandated benefit.

For benefit planning purposes, it is useful to view mandatory coverages as an employee's primary sources of income replacement with employer-sponsored plans serving as a secondary or supplemental source.

Tax Implications

Since certain benefits are not fully taxable, it is neither necessary nor advisable to design plans that replace an employee's total earnings during all periods of disability. To do so could result in an employee receiving a higher net income while disabled than while working — clearly a work disincentive.

Another important consideration for company benefit planners is the principle that employees generally are not taxed on the portion of disability benefits that have been paid for by their own contributions. For example, if an employee were required to contribute five dollars a month for long-term disability coverage and this represented half of the group premium rate, only half of any plan benefits received by that employee would be considered taxable. This suggests that contributory or employee-pay-all financing arrangements, which obviously conserve employer funds, can be quite acceptable to employees on the basis of tax effectiveness.

A summary of the current tax status of various forms of disability benefits is shown in Exhibit 4.6.

Current Practice

The form of income protection that employees receive from their employers during periods of disability is largely determined by their major occupational group placement. As shown in Exhibit 4.7, there are sharp distinctions between white-collar workers (professional, administrative, technical, and clerical) and blue-collar production workers. And within the former category there are further distinctions, often based on organization level.

Professional and *administrative* employees tend to fare the best in terms of adequacy of coverage. This is in part due to the cultural expectation called R.H.I.P., or "rank has its privileges." But it also results from the traditional management view that higher-level employees won't misuse generous allowances and are not frequently subject to disabling injuries or illnesses that would keep them from working.

Exhibit 4.6   Tax Treatment of Various Disability Payments

Type of Payment	Federal Income Tax	F.I.C.A.
1. Workers' compensation	No	No
2. Social Security	No[a]	No
3. Sick pay	Yes	Yes (for 6 months)
4. Temporary disability benefits (up to 6 months)	Yes[b]	Yes[b]
5. Long-term disability benefits (after 6 months of disability)	Yes[b]	No

[a]As long as adjusted gross annual income does not exceed $25,000 (single) or $32,000 (married and filing jointly); partially taxable above these thresholds.
[b]Except to the extent that the employee contributes for coverage.

Exhibit 4.7   Prevalence of Disability Coverages

Percentage of full-time employees by participation in employee benefit programs:

		Type of Employees		
Type of Plan	All	Professional and Administrative	Technical and Clerical	Production
Paid sick leave	70	93	93	45
Sickness and accident	49	28	35	69
Long-term disability	48	68	60	30

Source: U.S. Department of Labor, Bureau of Labor Statistics, *Employee Benefits in Medium and Large Firms, 1986,* (Washington, D.C.: U.S. Government Printing Office, June 1987).

Employees in this category normally receive their full pay under a sick-leave plan that covers both single and consecutive days of absence up to a scheduled annual or per-disability limit. This type of plan, sometimes called salary continuation, is usually not insured and the total number of days allowed is often a function of company service. The annual limit, for example, might be twenty days during the first year of service; this could increase to twenty-five in the next year, thirty in the following year, etc. In companies that do not have a sickness and accident insurance plan, sick pay coverage often continues for up to six months or longer for high-level and long-service employees. In such cases, however, the individual may receive full pay for a limited time and then a percentage of salary for the balance of any disability.

Sickness and accident plans are insured arrangements that replace a portion of pay (for example, 50 to 65 percent) after an employee has been absent for a week or so. In most cases, benefits are payable for a per-disability maximum of twenty-six weeks. While these kinds of plans are not widely used to cover the professional and administrative group, some benefit plan managers believe that they offer an effective means of supplementing sick pay allowances to fill gaps in income protection, particularly for short-service employees.

Whenever a professional and administrative employee has been continuously disabled for three to six months, and other company income replacement benefits have expired, long-term disability (LTD) plan benefits typically become available. These plans, which are usually insured, provide payments in the range of 50 to 60 percent of salary up to a maximum of about $5,000 (which is reduced for any statutory plan payments received). Unquestionably LTD plans are most meaningful to higher salaried employees, who are least likely to receive workers' compensation payments and who receive a low percentage of income replacement from Social Security.

Most LTD plans use a two-stage definition of disability. Initially, the test involves the ability of the employee to perform his or her regular job. If the disability precludes this, benefits are usually paid for two to three years. At that point, the definition of disability changes to the inability to perform any occupation for which the person is qualified by education, training, or experience. This split definition, often called "his occ/any occ," is intended to encourage rehabilitation and possible career redirection as well as to limit the employer's liability.

When a disability meets the "any occ" standard, LTD benefits ordinarily continue until recovery, death, or age sixty-five, when unreduced company pension plan benefits become available. In most defined-benefit pension plans, a participant's benefit accruals continue throughout the period of disability based on the salary being paid when the disability began.

Since *technical* and *clerical* employees are considered part of the white-collar work force, they frequently participate in the same plans as those that cover the professional and administrative group. However, based on management culture, economic considerations, or both, some companies do not fully extend all coverages to the former group. Evidence of such disparate treatment can be seen in Exhibit 4.8. At all levels of service, paid sick leave allowances average lower for the technical and clerical group. It is also noteworthy that short-service employees in this category typically receive allowances only slightly higher than those provided to production employees.

As indicated in Exhibit 4.7, sickness and accident insurance plans are slightly more prevalent here than in the professional and technical category. This is another manifestation of the tendency to provide somewhat less complete coverage for this type of employee since these plans only replace a portion of pay.

Among the three major occupational groups, blue-collar production workers receive the least comprehensive income replacement coverage from their employers. This results from several factors:

> The traditional view is that these employees are paid for hours worked or units produced and any other considerations result from employer beneficence, union power, or legal requirement.

Exhibit 4.8   Paid Sick Leave

Length of Service	All	Professional and Administrative	Technical and Clerical	Production
		Type of Employees		
6 months	11.7[a]	16.4	9.0	9.3
1 year	15.2	21.6	12.8	11.1
3 years	19.1	27.2	17.1	12.8
5 years	25.1	36.4	23.6	15.1
10 years	32.2	46.2	31.9	18.2

[a]Average number of days at full pay (annual allowance).
Source: U.S. Department of Labor, Bureau of Labor Statistics, *Employee Benefits in Medium and Large Firms, 1986,* (Washington, D.C.: U.S. Government Printing Office, June 1987).

Production employees have been the major beneficiaries of workers' compensation payments, and many receive a substantial percentage of income replacement from this source, Social Security, and other statutory coverages.

Wage structures for production employees are predominantly determined by market factors, and less weight is given to pay comparisons with employees in the two other occupational groups. To a large extent, this also applies to the benefits area, especially regarding wage replacement practices.

Characteristically sick pay allowances for production employees are limited to a maximum of about twenty days per year at full pay after ten or more years of service. In addition, plans for this group frequently contain restrictive conditions such as no coverage for one-day absences and required physician statements.

Blue-collar workers are normally covered by sickness and accident plans providing partial income replacement for up to twenty-six weeks, but employer-paid disability benefits beyond that are not common. In most instances employees in this category who suffer extended disabilities must rely on statutory plans, pension plans, or individually financed coverage for income replacement benefits.

Solving the Sick Pay Dilemma

In most organizations paid sick leave plans present ongoing problems for employee benefit and human resource managers. Management tends to view these plans as a form of "insurance" against a specific risk and expects them to be used only for that purpose. But many employees perceive the allowances as earned entitlements to be used as if they were vacation days. Although effective communication can help to resolve conflicts caused by these divergent positions, some organizations have found that there may be better resolutions through benefit plan redesign.

Federal government employees, for example, receive thirteen days of sick leave each year. Unused sick leave is carried over from year to year without limit during an employee's career. Before 1969, employees forfeited any unused sick leave at the time of their retirement, so they had an incentive to use all of their leave before retiring. It was estimated that about half of all retiring federal employees left with a zero sick leave balance prior to 1969.

In 1969, Public Law 91-93 granted future retiring federal employees service credit for accumulated sick leave in computing their retirement benefits. To help pay for the costs of these added credits (and other retirement enhancements), employee pension contributions were increased slightly. The primary intent of this change was to influence employees (especially those nearing retirement) to use sick leave allowances more prudently.

A report issued by the General Accounting Office in June, 1986, revealed that federal employees who retired in 1984 and 1985 had significantly higher average balances of unused sick leave than those who retired in 1968. The increases (38 percent and 46 percent respectively) were attributed largely to the effect of the retirement service credit for unused sick leave enacted in P.L. 91-93.[16]

Another way to solve the sick pay dilemma is to eliminate the plan as a discrete disability coverage. In 1983, the Cleveland Clinic Foundation (Cleveland, Ohio), after surveying and analyzing employee opinions, combined sick days, vacations, and holidays into a total time-off package.[17] Employees were given broad choice within certain limits of how to use the allowable time off without regard to "labels." At the same time, management gained better control over the timing of absences because of greater emphasis on advance scheduling. This concept of "total time-off" is becoming increasingly popular, particularly in hospitals and other organizations that need to operate continuously and are especially vulnerable to unscheduled absences and cannot close for holiday observances or vacation shutdowns.

A Total Perspective

Because there is almost always more than one group plan and several statutory programs addressing a wide range of situations, employees often become confused about their disability protections. By highlighting the applicability of specific coverages to the length of a disability, an employer can alleviate some of the confusion. Exhibit 4.9 is based on an illustration used by a major manufacturer to demonstrate the continuity and interrelationship of disability coverages for its professional and administrative employees.

Benefit plan managers also need to address the effect of disabilities on other benefit plans. Although income loss is the principal worry of most employees, there are also concerns about the status of group health and life insurance coverages. Most firms continue to maintain these benefit protections for disabled employees, and in many cases employee contributions (if any) are suspended. Whatever policy the employer follows, it is important to communicate essential conditions and requirements to employees so they have a realistic understanding of their benefit coverages throughout periods of disability.

Survivor Benefits

In 1979 compensation consultant and author David Thomsen observed, "I don't believe there is any other pay practice area that is as poorly matched to individual needs as group life insurance."[18] Thomsen saw the source of the problem as employers' overemphasizing the competitiveness of their group plans rather than stressing their social value. For the most part it appears that his analysis is still valid.

A typical group survivor benefit program for salaried employees in the late 1980s offers an array of uncoordinated coverages that produce benefits related more to the cause of death than to the status and circumstances of survivors. Employer-financed benefits payable in behalf of an employee killed while traveling on company business, for example, could be ten times greater than payments in behalf of a colleague at the same salary who died from an illness. This would be the case even if the latter person were survived by a dependent (nonworking) spouse with several young children and the accident victim had been single with no dependents.

Despite this continuing pattern, some employees have gained more control over their survivor protections as a result of the recent growth of flexible

Exhibit 4.9 Disability Income Protection Continuum: A Summary of a Company Program and Statutory Coverages for Professional and Administrative Employees

100%	66.67%	60%	
Salary Continuation	Short-term disability plan	Long-term disability plan	Pension Plan (or long-term disability plan depending on age when disability began)
	Workers' compensation	Social Security	
Workers' compensation	State-required nonoccupational disability	Workers' compensation	Social Security
State-required nonoccupational disability (where applicable)			Workers' Compensation
Up to 30 days a year →	After expiration of salary continuation up to 6 months →	After 6 months up to age 65 →	Thereafter

benefit programs. In most of these arrangements, employees receive a base level of protection and can elect to have additional life insurance coverage, which is paid for with flexible "credits," with payroll deductions, or some combination of the two. In some plans, employees can trade unwanted life insurance for other benefit coverage. Also, more specialized forms of group insurance, such as dependent life and survivor income benefits, are being offered now to employees on a voluntary or contributory basis.

If group life insurance and other survivor benefits are to become increasingly responsive to individual needs, benefit plan managers will need to work closely with their counterparts in company insurance departments. Failure to resolve differences in objectives or to share expertise can result in the selection of inappropriate coverages and wasteful expenditures.

The Role of Mandatory Coverages

Both the workers' compensation laws and Social Security have been designed to address the social responsibility issue in survivor benefits. As described in Chapter 3, eligibility for these mandatory coverages depends on such need-related factors as the age, marital status, and parental responsibility of the employee's survivors. Since employers are responsible for the entire cost of workers' compensation benefits and half of the Social Security payroll tax, it seems fair to cite these coverages as contributing to the social value of company-provided protections. Certainly they represent a foundation upon which to build a program.

Tax Considerations

The Internal Revenue Service (IRS) specifies that the cost of employer-paid group term life insurance coverage exceeding $50,000 must be included in an employee's taxable income. For blue-collar employees, who typically receive flat dollar protection of $5000 to $10,000, this means that their coverage is tax-free. And white-collar employees earning $25,000 or less in a year are not apt to have taxable income since their company-paid life insurance is rarely more than twice their annual salary.

The IRS publishes a Uniform Premium Rate Table that employers must follow in determining imputed income subject to tax. This table, which is similar to those used by insurance companies in setting individual premium rates, uses age classes, so older employees are assigned higher "charges" for their coverage. Exhibit 4.10 is an example of a company form, completed

Exhibit 4.10   Group Insurance Income Tax Information for Employees

---

**Analysis of Basic Group Life Insurance Imputed Income,
for Federal Income Tax Purposes, for** _____ Leslie Monet

Your Age As of December 31, _____ 47

[A] Your Annual Contribution for Group Life Insurance $ _____ 180
Taxable Year Ending December 31,

Gross Amount of Basic Group Life Insurance . . . . $ 120,000

Annual Exemption from Gross Coverage . . . . $ – 50,000

NET TAXABLE COVERAGE $ 70,000

Uniform Premium Rate,* selected from the Table below for your age,

$3.48 _____ times NET TAXABLE COVERAGE, ___ 70 ___ equals

VALUE OF COMPANY CONTRIBUTION PER IRS TABLE . . . . $ 243.60

Minus your Annual Contribution . . . . $ – 180.00

Equals IMPUTED INCOME SUBJECT TO TAX . . . . $ 63.60

UNIFORM PREMIUM RATE TABLE

Age Class	Per Each $1,000 of Insurance Annual	Monthly
Under Age 30	$ .96	$ .08
Age 30 to Age 34	1.08	.09
Age 35 to Age 39	1.32	.11
Age 40 to Age 44	2.04	.17
Age 45 to Age 49	3.48	.29
Age 50 to Age 54	5.76	.48
Age 55 to Age 59	9.00	.75
Age 60 and Over	14.04	1.17

*If you were insured for 12 months of the taxable year then the annual rate would be used; otherwise the monthly rate times the number of months insured would be used.

Source: Form courtesy of Pfizer, Inc.

by the benefits department, used to inform employees of imputed income resulting from group life coverage. It is distributed prior to the annual issuance of W-2 forms, which include the imputed income in "wages, tips, and other compensation" without further explanation.

As demonstrated in Exhibit 4.10, the value of the *company* contribution per the IRS table is reduced by the amount (if any) of the employee's contribution in determining taxable income. This is a very important factor in the design of a group insurance plan, and it has influenced a growing trend towards structuring plans on a contributory basis. For example, recognizing that younger single employees tend to have minimal needs for coverage and that married employees with young children and large home mortgages need a lot of insurance, many companies now offer core coverage plus optional supplements. If the core equals annual earnings, it will satisfy the needs of many single workers and not create taxable income for most employees even if it is fully company-paid. The supplements are usually available on a contributory or employee-pay-all basis, but at a generally favorable group rate. Employees who perceive a need for more than the core coverage can purchase supplemental insurance (one or two times salary), and by contributing to the cost avoid or minimize the creation of imputed income.

Another tax consideration for benefit planners is that the $50,000 exclusion is not available to executives who receive special supplementary group term life coverage based on their organizational rank or position level. Because they participate in a discriminatory plan, the cost of *all* their employer-paid term coverage must be included in imputed income calculations, according to the IRS.

Other Regulatory Considerations

Although the Age Discrimination in Employment Act (ADEA) generally prohibits mandatory retirement based on age, it does allow certain cost-justified reductions in benefits for older workers. A specific provision in ADEA permits reductions in group term life coverage for those who work past age sixty-five. Currently the "safe harbor" reductions that are sanctioned by the Equal Employment Opportunity Commission are:

1. '8 percent a year starting at age sixty-five, or
2. a one-time reduction of 35 percent at age sixty-five.

Some organizations have used more precipitous reductions, which they claim can be supported by internal and insurance carrier cost data.

Most states require, and virtually all group term life insurance plans include, a conversion clause. Typically this states that upon termination of employment an employee has the right to convert within thirty-one days all or a portion of the term coverage to an individual policy of permanent life insurance. There is no pricing advantage for the ex-employee, but anyone with a serious health condition might want to convert because no medical examination is required. Since this creates some adverse selection the employer is charged a fee, usually about $65 per $1,000 of converted insurance.

Types of Plans

In designing a complete group program of survivor income protections for employees, a benefit manager needs to consider all of the following types of plans:

1. Basic term life insurance
2. Supplemental term life insurance
3. Accidental death insurance
4. Business travel accident insurance
5. Survivor income benefit insurance
6. Paid-up life insurance
7. Universal life insurance
8. Surviving spouse's pension
9. $5,000 tax-free death benefit

Basic term life insurance is the most broadly applicable form of coverage. It represents the core of employer-provided insurance benefits. Because term insurance is intended purely for protection and does not accumulate cash values for the covered person, it is relatively inexpensive. According to the BLS Employee Benefits survey for 1986, virtually all medium and large firms provided this benefit. Coverage for two-thirds of all participants was based on their earnings. About one-half of these participants had coverage equal to annual earnings and two in five were covered for at least twice their annual rate of pay.[19] As stated earlier, production workers typically received a uniform amount of group term insurance averaging $10,000.

Supplemental term life insurance has become increasingly common as an optional benefit available to employees through group enrollment on a contributory basis. Because an employed group is rated a better risk than the general population, premiums for this type of coverage are less than individual rates. However the premiums are not as low as those for a noncontributory basic plan since the insurance carrier must make some allowance for adverse selection. This is based on the expectation that a disproportionately large number of employees with high-risk health profiles will opt for maximum supplements because of the low premiums and absence of medical examination requirements.

Accidental death insurance is a standard component in group survivor packages, and it is normally fully paid for by the employer. The most familiar arrangement, called "double indemnity," is to make this coverage equal the amount of basic term life insurance for each employee. Organizations purchase this coverage because the rates seem to be low, and insurance companies market it as a traditional benefit that must be provided for competitive reasons.

But some benefit plan managers now question the logic and cost effectiveness of the coverage. Leonard L. Berekson, a risk management consultant and professor of finance at the College of Business Administration, University of Nebraska at Lincoln, has made the following arguments against including any accidental death benefits in a group program:

It is relatively expensive coverage for the benefit provided.

There is a low probability of accidental death compared to death from sickness.

A person's need for life insurance seldom doubles if he or she dies in an accident.

Premiums are misallocated. The accidental death insurance premiums could be better used to purchase additional amounts of group life insurance.[20]

Faced with competitive realities, it seems unlikely that many firms will soon eliminate this coverage completely. However, as part of the flexible benefits trend, the lockstep with basic term insurance is not always automatic, and some plans separate the coverage into core and optional amounts. A major manufacturer of health-care products, for example, provides coverage equal to basic term, but only up to $25,000. Employees then have the option of purchasing additional amounts of accidental death protection (in units of $10,000 each) up to $300,000 at group rates.

Business travel accident insurance is another group benefit that addresses the cause of death without considering survivor needs. It has become a common feature because it responds to the perceptions of many employees that they incur added risks of accidental death as a result of employer-required travel. It has also been suggested that organizations provide the coverage as a buffer against adverse public reactions to deaths related to business travel accidents. In reality, the added risks may be nonexistent, and as indicated by Professor Berekson, the needs of survivors are not multiplied by a discrete factor. Nonetheless most organizations provide a benefit of three to five times salary when an accidental death is related to business travel. Some plans, known as "twenty-four-hour coverage," protect the employee during the entire period that he or she is away from home. To control premium costs, many plans limit coverage to travel "to and from the assigned destination"; others impose specific exclusions such as time spent piloting an aircraft, taking vacations in conjunction with business travel, working at another company location, etc.

A natural extension of the need-related basis of statutory survivor income programs is *group survivor income benefits insurance* (*SIBI*). SIBI plans seem to be ideally suited as a supplement to basic group term insurance. They provide a regular monthly benefit to a surviving spouse and dependent children, but unlike group term insurance coverage, payments usually are not made to any other class of beneficiary. A typical plan would specify a spouse's annual benefit at 25 percent of the insured employee's final pay, with an additional 5 percent for each dependent child (under age nineteen) and a maximum benefit of 40 percent. Some plans set the maximum benefit level at a higher percentage (for example, 70 percent) but apply offsets for Social Security and workers' compensation payments. In most plans, the spouse's benefit is payable until remarriage, death, or attainment of age sixty-two, whichever occurs first.

In spite of the obvious logic of SIBI, its growth as an employee benefit has been surprisingly slow. Only 13 percent of participants in the 1985 BLS study were covered by this type of plan. One reason for this has been the relatively high cost of funding continuing payments to younger survivors. Because it is an expensive benefit and does not offer the same values to everyone, its greatest potential for growth will be as an option in flexible benefits plans.

Paid-up life insurance is an approach used by a small number of companies to provide continuing protection for employees in retirement or following termination of employment. These are times when individuals may encounter serious problems with their survivor protections because they may be underinsured because of overdependence on their group term coverages, which expire at termination of employment and usually decline drastically at retirement.

there is no accumulated cash value in group term coverage.

conversion from group term to individual coverage is restricted to forms of permanent insurance, which is more costly.

premiums for conversion policies are based on present age; rates for retirees can be very high.

Group paid-up life plans combine term and permanent insurance features. Initially the entire protection is term, but each year thereafter a portion of the premium is used to purchase paid-up coverage, which becomes a nest egg for the employee. As the paid-up portion increases, the term portion decreases. To illustrate:

Year of participation	Total coverage	Term	Paid-up
First	$50,000	$50,000	—
Second	$50,000	$49,500	$ 500
Third	$50,000	$48,900	$1,100
•	•	•	
Tenth	$50,000	$42,500	$7,500
Terminates after 10 years in plan	$ 7,500	—	$7,500

These types of plans are not very common due to the IRS position that the cost of employer-paid insurance with permanent benefits is taxable as imputed income to the employee. Also, because of the mixture of permanent and term insurance, the plans are difficult to administer and to communicate.

A newer form of insurance that is being used increasingly to address the issue of post-employment protection is a *group universal life plan* (GULP). Like supplemental term life, this is offered to employees on a voluntary basis, usually without employer subsidies, at favorable rates. A unique characteristic of GULP is the inclusion of a side fund in which a portion of the premium is invested at competitive rates. In this way the covered individual can accumulate tax-deferred savings while maintaining a targeted amount of term insurance during active employment. If the savings are ultimately paid out in death benefits they are tax free.

Surviving spouse's pensions were mandated by ERISA (1974) and substantially broadened by the Retirement Equity Act of 1984. The current requirements are extensive and complex, applying to all defined benefit plans and most defined contribution plans. In general they specify that

1. If a married plan participant dies before retirement and has vested benefits in the plan, his or her surviving spouse must receive a "qualified preretirement survivor annuity" (PSA), which must be equivalent to at least 50 percent of the participant's earned benefits. PSA payments need not begin prior to the date the participant would have become eligible for early retirement (typically upon reaching age fifty-five).

2. At the time of retirement, married plan participants must receive their plan benefits in the form of a "qualified joint and survivor annuity" (J&S), unless, with spousal consent, another form of benefit payments has been elected in writing. This legally required J&S option provides an annuity for the participant's life with a reduced amount (at least 50 percent) payable to the survivor for life. A qualified J&S annuity is actuarially equivalent to a single annuity for a participant's life.

In addition to these legal requirements, most pension plans offer participants several other survivor options. A common choice is a *term-certain arrangement* in which an actuarially reduced amount is payable until the retiree's death. After that, if the elected term (for example, fifteen or twenty years) has not ended, payments will be made to the designated beneficiary for the balance of the term.

The *$5,000 tax-free death benefit* is a relatively minor consideration, but it is an opportunity for organizations to assist survivors without incurring the added costs of insurance. To qualify up to $5,000 for exclusion from the recipient's taxable income, employer payments must conform with conditions specified in Section 101(b) of the Internal Revenue Code. Essentially these require that the payments cannot be related to nonforfeitable entitlements of the deceased — except for distributions from a tax-qualified retirement plan.

Summary

In managing welfare plans, a benefit manager can expect close scrutiny from both employees and senior management. Employees place a high value on the group plans that protect them and their families against such occurrences as a major illness, a disabling injury, and death. And company executives recognize the need to develop cost-effective strategies to avoid excessive payments and to control employer expenditures.

Health care is generally considered to be the most visible of all benefits to employees, and since the beginning of this decade many aspects of group programs have changed. New delivery systems such as health maintenance organizations and preferred provider organizations have grown in importance, and self-funding of health benefits is now common. The basic design of most group plans is different from what it was ten years ago. Today a typical comprehensive model plan requires a covered individual to pay for the first $100 or $150 of medical expenses in a year before becoming eligible for group benefits. A variety of cost-containment strategies have evolved. The most successful ones have balanced the imposition of stricter requirements and reduced allowances with the addition of wellness features, utilization incentives, and increased flexibility in coverage choices.

The enactment of COBRA in 1986 made it possible for employees and dependents to continue group coverage at their own expense for a limited period of time following certain "qualifying events" including termination of employment. The law also significantly increased administrative requirements for benefit departments.

Although Medicare is available to retirees beginning at age 65, many companies provide supplementary coverage to that program and a broader range of benefits under their group plans to early retirees. As the ranks of retired employees grow, the future liabilities for these obligations are beginning to become enormous for some organizations, especially older firms.

To be effective in designing company plans that protect employees against income loss during periods of disability, a benefit program manager must be fully conversant with the applicable mandatory coverages and current tax rules on disability payments. The former represent the primary source of income replacement for employees. The latter should influence decisions regarding both benefit levels and provisions for employee contributions in company plans.

Surveys of current practice reveal some significant differences in the form and extent of employer-provided disability benefits for different classifications of employees. For example, allowances are typically most generous for professional and managerial employees. In part this results from cultural expectation, but it also relates to the fact that these employees receive lower percentages of income replacement from the mandatory programs than either nonexempt white-collar employees or blue-collar workers.

Pay protection plans covering short episodes of disability are a special challenge for a benefit manager. They are extremely vulnerable to abuse by employees who may feign illness in order to avoid forfeiting an unused balance of an annual allowance of sick days. Remedies used to address this problem have included alternative rewards and recognition for not using the full allowance, and the elimination of designated sick days through absorption within a total time-off allowance program.

Survivor benefits in many organizations are often a patchwork of disconnected employer-provided plans that create benefits based on salary levels and the cause of death rather than in relation to a survivor's status or needs. Recently, however, employers have begun to allow employees to exercise greater control over the selection of survivor coverages. Most companies now offer employees at least several levels of choice for supplemental term insurance. Also many firms now offer such specialized forms of insurance as dependent life, survivor income benefits, and universal life on a contributory or employee-pay-all basis. Sponsors of flexible benefit plans typically include a variety of survivor benefit and life insurance options.

In addition to the various insurance benefits, spouses of deceased employees with vested amounts in pension plans are entitled to pension benefits in accordance with ERISA and the Retirement Equity Act of 1984.

Notes

[1]Mark J. Ugoretz, "Mandated Benefits May Impinge on Basic Benefit Coverage," *Journal of Compensation and Benefits* 2, no. 1 (July-August 1986): 60–61.

[2]Glenn Kramon, "Overpayments on HMOs," *New York Times*, October 20, 1987, p. D2.

[3]Paul Susca, "Preferred Provider Organizations: The Alternative Choice," *CFO (The Magazine for Chief Financial Officers)* 2, no. 10 (October 1986): 87ff.

[4]Arizona v. Maricopa County Medical Society, 102 S. Ct. 2466 (1982).

[5]As reported in "End of Fee-For-Service?" *Employee Benefit Plan Review*, 40, no. 9 (March 1986): 32.

[6]Hewitt Associates, *Salaried Employee Benefits Provided by Major U.S. Employers: A Comparison Study, 1979 Through 1984* (Lincolnshire, Ill.: Hewitt Associates 1985), p. 20.

[7]Bernard Handel, *New Directions in Welfare Plan Benefits: Instituting Health Care Cost Containment Programs* (Brookfield, Wis.: International Foundation of Employee Benefit Plans, 1984), p. 6. This 330-page book offers an exceptionally comprehensive treatment of a total strategy for health-care cost containment.

[8]"The One Plan Approach," *Benefits News Analysis* 6, no. 3 (March 1984): 15.

[9]Jim Hirsch, "What's New in 'Wellness' Programs," *New York Times*, October 5, 1986, p. F19.

[10]Peter D. Abarbanel, "Communicating Health Care Cost Containment Programs," *Benefits News Analysis* 5, no. 1 (January 1983): 38–39.

[11]"Health Care Coalitions Try to Provide a Concerted Effort to Control Costs," *Employee Benefit Plan Review* 39, no. 10 (April 1985): 121.

[12]"Case Management: Going Beyond Claims Payment," *Employee Benefit Plan Review* 41, no. 6 (December 1986): 10.

[13]Steven Markman. "Once and Future Retirement," *Across The Board* 22, no. 5 (May 1985): 43.

[14]Hansen v. White Farms Equipment Co. et al. (Nos. 84-3870/3986).

[15]Jerry S. Rosenbloom and G. Victor Hallman, *Employee Benefit Planning*, 2nd ed. (Englewood Cliffs, N.J.: Prentice-Hall, 1986), p. 29.

[16]United States General Accounting Office, "Retirement Credit Has Contributed to Reduced Sick Leave Usage," (Washington, D.C.: U.S. General Accounting Office, 1986).

[17]"Employee Input Shapes Benefit Plan," *Impact*, 2, no. 16 (August 1, 1984): 5.

[18]David J. Thomsen, "Compensation and Benefits," *Personnel Journal* (June 1979): 358.

[19]U.S. Department of Labor, Bureau of Labor Statistics, *Employee Benefits in Medium and Large Firms, 1986* (Washington, D.C.: U.S. Government Printing Office 1987), p. 32.

[20]Leonard L. Berekson, "Group Accidental Death Benefits — An Inherent Contradiction," *Benefits Quarterly* 1, no. 1 (First Quarter 1985): 65–68.

5

Retirement Income and Capital Accumulation Plans

"In summary, this report calls for a long term shifting of dependency on pay-as-you-go financed federal programs such as social security, welfare and in-kind benefit programs to a balanced program of employee pensions, social security and individual effort."[1]

This reaffirmation of the concept of a balanced "three-legged stool" providing adequate income for retirees was a key conclusion in the final report of the President's Commission on Pension Policy in 1981. To strengthen employee pensions, the Commission recommended that a Minimum Universal Pension System (MUPS) be established for all workers, fully funded by employer contributions. To facilitate individual efforts, the Commission called for more favorable tax treatment of employee contributions to pension plans and encouraged the development of alternative work options for older employees.

While MUPS is not yet a reality, as of 1986 91 percent of employees in medium and large firms were covered by some type of pension or capital accumulation plan.[2] Also, in addition to accepting employee contributions to most savings and thrift plans on a pretax basis, many employers now offer employees opportunities to participate in a variety of "stand alone" savings and investment arrangements — with tax advantages — through salary re-duction agreements and payroll deductions. Sections 401(k) and 403(b) of the Internal Revenue Code govern these plans. Also, a small but growing number of firms (notably Travelers Insurance Company, Motorala, Honey-well, and Control Data Corporation) have designed a variety of work options for retirees including temporary full-time and permanent part-time employment.

On a national scale it would appear that employers are carrying their fair share of the responsibility for providing employees with adequate retire-ment income. But the approaches vary, and within any organization the employee benefit manager often faces perplexing and frustrating challenges in trying to select and design plans to achieve human resource (HR) goals. One reason for this is the need for close coordination with several other organizational units, typically finance, tax, and law, each with its own ob-jectives and priorities.

A finance director, for example, may want to terminate an overfunded pension plan to recapture excess assets for other company purposes; a tax manager may advocate amending a qualified plan to add a provision that appears to favor only highly paid employees; and the general counsel may decline to support a plan revision proposed by HR because of the absence of "published" legal precedent. Each of these positions could thwart the efforts of a benefit manager to attain HR goals. Of course, objectives will often be consonant, and cooperation among the several units will synergistically en-hance the processes of plan development and revision. To be effective, how-ever, a benefits manager needs to acquire a basic grasp of the financial, tax, and legal aspects of pension and capital accumulation plans, and to always be aware that the goals and priorities of the managers who direct those functions may conflict with employee benefit program initiatives.

Qualified and Nonqualified Plans

In determining methods of generating retirement income for employees, an organization must decide whether its plans will be "qualified" or "nonqual-ified." In this context the term "qualified plan" means a pension plan that covers a broad class of employees, meets numerous other requirements of the Internal Revenue Code (IRC), and receives favorable tax treatment. When-ever an organization wants to cover its entire work force or any large diversified group of employees, the advantages of a qualified plan are compelling. This is principally because the employer receives an immediate tax deduction for the amount contributed to the plan and the participants pay no current income taxes on that amount. On the other hand, there is no special tax treatment for a nonqualified plan. Employer contributions cannot be deducted until benefits are paid, and the participant is taxed at that time — or earlier if the plan is funded.

Whenever an employer wishes to implement a pension plan for a select group of employees such as key executives, the plan must be nonqualified. Although there are no special tax advantages for nonqualified plans, neither are there many regulatory requirements, and this approach is used quite frequently to provide supplemental retirement benefits for executives.

Defined Benefit and Defined Contribution Plans

The form of pension plan or combination of plans that an organization sponsors often mirrors the organization's culture. Strongly paternalistic employers favor defined benefit plans that produce predictable, secure, and continuing income for retirees. Firms that are highly risk-oriented tend to offer capital accumulation plans with a multiplicity of investment options. Companies committed to a participatory management style are closely associated with deferred profit-sharing plans.

Before any organization decides which approach to take, it needs to carefully explore the fundamental differences between defined benefit and defined contribution plans. In some cases, this will entail an either-or decision. Normally a company in its start-up phase will sponsor just one plan to provide retirement benefits. Financially stressed and opportunistic firms may consider substituting a less costly defined contribution plan for a defined benefit plan. But successful, growing organizations, are more likely to consider supplementing an existing plan with another type of plan and balancing the combination to achieve organizational objectives.

Statistics compiled by the Internal Revenue Service, particularly since the enactment of ERISA in 1974, show that a high proportion of new pension plans each year are of the defined contribution type. The Pension Benefit Guaranty Corporation (PBGC) and IRS data also show that terminating plans are more often defined benefit than defined contribution.[3] There can be little doubt that these trends relate closely to the more stringent and costly regulatory requirements placed on defined benefit plans by ERISA (see pages 55–62 and Exhibit 3.4). In addition to this discouragement through public policy, some employers have been enticed to terminate overfunded defined benefit plans to recapture excess assets resulting from greater-than-projected investment gains.

A manifest theme in the Tax Reform Act of 1986 was that qualified plans should focus on retirement income and retirement savings and not lump-sum distributions and early withdrawals. These objectives were reflected in numerous restrictions and tax penalties on premature employee withdrawals from defined contribution plans and in a 10 percent excise tax on employer reversions of excess assets from defined benefit plans. These actions have already changed management perceptions about the relative viability of the two types of plans and created renewed support for the defined benefit approach.

Another factor with human resource management implications is that unions historically have favored the defined benefit approach. In 1982, Thomas F. Duzak, director of insurance, pension, and unemployment benefits for the United Steelworkers of America, provided the following insights:

> Regardless of the implications of the employer, or any individual employee, defined benefit plans are clearly best suited and most compatible with the concept of employee benefits as a form of income replacement. . . . defined contribution plans which determine the amount of income to the employee as a function of the employer's profit, or the price of the company's stock, or the investment yield of a fixed pool of assets are not compatible with the concept of a wage versus income security trade-off.[4]

Defined Benefit Plans: Issues and Characteristics

In formulating a defined benefit plan, a benefits manager needs to resolve a number of basic questions:

1. What are the desired levels of income replacement?
2. To what extent, and how, will the plan be integrated with Social Security benefits?
3. What is the "normal" age of retirement?
4. At what age will early retirement benefits become available and what reduction factors will be used?

5. What factors will be considered in determining benefits?
6. How will benefits be financed?
7. What about benefits after retirement?

Income Replacement

The President's Commission 1981 report contained estimates of the income replacement rates necessary to maintain the preretirement standard of living for retiring workers at various income levels (see Exhibit 5.1). These rates were developed by reducing gross preretirement income by the amount of federal, state, and local taxes and by work-related expenses, savings, and investments that would not be applicable in retirement. Also, as Exhibit 5.1 shows, it was noted that Social Security provides significant income replacement in relation to covered wages, with the percentage levels being inversely proportional to earnings.

Although the percentages need to be adjusted periodically because of changes in tax laws and Social Security benefits, this model can be a useful tool for setting and explaining income replacement goals for retirees. The model also provides a perspective for addressing the question of integration with Social Security.

Integration

Integration is the process of coordinating pension plan benefits with Social Security to produce a total payment that replaces a targeted level of preretirement income. The Social Security benefits formula favors lower paid workers, and integration offers employers an opportunity to counterbalance that effect by discriminating in favor of the more highly paid groups. This consideration is given because employers pay for half of Social Security costs. Of course, IRS regulations restrict the degree of discrimination according to the method of integration. There are two basic methods.

1. *Offset* integration is the most commonly applied method for defined benefit plans, but it is not appropriate for defined contribution plans. It involves two steps: (a) the calculation of a targeted amount based on the plan formula, and (b) the subtraction from that amount of a portion of the employee's Social Security benefit. This determines the plan benefit, which, in combination with Social Security, should meet the organization's income replacement goals.

Exhibit 5.1 Hypothetical Social Security Replacement Rates Compared to Replacement Rate for Maintaining Pre-retirement Standard of Living at Three Alternative Earnings Levels[a]

	Maximum		Average[b]		Minimum	
	Social Security	Maintain Standard of Living	Social Security	Maintain Standard of Living	Social Security	Maintain Standard of Living
1. Never-married person.	28%	58%	42%	65%	53%	80%
2. Married couple. Only one spouse has earnings.	42	63	63	70	80	85
3. Married couple.[c] Both spouses have the same earnings.	40	63	54	70	77	85
4. Widowed person. Only one spouse has earnings.	28	47	42	53	53	64
5. Widowed person. Both spouses had same earnings.	20	47	27	53	38	64

[a]The three alternative levels of earnings are defined as follows. The *maximum* level is the wage base (i.e. the maximum taxable earnings) under the OASDI system, beginning with 1981 (after which time the wage base is automatically indexed). The *average* level is the level of the average male worker beginning with 1981. The *minimum* level is the level of a worker who always earns the federal minimum wage, beginning in 1981.

[b]Male worker's earnings level.

[c]Both spouses together earn this level.

Source: Office of the Actuary, Social Security Administration, U.S. Department of Health and Human Services.

To illustrate, suppose that the normal pension benefit for an employee in Company Y with thirty years of service at age sixty-five is 50 percent of final average pay (highest three consecutive years) less an offset of 50 percent of the employee's Social Security benefit. The benefit calculation for an employee retiring with final average pay of $40,000 and a Social Security benefit of $9,500 a year would be:

$20,000 − $4,750 = $15,250 + $9,500 = $24,750
(50% of   (50% of   (Annual   (Annual   (Total
$40,000) $9,500)   lifetime   benefit   annual
                    plan   from SS) retirement
                    benefits)   income — 62%
                                         of final avg.
                                         pay)

The current IRS rules specify that the offset cannot be more than 83⅓ percent of the primary Social Security benefit. But after 1988 the offset cannot reduce the original pension benefit (for example $20,000 in the calculation above) by more than half and may not be more than .75 percent of final average pay for each year of plan service.

2. The *step-rate* or *excess* approach can be applied to either a defined contribution or a defined benefit plan. Profit-sharing or money purchase plans may be integrated by making contributions at a certain percentage of salary up to a stated level and then having a "step up" to a higher rate of contributions for pay above that level. The IRS does not permit the spread between the two percentages to exceed the employer's contributions for old age, survivors', and disability insurance (currently 5.7 percent); and the integration point, or "breakpoint," cannot be higher than the Social Security tax base. A further restriction that becomes effective in 1989 is that the contribution percentage for the amount above the integration point may not be more than twice the percentage of the amount below.

In defined benefit plans, step-rate integration is used primarily when benefits are being accrued in relation to career earnings. For example, a participant's annual pension credit could be 1 percent of pay up to $15,000 and 1.5 percent on earnings in excess of that level. Thus, an employee who received $25,000 in 1988 would, for that year, accrue an annual pension benefit, payable at normal retirement, of $300 (1% × $15,000 + 1.5% × $10,000).

Currently the maximum spread between steps in defined benefit plans allowed by the IRS is 1.4 percent per year or a total of 37½ percentage points for career service. In 1989 those limits become ¾ of a percentage point per year of service and a maximum of 26¼ points.

Some of the pros and cons to be weighed in deciding which integration method is best for a particular plan are:

Offset integration generally produces larger credits for Social Security because it automatically recognizes increases in benefits from that program. Also, it ties in more closely with the concept of combining the two sources of retirement benefits to achieve a targeted percentage of preretirement income replacement. Among major employers, it is used more than twice as often as the step-rate approach.[5]

Step-rate integration is easier to explain to employees since they can visualize their pensions building each year by a discrete amount. Also, there is no need to introduce the "minus factor," which complicates offset-method communication. Step-rate integration permits more predictable cost projections and it is easier to administer since there are no Social Security calculations required.

Normal Retirement Age

The normal retirement age in a pension plan is the earliest age when participants can retire with full benefits. Since unreduced Social Security benefits are available at sixty-five (until 2003, when the eligibility age starts to gradually increase to sixty-seven), that continues to be the most common normal retirement age in private plans. The identification of this age is a key actuarial factor in funding a defined benefit plan, and although mandatory retirement is not generally prohibited, the term "normal" conveys a message of "expected retirement" to employees. In fact, prior to 1988 employers were permitted to cease benefit accruals for participants who continued to work past their normal retirement age, and most companies followed that practice. Federal law now prohibits a qualified retirement plan from reducing or freezing the rate of benefit accruals because of age.

Early Retirement

Early retirement provisions allow eligible employees to retire before the normal retirement age (usually sixty-five) and receive an immediate, reduced lifetime benefit. Virtually all private pension plans have such provisions, and most offer the option of deferring the pension and receiving an unreduced benefit at the normal retirement age.

The service requirement for early retirement is usually ten years, and the most prevalent minimum age is fifty-five. A policy permitting retirement before age fifty-five could cause employees to leave while still in their peak productive years. Yet the military and many public organizations use years of service as the only retirement criterion, thereby allowing employees to retire after twenty-five or thirty years of service while still in their forties, and sometimes with an unreduced benefit.

Initially, most defined-benefit plans applied standard actuarial reductions to benefits commencing prior to age sixty-five. This produced rather low benefit levels (for example, typically about 40 percent of accrued benefits at age fifty-five; 61 percent at sixty; 74 percent at sixty-two) and tended to discourage early retirement. Today, it is more common for plans to have subsidized early retirement schedules. Many large company plans, for example, now pay unreduced accrued benefits at age sixty-two. A more widespread practice is to use a uniform reduction schedule, usually 4 percent or 3 percent a year for each year prior to age sixty-five, so that benefits at age fifty-five are 60 percent or 70 percent of accrued amounts.

Early retirement provisions exist for the mutual interests of employees and employers. An employee who is not in good health, who has lost interest in a job, who wants to relocate, or who sees an opportunity for self-employment need not mark time until age sixty-five. Since Social Security retirement benefits become available at age sixty-two, that is a popular retirement age for many employees. Also, some company plans have a Social Security adjustment option that permits the employee to receive a larger-than-computed pension before the receipt of Social Security benefits, which is paid for by reducing plan benefits afterward.

Employers, too, welcome early retirement as an alternative to layoffs because of adverse business conditions, technological changes, or plant relocations. When companies have found it necessary to spur attrition through early retirement, common practice has been to specify a combination of age and service. This figure is frequently seventy or eighty, but the precise number will depend on the depth of the desired reduction in staff. Usually, no actuarial reduction factor is applied under programs of this type, and supplementary benefits are frequently provided at company expense until the employee qualifies for Social Security benefits. In recent years, most early retirement incentive programs have been offered for a limited time. (For example, the company offers a bonus to any one who retires within the next two months.) Such programs are called open-door policies or open-window policies. The major national union contracts guarantee special supplements to workers who are retired early at the company's option or under mutually satisfactory conditions.

Factors in Determining Benefits

One perception of pension benefits is that they are simply a reward for company service. Based on that one-dimensional view, some plans, mostly those that are negotiated or otherwise provided for blue-collar workers, accrue benefits as a flat dollar amount for each year of service. For example, if the plan specified accrual of a $15 monthly pension for each year worked, a thirty-year employee would receive a $450 monthly benefit at normal retirement. While this type of plan may satisfy union goals of worker solidarity and membership equality, it fails to relate the benefit to maintaining the employee's standard of living at the time of retirement. As a partial accommodation to that consideration, some plans for blue-collar workers now have split schedules in which participants earning above a stated pay level receive a higher monthly accrual per year of service.

Most pension plans for white-collar employees determine benefits according to a formula that includes earnings as well as service; examples were shown in the preceding section on integration. A key design issue in these plans is the definition of "earnings." For many years the term was equated with base pay, but there is a continuing trend toward including bonus payments, especially in organizations with many sales representatives who receive this form of compensation. Also, in recognizing service in the benefits formula it is now common to weight the computation to favor the final three to five years of service when earnings are usually the highest. Both of these considerations, while costly, are intended to make pensions replace realistic amounts of preretirement income.

When an organization installs a defined benefit plan it needs to consider the issue of crediting current employees for service before the plan was in effect. Although there are no legal requirements for granting any past service benefits, the employee relations advantages of recognizing preplan service convince most firms to provide some benefit credits. Unless this is done, current employees tend to perceive an inequity in being treated as if they were newly hired.

Of course, if the organization has a large number of long-service employees, the past service funding liability can be extraordinary. However, the

ERISA minimum standard allows up to thirty years to meet the obligations, and the benefit formula need not be as liberal as the future service formula. If, for example, the benefit for each year of future service was based on 1.5 percent of final average pay, the benefit for each year of creditable past service might be 1.0 percent of final average pay.

Financing Pensions

Approximately 93 percent of defined benefit pension plans in the private sector are noncontributory.[6] This is largely because most employer contributions to these plans are tax deductible, while employee contributions must generally be made on an after-tax basis. Only in certain public-sector organizations that *mandate* plan participation are pretax employee contributions allowed.

Another reason why contributory financing occurs so infrequently is the traditional position of organized labor. Unions tend to perceive income from defined benefit plans as deferred wages for which employers should be fully responsible. This position has generally prevailed in collective bargaining and has had a major influence on plans in organizations that seek to preserve a nonunion status.

Postretirement Increases

The specter of inflation eroding the purchasing power of retirement income is a constant concern of retirees and such organizations as the American Association of Retired Persons (AARP). Some of these fears have been allayed since 1975, when Social Security benefits were indexed to the Consumer Price Index (CPI). Since that time, annual adjustments have ranged from 14.3 percent in 1980 to 1.3 percent in 1987. Also, ERISA prohibits defined benefit plans from recognizing any postretirement Social Security changes as a means of reducing plan benefits.

For cost reasons, very few companies have indexed pension plan benefits with the CPI or any other automatic escalator arrangement. Alternatively, most firms with defined benefit plans grant postretirement increases on an ad hoc basis. A 1986 survey of fifty of the largest U.S. industrial firms conducted by the Wyatt Company revealed that forty-three companies had increased pension plan benefits at least once during the past ten years, with a median frequency of three times.[7]

In recognition of the compounding effect of inflation on pensions, most companies give larger increases to older retirees. For example:

Retired prior to:	Pension Increase
1980	10%
1984	7%
1988	4%

Guaranteed Account Balance Plans

A recent development in pension plan design is the guaranteed account balance plan, which some benefits authorities have called a defined benefit plan that looks like a defined contribution plan. In this hybrid design, benefits accrue in individual accounts as if specific contributions were being made each year. For example, the annual benefit accrual could be 4 percent of pay. In addition each account grows at a predetermined rate of interest. Benefits become payable at retirement or separation as either an annuity or a lump sum. For employees, this is very similar to a standard money purchase type of defined contribution plan, but in this case the account balance is guaranteed and the employee bears no investment risk. Since the plans are subject to defined benefit plan regulations, benefits must be "determinable." Although employers must satisfy ERISA funding standards, future costs are more predictable in this type of plan because benefits are based on each year's pay rather than being related to final earnings. The first major plan of this type was introduced by Bank of America in 1985, and the approach is expected to be influential in pension planning within the next decade.

Defined Contribution Plans as an Alternative to a Defined Benefit Plan

Defined benefit plans continue to be the most prevalent type of retirement plan. Employees cite their advantages in offering a known level of retirement income and the peace of mind obtained from the expectation of a "guaranteed" benefit. Employers favoring this approach observe that it permits orderly funding over many years, rewards the loyalty of long-term employees (including their preplan service), and integrates well with Social Security in a cost-efficient way.

But a minority of organizations have elected to use a defined contribution plan as the primary vehicle for providing retirement income benefits. In some cases this decision has been based mainly on financial considerations and an unwillingness to take the risk of being able to meet future funding obligations. In other situations, the reasoning reflects philosophical beliefs in how retirement credits should be earned and who should bear the risk of investment performance. The two most common forms of defined contribution plans that serve as a primary or major source of employer-funded retirement benefits are the money purchase type and profit-sharing plans.

Money Purchase Plans

These are plans in which the employer makes fixed and regular contributions for participants, usually as a percentage of pay. A typical plan would specify an annual employer allocation of 4 to 7 percent of pay. In addition, there may be provisions for voluntary employee contributions on an after-tax basis. The IRS limits total contributions to 25 percent of earned income and a maximum of $30,000 per year for *all* defined contribution plans in which the employee participates. All contributions are held in trust funds and the employee can usually choose from among several investment options with different degrees of risk and growth potential. At retirement, accumulated funds are used to provide annuities, although most plans also offer a lump-sum distribution option. For participants who terminate their employment prior to retirement, vested benefits are held in trust, continuing to appreciate in value until the date of early retirement eligibility. At that time an annuity can be payable or a lump-sum distribution elected. When the latter occurs prior to age fifty-five, there is an additional federal income tax of 10 percent. To avoid this penalty, recipients can roll over the distribution into an IRA or another qualified retirement plan within sixty days of receipt. Subsequent withdrawals after age fifty-nine and a half escape the tax penalty.

A notable example of the money purchase plan approach is the retirement system utilized by most colleges, universities, and private schools, and by some tax-exempt research institutions in the United States. This pension system is administered for approximately 900,000 individuals employed in nearly 4,000 organizations by the Teachers Insurance and Annuity Association–College Retirement Equities Fund (TIAA-CREF) headquartered in New York City. The employers make fixed contributions to employee accounts according to the terms of the participating organization's money purchase pension plan. These contributions are fully and immediately vested and totally portable within the TIAA-CREF system. Each participant allocates the employer contributions (and any employee supplements) on a percentage basis between two investment accounts, TIAA and CREF. The most common arrangement is 50 percent to each.

An allocation to TIAA is a premium payment for a contractually guaranteed amount of future lifetime annuity income. This benefit cannot decrease, and it will almost certainly increase through the addition of dividends. CREF allocations are used to purchase accumulation units representing shares of participation in a common stock investment fund. The value of a unit in this fund is adjusted monthly to reflect changes in market value of the investment portfolio. Short-term fluctuations can cause accounts to drop as well as rise in value, but between 1952, when the fund was introduced, and the end of 1986, the unit value increased from $10.43 to $101.49, with additional appreciation in accounts resulting from dividend additions.

At retirement, CREF *accumulation* units are converted into *annuity* units according to actuarial factors, and the value of a unit is then adjusted annually to reflect market changes. In most instances the variable annuity from the CREF fund provides inflation protection to the extent that stock values rise at least as sharply as the Consumer Price Index (as they have tended to do over the long run). Participants can of course provide their own hedge against a decline in the annuity unit value by balancing their retirement income with fixed payments from TIAA.

All money purchase plans do not offer the wide range of flexibility and portability inherent in the TIAA-CREF system. However, the features of fixed employer contributions, choice in investment of contributions, alternatives for receiving benefits, and opportunities to achieve portability through rollover of lump-sum distributions are common characteristics in many plans of this type.

Profit Sharing

Among employees in medium and large firms who are covered by some form of retirement or capital accumulation plan, approximately 22 percent participate in a profit-sharing plan, and for more than one-third of these employees that represents the sole source of employer-funded retirement income benefits.[8]

Profit sharing in the United States dates back to 1794 when Albert Gallatin, secretary of the treasury under Presidents Jefferson and Madison, introduced it into his glassworks in New Geneva, Pennsylvania. Initially profit sharing was viewed as an extension of democracy in industry and, somewhat later, as a means for stimulating workers to be more productive by offering incentives in the form of participant "shares" in growth. To reinforce the incentive aspects with timely and meaningful rewards, most of the early plans were of the cash type, providing payments soon after profits could be determined. There are still plans of this type being utilized by some firms with fully taxable cash payments issued quarterly, semiannually, or annually.

After 1940, when deferred profit-sharing plans were given special recognition and favorable tax treatment in the Internal Revenue Code, the advantages of this approach for creating retirement income began to appeal to a number of organizations. Tax-qualified deferred profit-sharing plans provide for employee participation in profits according to a predetermined formula for allocating contributions among the eligibles and for distributing accumulated funds at retirement or upon termination. The IRS allows employers annual tax deductions of up to 15 percent of participants' compensation (recognizing individual compensation up to $200,000 a year starting in 1989) for profit-sharing contributions. Many plans also accept employee contributions, some on a pretax basis. Most plans specify a uniform percentage of pay for all participants with the percentage varying from year to year based on profits. In such plans the maximum annual award is 15 percent (the deductible limit), and in unprofitable years there are no awards. Some plans weight the contribution level for participants according to company service, the amount of the individual's plan contribution, or both.

Typically, participants in deferred profit-sharing plans can choose among several investment funds for their allocations, with periodic opportunities for reallocations. Many plans also permit loans and hardship withdrawals subject to IRS limitations and sometimes more restrictive company rules. Benefits are distributed according to plan vesting and retirement eligibility provisions, and the employee can choose among several methods of payment including annuity, lump sum, and installments, depending on the type of termination and individual preference.

Exhibit 5.2 illustrates the use of deferred profit sharing, combined with an IRC Section 401(k) savings and investment plan as a key component in the overall retirement and income security program at Motorola in 1987. Introduced in 1947, the profit-sharing plan provides for company contributions based on profits, employee (basic) contributions, and reallocation of forfeitures (relinquishments) to participant accounts. In addition, employees may defer salary payments into the savings and investment (SIP) plan, and these amounts are added to their accounts in the profit-sharing trust fund.

Exhibit 5.2   Motorola Profit Sharing and SIP

```
┌─────────────────────────────────────────────────────────────────────────┐
│  ┌──────────────────────────┐            ┌──────────────────────┐         │
│  │   Basic Contributions,   │            │        SIP           │         │
│  │  Company Contributions,  │            │    Contributions     │         │
│  │     & Relinquishments    │            │        Only          │         │
│  └──────────────────────────┘            └──────────────────────┘         │
│                                                                           │
│  ┌──────────────────────┐  ┌──────────┐  ┌──────────────────────┐         │
│  │        Loans         │  │          │  │     Withdrawals      │         │
│  │ • Only for           │  │  Profit  │  │ • Only for           │         │
│  │   reasons allowed    │  │ Sharing  │  │   reasons allowed    │         │
│  │   by plan            │  │  Trust   │  │   by plan            │         │
│  │ • Amount based       │  │  Fund    │  │ • SIP money only     │         │
│  │   on combined        │  │          │  │ • 1 per year         │         │
│  │   vested value       │  └──────────┘  └──────────────────────┘         │
│  │   of p/s & SIP       │                                                 │
│  └──────────────────────┘                                                 │
│                                                                           │
│  ┌─────────┐  ┌────────┐  ┌──────────┐  ┌──────────────┐                  │
│  │ General │  │  Bond  │  │ Motorola │  │Preretirement │                  │
│  │  Fund   │  │  Fund  │  │  Stock   │  │    Fund      │                  │
│  │         │  │        │  │  Fund    │  │              │                  │
│  └─────────┘  └────────┘  └──────────┘  └──────────────┘                  │
│                                                                           │
│  ┌─────────────────────────────────────────────────────────┐             │
│  │                    Distributions                        │             │
│  │ • Full payment of profit sharing at retirement,         │             │
│  │   disability, death or termination after 11             │             │
│  │   years of service                                      │             │
│  │ • Full payout of SIP if you leave Motorola              │             │
│  │   for any reason                                        │             │
│  │ • Vested portion of profit sharing paid out             │             │
│  │   if you leave Motorola with less than                  │             │
│  │   11 years' service                                     │             │
│  └─────────────────────────────────────────────────────────┘             │
└─────────────────────────────────────────────────────────────────────────┘
```

Source: Courtesy of Motorola, Inc.

Participants have four investment funds from which to choose, and loan and withdrawal opportunities subject to plan rules. Distribution of vested benefits occurs at retirement or termination; there are a variety of payment options.

In addition to this program, Motorola employees have been covered since 1978 by a noncontributory defined benefit pension plan that is integrated with Social Security benefits. Prior to that time, the company offered employees the opportunity to participate in a supplementary contributory retirement plan.

The opportunity to include motivational features in a tax-favored plan appeals to the many employers who use profit sharing as a primary pension plan or a significant component in their total retirement benefits package. Profit sharing has been especially popular with nonunion firms. In a major study of personnel practices in twenty-six large nonunion companies published in 1980, it was noted that five firms used profit sharing as their primary retirement benefit and eleven had supplemental plans. A leading behavioral scientist at one of the companies observed:

> Through this system more people come to understand criteria of organizational effectiveness and the interdependence of individual and organizational goals. When all members of the group benefit from profit sharing, group involvement in increasing profits is encouraged. Profit sharing constitutes a lesson in economics supporting the free enterprise system.[9]

The Profit Sharing Research Foundation in Evanston, Illinois, is an excellent source of further information about profit sharing. Exhibit 5.3 is a list of advantages and disadvantages of profit sharing as a source of retirement income prepared by the Foundation.

Defined Contribution Plans as Supplements to a Defined Benefit Plan

The more familiar role for defined contribution plans is that of supplementing a defined benefit plan. This is a common combination in large firms, and it enables employees to consider the defined contribution plan as either the third leg of their retirement income stool or a source for accumulating funds to be used for shorter-term needs and goals.

The three most widely adopted forms of supplemental defined contribution plans in the private sector are savings (thrift) plans, employee stock ownership plans (ESOPs), and freestanding cash-or-deferred arrangements qualified under Section 401(k) of the Internal Revenue Code. Another type of plan, available only to certain nonprofit organizations and public school systems, is a tax-sheltered annuity, or 403(b) plan.

Exhibit 5.3   Advantages and Limitations of Deferred Profit-Sharing Programs

Advantages		Disadvantages	
Company Point of View	Employee Point of View	Company Point of View	Employee Point of View
• Company contributions directly reflect corporate performance. Plan is *funded within the company's ability to pay.* • Enhances feeling of partnership, encourages *teamwork and productivity,* recognizes worth of individuals. • Provides a good reason for *periodic communication* about the company, its progress, plans, and problems. • Is, by its nature, *a fully funded plan.* • Improvements *affect future benefits* but do not increase past service liabilities.	• *Opportunity to share directly in success of the company.* • Chance to *affect size of benefits through effective work performance.* • Develops sense of *belonging.* • Account is in *name of* individual employee. • *Good investment returns augment participants' accounts.* • Is *financial reservoir for* loans/withdrawals for hardship, home purchase, college education of children.	• Can only inadequately recognize *past service* (before plan was in effect). • Takes *time* for accounts to build up significant amounts. Favors younger workers, discriminates against older, long-service employees. • *Variability in company* contributions and investment returns makes income replacement planning difficult.	• Company *contributes little* to profit sharing in a poor year. • *Employees bear burden* of poor investment performance. • *Market depreciation* can more than offset gains from company contribution and fund earnings. • Rewards or penalizes employees for factors *not under their direct control.* • Fails to recognize properly *prior service* before plan was established.

continued

Exhibit 5.3 *Continued*

Advantages		Disadvantages	
Company Point of View	*Employee Point of View*	*Company Point of View*	*Employee Point of View*
• Accrues benefits today in relation to today's pay. *"Career average" plan* reflecting the member's current contribution to company performance, not his or her contribution at point of retirement. • *No termination insurance premiums or 30% net worth exposure.* • Less need for *actuarial reviews.* • Is a *multipurpose plan* — i.e., investment/capital accumulation, system incentive, severance pay, and benefits during employment.	• *Flexibility inherent* — i.e., employee contributions, cash-deferred options, employee investment choices, transfer privileges, range of disbursement alternatives. • Nonintergration with Social Security, *no offset feature.* • *Rapid vesting.* • *Participation in risk/ reward free enterprise* system.	• Philosophy of profit sharing *may not mesh well* with a company's particular management style. Many managers are not ready to share information, responsibility, and profits with their people.	• Does not provide *guarantees or known* level of retirement income.

Source: Courtesy of Profit Sharing Research Foundation, 1718 Sherman Ave., Evanston, Ill. 60201.

Savings Plans

These are the oldest and most prevalent of the supplemental type of plans. Instituted in the petroleum industry during the 1920s, they receive special tax treatment under Section 401(a) of the Federal Revenue Code and now cover more than one-fourth of all employees in medium and large companies.[10] The key characteristics of a savings plan are individual participant accounts, employee contributions, employer matching contributions, several different investment options, limited in-service withdrawal and loan provisions, and lump-sum distribution provisions upon retirement or termination.

The essential ingredient in a savings plan is employee initiative. Unless the employee elects to participate, there will be no employer-provided benefit. In most plans, an employee can elect to contribute (through payroll deduction) up to 6 percent of pay to an individual account administered by an outside trustee. That amount will be matched in some proportion by the employer. Most plans also permit employees to make unmatched voluntary contributions of up to an additional 10 percent of pay.[11] Since the issuance of proposed regulations for Section 401(k) in late 1981, virtually all savings plans accept salary reduction amounts as plan contributions, thereby enabling employees to reduce their current tax obligations. This advantage has increased the appeal of savings plans to employees and led to a surge in the adoption of new plans. All employee contributions, whether before or after taxes, must vest immediately.

The most common proportion of employer matching contributions in a savings plan is 50 percent. However, some firms believe in rewarding seniority and increase the rate of match according to years of service. Others have incorporated profit-sharing features by providing for higher rates of matching based on profit performance. Another variation, sometimes used to stimulate plan participation among lower paid employees, is to match smaller rates of employee contributions at a higher percentage, for example, 100 percent on the first 2 percent of pay contributed and 50 percent on the next 4 percent of pay contributed.

Employer contributions are subject to ERISA minimum vesting standards but most plans have more liberal provisions. This is because they are intended to serve as a recruitment attraction and to produce early rewards. It is not unusual for a plan to provide for full and immediate vesting of employer contributions, and a very typical schedule specifies 20 percent vesting after one year of participation, 40 percent after two years, etc.

Two benefit plan design issues for setting up a savings plan are the number of investment options and the frequency of reports and reallocation opportunities. Because these are by nature *contributory* plans, they tend to create high employee expectation levels. The feeling that "since it is my money I should be able to control it as a personal investment" is bound to surface. Realistically, a multiplicity of options and monthly account statements could create huge costs and burdens. Currently a range of three to five investment choices and quarterly reports are considered reasonable.

Withdrawal and loan features in savings plans are similar to those in profit-sharing plans. Companies often impose time limits and periods of suspension from plan participation for withdrawals of employer contributions, but they do not place the same degree of restriction on employee contributions. Of course employees are also discouraged from gaining access to all accumulated funds prior to retirement by various excise tax provisions.

At retirement, the normal benefit is a lump-sum distribution. Although the tax advantages of this form of payment were curtailed after 1986, recipients continue to retain much flexibility in how they use the funds, and this method is consistent with the character of a supplemental capital accumulation plan. Also, most savings plans offer retirees, but not other terminating employees, annuity options.

ESOPs

Employee stock ownership plans, which first appeared in the 1950s, are based on the so-called people's capitalism theories of Louis Kelso, an attorney and economic theorist. Kelso conceived a system that combines leveraged financing with a qualified stock bonus plan. In a prototypal arrangement, an employer establishes a tax-exempt trust that borrows funds from a bank based on the sponsoring organization's credit. The funds are then used to purchase employer stock, which is held in the trust. On an annual basis the employer makes tax-deductible payments through the trust to repay the bank loan. At that time the trust distributes stock of equivalent value to the accounts to employee participants in a stock ownership plan, which it directs and administers.

This type of plan, known as a leveraged ESOP, appeals to some employers as a tax-efficient way to raise capital. It has not been favored by closely held corporations or those that do not wish to give employees too much control of the business. In the years from 1975 to 1986 Congress sanctioned another type of employee stock ownership plan that produced relatively small benefits for employees and tax credits for employers. The early versions of these tax reduction plans were based on capital investment and were known as TRA-SOPs. They were superseded in 1982 by payroll-based plans (PAYSOPs), and by 1986 28 percent of employees in medium and large firms were covered by such plans.[12] The Tax Reform Act of 1986 eliminated tax credit ESOPs but preserved and extended some advantages for other types of employee stock ownership plans. Until 1990, for example, ESOPs in general are exempt from the 10 percent excise tax on early distributions from defined contribution plans, and there are special estate tax advantages if employer securities in the estate of a deceased participant are sold to an ESOP.

ESOPs have a major disadvantage in comparison with other forms of defined contribution plans in their inherent lack of investment choice and diversification. All the benefit eggs are in one basket. While proponents cite the motivational aspects of this feature, it places participants' accumulations at considerable risk. The success of an ESOP depends heavily on business results and the valuation of employer stock in the market, but employees do not have full control over either of these factors. Despite the temporary upswing in the plan adoptions during the period that tax credit plans were allowed, ESOPs have received relatively limited attention as an employee benefit. A 1986 survey by the National Center for Employee Ownership revealed that there were 7.4 million employees participating in non-tax credit plans, mostly in smaller firms.[13]

Freestanding 401(k) Plans

A provision allowing employees to reduce a portion of pay and to have that amount contributed to a deferred compensation plan was included in the Revenue Act of 1978. Specifically, Section 401(k) was added to the Internal Revenue Code to become effective in 1980 subject to issuance of regulations. Proposed regulations were not published until November 10, 1981, but many employers found this to be sufficient authority to implement cash-or-deferred arrangements (CODAs), and within the next year the term "401(k)" became part of our popular culture.

As discussed earlier, the application of 401(k) provisions to savings plans with employer matching contributions is now nearly universal. But some of the first 401(k) plans were of the freestanding type, consisting entirely of elective deferrals by employees. One such plan was adopted by Honeywell in 1982. It provided for "pay conversion" of up to 4 percent of pay and three choices of investment funds. Although there was no employer match, the plan proved attractive to employees because of the opportunity it offered to reduce current income taxes and to have investment earnings be tax-sheltered. Freestanding CODAs are now sponsored by only 8 percent of major U.S. employers,[14] but they continue to be a viable alternative to a subsidized savings plan, particularly for small organizations and new ventures that wish to conserve employer funds.

Whether operated separately or joined with a matched savings plan, 401(k) arrangements are subject to special IRS regulatory conditions and limitations. Key among these are:

1. The maximum annual salary deferral allowed for any employee as of 1988 was $7,313. This amount is subject to cost-of-living adjustments in future years.

2. Plans must pass a special nondiscrimination deferral test that is designed to prevent highly paid employees from taking substantially greater advantage of this tax shelter than lower-paid employees do (see Exhibit 5.4).

Tax-Sheltered Annuities (TSAs)

Since 1942 the Internal Revenue Code (IRC) has permitted arrangements in which employees of certain nonprofit groups and public school systems could purchase annuities on a pretax basis. Millions of such employees participate in these TSA plans, which are mostly administered by large insurance companies, and in a small number of plans there are also employer contributions.

Until 1987 TSAs were minimally regulated through section 403(b) of the IRC, but the 1986 tax act imposed numerous restrictions designed to make them more closely comparable to 401(k) plans. Among these were:

1. Annual deferrals of salary are limited to $9,500.

2. Catch-up deferrals (attributable to preparticipation service) are subject to a $3,000 yearly limit and a $15,000 lifetime maximum.

3. Coverage and participation rules for qualified pension plans will apply to TSAs with employer contributions starting in 1989.

4. TSA contributions are reduced by any elective deferrals to a 401(k) plan.

In spite of these limitations, TSAs continue to be a tax-effective and flexible vehicle for eligible employees to supplement the primary pension plan sponsored by their employers and to build additional retirement income.

Exhibit 5.4 401(k) Nondiscrimination Rules

Basic Requirements

Plan sponsors must calculate the average deferral percentage (ADP) of salary for all eligible employees, including those who defer no portion of their pay. Then the ADP for the highly compensated group must be compared with the ADP for the lower paid.

Definition of Highly Compensated Employees

- 5 percent owners of the enterprise
- employees earning more than $75,000 in the current or preceding plan year
- the top one-fifth of all employees ranked by compensation and earning more than $50,000 in the current or preceding year
- officers who earn more than $45,000

The Test

The ADP for the highly compensated group is limited to the higher of:

1.25 times the ADP of the lower paid

or

2 times the ADP of the lower paid but
not to exceed 2 percentage points

Application

Average Salary Reduction for Lower Paid	Which Test Gives Maximum Benefits for Highly Compensated?	Reduction Allowed for Highly Compensated
1%	2 times ADP	2%
2		4
3	2 percentage point limit	5
4		6
5		7
6		8
7		9
8		10
9	1.25 times ADP	11.25
10		12.5

Consequences of Failing the Test

If at the end of a plan year there are excess deferrals in the accounts of employees in the highly compensated group the amounts must, within 2½ months, be recharacterized as after-tax plan contributions, or distributed in cash. Otherwise the employer will have to pay a 10% excise tax on the excess amounts.

Summary

The traditional model depicting sources of retirement income in the United States is a stool with three legs: (1) Social Security benefits, (2) individual effort, and (3) pension plan payments. Employers pay a major role in securing each of these legs. They pay half of all Social Security taxes, provide a variety of part-time and temporary work options for retirees, and sponsor pension plans in which employees accumulate retirement benefits during their active working years.

Because of the intricate financial, legal, and tax aspects of pension plans, a benefit program manager needs to work closely with organizational counterparts responsible for those functions, and become familiar with the fundamentals of plan qualification, design, and funding.

In order to be "qualified" a pension plan must conform to stringent requirements contained in the Internal Revenue Code. Except for special plans for executives that exclude other employees, thereby failing the discrimination standards for qualification, most pension plans are qualified. Qualified plans offer significant tax advantages for both employers and employees.

A basic decision in any organization is whether to emphasize a defined benefit or a defined contribution form of pension plan. There are numerous variations of each type, and it is becoming increasingly common, particularly in large firms, to have a combination of plans. Regardless of the type of plan selected it is important to focus on income replacement goals and to consider how much of the goals will be satisfied by Social Security benefits at different income levels.

Defined contribution plans, particularly savings arrangements in accordance with I.R.C. Section 401(k), have expanded very rapidly in recent years. However the Tax Reform Act of 1986 may have removed some strong attractions to these plans for employees by restricting the amount of annual contributions and penalizing early withdrawals.

Guaranteed account balance plans are a hybrid form of pension plan introduced by a major bank in 1985. For employees these plans offer many characteristics of a defined contribution plan but without the risk of investment loss. For employers they are classified as defined benefit plans, therefore annual additions to the fund can be based on actuarial considerations.

Notes

[1]President's Commission on Pension Policy, *Coming of Age: Toward a National Retirement Income Policy* (Washington, D.C.: President's Commission on Pension Policy, 1981), p. 9.

[2]U.S. Department of Labor, Bureau of Labor Statistics, *Employee Benefits in Medium and Large Firms, 1986* (Washington, D.C.: U.S. Government Printing Office, June 1987), p. 81.

[3]Charles Lambert Trowbridge, "Defined Benefit and Defined Contribution Plans: An Overview," in *Economic Survival in Retirement: Which Pension Is for You?*, ed. Dallas L. Salisbury (Washington, D.C.: Employee Benefit Research Institute, 1982), p. 16.

[4]Thomas F. Duzak, "Defined Benefit and Defined Contribution Plans: A Labor Perspective," in *Economic Survival in Retirement*, ed. Salisbury, p. 69.

[5]*Salaried Employee Benefits Provided by Major U.S. Employers in 1986* (Lincolnshire, Ill.: Hewitt Associates, 1987) showed that 91 percent of 812 employers had pension plans; 64 percent of the plans used the offset method and 24 percent used the step-rate excess approach.

[6]*Salaried Employee Benefits.*

[7]*A Survey of Retirement, Thrift and Profit Sharing Plans Covering Salaried Employees of 50 Large U.S. Industrial Companies as of January 1, 1986* (Washington, D.C.: Wyatt Company, 1986), p. 9.

[8]*Employee Benefits in Medium and Large Firms, 1986*, p. 81.

[9]Fred K. Foulkes, *Personnel Policies in Large Nonunion Companies* (Englewood Cliffs, N.J.: Prentice-Hall, 1980), pp. 229, 248.

[10]*Employee Benefits in Medium and Large Firms, 1986*, p. 81.

[11]Both the 6 percent and 10 percent levels are limits set by the IRS to prevent this type of plan from discriminating in favor of highly compensated employees (who are presumed to have more discretionary income available for tax-favored savings plans).

[12]*Employee Benefits in Medium and Large Firms, 1986*, p. 81.

[13]"Survey Tracks ESOP Surge," *Employee Benefit Plan Review* 41, no. 5 (November 1986): 36.

[14]*Salaried Employee Benefits.*

6

Paid Time Off

Employee benefit practitioners tend to be ambivalent in dealing with issues related to paid time off. Although information on paid vacations, holidays, and other eligible days is prominently communicated in annual personalized benefits statements and in the benefits sections of recruitment brochures, a typical response from a benefits manager to a question about a particular coverage is "check that with Personnel." Still, the cost of paid time off consistently ranks as one of the highest benefits expenses in the annual U.S. Chamber of Commerce surveys, and most internal company reports categorize the expense as "indirect compensation," an equivalent term for employee benefits.

Perhaps the best evidence of the benefit profession's less-than-enthusiastic attitude about this subject is its treatment in one of the leading handbooks in the field. This reference consists of nearly 1,500 pages of detailed information about all forms of benefit plans. Paid time off is briefly discussed in a section covering fewer than four pages.

Although the management of paid time off does not require the level of skills needed to design health cost strategies or to do pension planning, it is an important area calling for effective cooperation between benefit planners and human resource administrators. Many of the newer types of flexible benefit programs (to be discussed in Chapter 8) offer employees choices to "buy" and "sell" vacation days with flexible credits that alternatively can be used to obtain other kinds of benefits or cash. The design of such programs requires a clear understanding of employee preferences, the impact of time off on organizational operations, competitive considerations, and costs. It is likely in the future that benefit managers will be paying more attention to the paid time off category and utilizing input from employee relations and personnel administration in the planning process.

The Shrinking Work Week

When the United States was an agrarian society, work for many was practically continuous. It could be characterized by the familiar rhyme: "Man works according to the sun but woman's work is never done." Very simply, hours were long and no one was paid for not working.

As the nation moved into an industrial age in the mid nineteenth century, employer awareness developed about the effect of time off on productivity, and some humanistic firms recognized individual needs for rest and relaxation. Also, more time off without loss of pay became a major goal of the emerging trade unions. Because of these factors, between 1890 and 1940 the standard work week in the manufacturing sector dropped from sixty hours to forty-two hours, or by 30 percent.[1] Today the typical production worker is scheduled to work forty hours and white-collar office employees, particularly those working in large cities, often have thirty-five or thirty-seven-and-a-half hour schedules.

It is important to recognize that as organizations shortened their work hours, employee base weekly income almost always remained the same. This means that employee's hourly rate of pay increased and the employer was effectively providing pay for time that was no longer being worked. This has definite cost, productivity, and capital utilization implications for the organization, but employees rarely perceived the change in that context. Since their take-home pay did not change, employees did not recognize that they had made an economic gain.

Paid Time Off Allowances

Most economic forecasters believe that any future expansion of paid non-working time is more likely to result from an increase in the number of paid time off allowances than from any shrinking of the work week. Companies now vigorously resist such increases, however, and there are recent examples of reductions, both unilateral and negotiated. Notably, the latter occurred in the automobile industry in the early 1980s when the United Auto Workers union accepted "take backs" of paid personal allowances in order to gain greater job security. A persuasive employer argument at the time was that their Japanese counterparts had a significant competitive advantage in productivity because employees in Japan were receiving far less generous paid time off allowances.

Payments for time not worked in U.S. industry are now reported by the U.S. Chamber of Commerce to average 13.6 percent of payroll.[2] Included in this calculation are vacations, holidays, personal time off allowances, guaranteed pay plans, and paid rest periods. Realistically, the challenge for benefit and human resource managers is to contain the costs for these items while continually seeking better ways to arrange and package the allowances to balance the often-competing factors of operational requirements, costs, and employee interests.

Vacations

Traditionally, there have been two basic reasons for granting vacations. One is the employee's need for time away from the physical demands and mental stresses of work. The other is the belief that employees should be rewarded with vacations in exchange for their commitment of service to the organization. Lately, two other reasons have been receiving increased attention. The sabbaticals, or extended vacation programs, first negotiated by the United Steelworkers Union in the 1960s were designed to create additional jobs. This confirmed the view that unions recognize that employers often find it necessary to hire more workers to replace vacationers and, as a strategy, bargain for kinds of arrangements that produce long periods of absence.

Also, a small but growing number of firms are voluntarily offering sabbaticals to employees after stated periods of service, but with the condition that the extended time off be used for self-improvement purposes. This type of plan is patterned after the traditional sabbatical for tenured university faculty members. Other programs have been tied to social service. For example, IBM and Xerox have granted paid leaves of up to one year for employees who perform community work or teach.

In 1977, Tandem Computers of Cupertino, California, asked its employees which benefits they wanted most. Workers rated sabbaticals ahead of pensions. By 1986 nearly one-quarter of Tandem's work force, having met the four-year service requirement, had taken six-week sabbaticals plus normal vacation time at full pay. At that time the head of human resources summarized the company view: "Short-term you could say there is a negative productivity impact. Long-term, we believe there is productivity enhancement."[3]

Service Requirements   The service requirements for vacation eligibility tend to vary by industry, locale, and company size. Although the gap between professional and administrative and production employees has closed substantially over the years, the latter still must wait longer to earn vacation time, especially the first and second week of eligibility, in many companies (see Exhibit 6.1).

Obviously an organization needs to weigh its obligations to senior employees against the recruiting incentive of early eligibility whenever it considers altering service requirements for vacations. Whenever there are salary compression problems, real or perceived, a clear advantage in vacation entitlement is an effective counterbalance to help preserve positive morale among long-service employees. At the same time, an employer is disadvan-

Exhibit 6.1   Paid Vacation by Length of Service 1986

	Average Number of Days Per Year	
Years of Service	Professional and Administrative Employees	Production Employees
6 (months)	6.0	5.0
1	10.1	7.5
3	11.0	10.2
5	13.5	12.0
10	16.5	15.3
15	19.0	17.9
20	21.2	20.3
25	22.7	21.7
30	23.4	22.1

Source: U.S. Department of Labor, Bureau of Labor Statistics, *Employee Benefits in Medium and Large Firms, 1986* (Washington, D.C.: U.S. Government Printing Office, June 1987).

taged in trying to hire experienced workers if they are going to lose paid vacation eligibility by changing employment. For this reason some companies use an age factor or credit years of prior experience in their vacation policies.

Pay Considerations   When a vacation check was viewed as an act of employer beneficence, pay administration was simple. Today the expectation of vacation pay as an earned right is dominant, and challenges and questions concerning the rate of pay, qualifying conditions, and timing of eligibilities create the need for precise policy statements and consistent administration. Some of the issues that need to be addressed are:

1. Will vacation pay calculations recognize any employee compensation other than base pay? For example, shift differential payments, overtime earnings, or incentive compensation?

2. Will vacation pay be based on scheduled hours or hours actually worked during the preceding twelve months (or calendar year)?

3. Under what circumstances, if any, can an employee be paid in lieu of a vacation?

4. How does a disabling accident or injury that occurs during a vacation period affect vacation pay?

5. What is the effect on an employee's vacation pay if, during the vacation period, an immediate family member dies? the employee is required to serve on a jury?

6. What pay rate applies if an employee is required to come in to work during a vacation?

7. What is the basis for granting pay for unused vacation at the time of retirement? death? other terminations?

Where collective bargaining agreements are applicable, these kinds of subjects are specifically covered in a contract book. Managers in nonunion firms need to ensure that they are spelled out in supervisory guides and employee handbooks. Otherwise uneven applications and perceptions of discriminatory treatment are certain to occur.

A pattern established in the steel industry in 1969 that has had limited growth to date in other industries is the vacation bonus. This is an extra amount of pay, which the employee receives on top of the regular rate, to help cover the added expenses associated with travel and recreational vacations. In most cases this is a flat dollar allowance, say fifty dollars a week.

A variation applied by at least one firm is to pay for vacations at the rate of time-and-a-half.

Vacation Deferrals   Most vacation policies state or imply that if all allowances are not taken in the year earned, or at least by the end of the following year, they are forfeited. The message to employees, in other words, is "use it or lose it." Lately, some organizations have recognized that such an inflexible policy can be counterproductive. As increasing numbers of employees become eligible for four or more weeks per year, some individuals find it difficult to schedule so much time, and being "forced" to take vacation time causes negative feelings. The option these organizations offer is known as vacation deferral, or vacation banking.

Philosophically, the alternative of converting vacation time to deferral of income is a departure from the traditional view that an annual vacation is necessary for rejuvenation and productive performance. However, proponents of this feature point out that most plans limit the amount of the annual eligibility that can be deferred. For example, one large firm allows banking of each year's vacation allowance in excess of three weeks. Another employer permits employees with six weeks of eligibility to defer just one week. With such limitations, the plans can continue to fulfill their primary purpose while offering greater flexibility to employees.

In most instances, vacation banking arrangements have been handled as nonqualified plans, with the employer simply agreeing to pay for the banked time at a later date. However, because of accounting accrual restrictions, employee expectations that future payouts should be at higher rates, and the lack of tax advantages, some firms now combine vacation deferral with a qualified savings plan. One manufacturing company, for example, permits long-service employees to roll over up to seven days of unused vacation each year (with a cumulative maximum of thirty days) into its savings investment plan. In this way the employer has effectively made a tax-deductible defined contribution to the plan and the employee can direct the tax-deferred amount and earnings for future needs.

Holidays

Although a number of traditional holidays have been observed by American employers for many years, pay for what is essentially involuntary time away from work was largely limited to salaried employees prior to World War II.

For example, 88 percent of 2,200 manufacturers surveyed by the Conference Board in 1939 provided certain holidays with pay to the salaried group, but only 12 percent did so for hourly workers.[4] This disparate treatment changed during the war years, when improvements in holiday payments were classified as "fringes" and therefore exempt from the federal government's wage controls. By 1945 paid holidays were for the most part provided to both types of employee on an equal basis.

Today employees in the United States average about ten holidays per year,[5] although the actual number in any one organization is influenced by both industry characteristics and geographic patterns. Banks are controlled by state laws that specify certain closing days and frequently prohibit closing on two consecutive weekdays. Retailers must be sensitive to the fact that many potential customers are off from work on such traditional holidays as Washington's birthday, Columbus Day, and the Friday after Thanksgiving. Store closings on those days are rare. Contrastingly, manufacturers favor these holidays because they are weekend extenders and do not create the operational inefficiencies of a midweek observance. Hospitals exemplify the type of organization that can never suspend operations to recognize a holiday. Because they must provide continuous patient and emergency service, they need to create arrangements that permit an equitable allocation of traditional holidays and substitute days to all employees.

Geographic variations include a slight lag behind East Coast practice in the number of holidays provided by West Coast employers. There are also some unique observances in certain states. For example, in a number of southern states Jefferson Davis's and Robert E. Lee's birthdays are observed, and in Massachusetts and Maine, Patriot's Day is a standard holiday. In Alaska, Seward's Day is widely recognized.

Observances and Employee Interests   Regardless of industry or area, six holidays are recognized and paid for by virtually all employers in the United States:

New Year's Day

Memorial Day

Independence Day

Labor Day

Thanksgiving Day

Christmas Day

These are the core holidays and it is reasonable to assume that their designation in any organization will be acceptable to the vast majority of employees. In selecting observances beyond this core, and subject to legal, operational, and competitive considerations, an employer should weigh employee interests. Indeed, a few companies have even allowed employees to vote on the selection of an annual floating holiday.

A Thanksgiving Friday observance, which creates a four-day "minivacation," is an example of a holiday that ideally matches employee preferences with operational efficiencies, at least in manufacturing industries. Similarly, Washington's Birthday, Martin Luther King Day, and Columbus Day, all designated by federal law and in most states as Monday holidays, satisfy mutual interests of employees and employers.

Good Friday and Christmas Eve are two days frequently included in company holiday schedules. They generally prove to be popular choices with employees because of the extended time off that they create. However, although the reasons for their selection are mostly secular, employers need to analyze their work force demographics and attitudes to determine if these observances are appropriate in relation to employee religious affiliations and beliefs. If there are significant numbers of non-Christian employees in the organization it may be preferable to substitute floating holidays or personal holidays for these designated dates.

Floating holidays are those that are selected for observance on a year-by-year basis. For example, if a company and a union were negotiating a three-year contract and agreed to add one holiday in each of the years, they might designate a "floater" to be observed as follows:

First year — Friday after Christmas

Second year — Columbus Day (Monday)

Third year — July 5th (Friday)

In each instance, the selection reflects union (employee) preference and employer objectives.

Personal holidays can range from special recognition of the employee's birthday to a day or more that can be used by each employee, subject to certain prior notification and approval rules, for any reason. Advocates of this type of holiday cite its appeal to individual needs as well as the advantages of spreading observances over the entire year while avoiding operational suspensions. Detractors point out the administrative burdens of year-round activity plus the difficulties of limiting approvals of requests for popular dates such as Good Friday if it is not a company holiday.

Holiday Pay   In addition to providing extra pay for time worked on a holiday (which is considered to be a form of overtime premium, not a benefit), companies find it necessary to specify a number of rules governing the granting of holiday pay. From management's viewpoint, one of the more important factors is some qualification on work in the holiday week. A familiar statement in union contracts and employee handbooks is "In order to be eligible for holiday pay, an employee must perform work on the day before and the day after the holiday."

Such clauses are intended to deter absenteeism, particularly on days surrounding a midweek holiday. Usually, when absences are for illness and specified personal reasons, compliance with these rules is waived.

Although most companies consider all employees immediately eligible for holiday pay, it is not unusual to withhold this benefit from temporary hires and summer replacements. And inevitably, employees or their unions question the basis of holiday pay. As with vacation pay, employers need to consider recognizing shift differential payments, overtime earnings, and incentive compensation in the calculation of holiday allowances.

Paid Personal Absences

Employers recognize that at one time or another, employees will be affected by events beyond their control that will cause absences. Some of these events, such as mandatory jury service and short-term military duty, are part of citizenship responsibility. Other causes of absence, such as death of a close relative and religious observance requirements, are personal in nature. Most companies now try to provide employees with protection against loss of income from these kinds of absences through a combination of *specified* and *general* allowances.

Specified Allowances   Among the more common provisions are:

1. Jury duty — Most firms continue full pay when employees miss work because of a summons for jury service. Employees are advised that they are required to report to work whenever they are excused for a substantial part of any day (typically on Fridays and summer afternoons). Also, some companies offset pay by a portion of the stipend paid by the court to jurors.

2. Witness duty — Although this normally does not require more than a day, it is often covered when an employee is subpoenaed to serve as a witness in a court appearance.

3. Family death — The most typical allowance following the death of an immediate family member is three days' pay. For clarity, most policies list the relationships covered, for example, "mother, father, wife, husband, son, daughter, brother, sister, in-law, or blood relative living in the same household." Some policies also provide for up to one day to attend the funeral of any other relative.

4. Military duty — Although there is no statutory requirement to pay military reservists and National Guard members during annual periods of training (normally two weeks in the summer), most employers grant some allowances. For the most part, employers pay the difference between normal wages or salary and the base military service pay. Some companies also include clothing, quarters, and sustenance allowances as part of military compensation for offset purposes.

General Allowances Requests from employees for time off can range from illness in the family and eye examinations to graduation ceremonies and divorce hearings. One approach to handling the variety of occasions for which employees need or desire time off is to have a published list of approvable reasons. However, no list, no matter how lengthy, can cover every legitimate employee request, and in some instances employees want to keep the reason confidential.

To avoid prejudging which causes should be listed, companies now provide a small pool of personal days for each employee to cover any reason whatsoever each year. An employee may be allowed two to five days per year and becomes the sole judge of whether any particular occurrence is important enough to be charged against the allowance. Once the pool is depleted, any further absences in the year are unpaid, or may be charged against vacation eligibility.

An extension of the pool approach is the total time off (TTO) concept introduced in the early 1980s by several large West Coast employers and referred to as an alternative to sick pay in Chapter 4 (see page 92). In the TTO model, a "bank account" of days is awarded to each employee as a replacement for the traditional time-based benefits including vacations, holidays, sick pay, and paid personal absence. Employees can then make "withdrawals" from their personal accounts to receive pay for any time away from work subject to company scheduling requirements.

Guaranteed Pay Plans

A key provision in the 1985 agreement negotiated between General Motors (GM) and the United Auto Workers (UAW) for the Saturn plant in Spring Hill, Tennessee, was that there would be no hourly workers; all employees would be paid on a salaried basis. This landmark contract also contained many other employment security features, which GM was willing to grant in exchange for flexible job classifications and a wage scale that was 80 percent of the industry average.[6] This was not exactly the guaranteed annual wage that the UAW had been seeking since the 1950s, but it signaled a fundamental change in pay protection policy for blue-collar workers by a major employer.

Historically employers have treated the pay of exempt employees as virtually irreducible, and nonexempt white-collar employees are generally assured of receiving their regular periodic payments (weekly or biweekly) without being docked for brief absences and tardiness. But traditionally, blue-collar workers are paid by the hour, and except for specifically covered situations, they have been conditioned to expect "no pay for no work." It is likely that the Saturn agreement, and the unilateral actions of some progressive nonunion firms, will result in this pattern changing in the United States. Eventually the term "hourly employee" should become obsolete.

Reflecting another dimension of guaranteed pay are the various provisions employers make to protect employee income during periods of involuntary unemployment. In steel, automobile, and some related industries, this protection is in the form of supplemental unemployment benefit (SUB) plans. These plans are prefunded with employer contributions and are coordinated with state unemployment compensation benefits. Initially their primary purpose was to replace employees' pay during seasonal layoffs, but the provisions also apply in the event of permanent layoffs. A typical SUB plan, combined with unemployment compensation, will replace nearly all of after-tax base wages for six months, with extensions under certain conditions.

Only 8 percent of employees in medium and large firms are covered by SUB plans, but most others are protected by some form of severance pay, either a formal plan or an informal practice. It should be noted that SUB and severance pay plans are considered employee welfare benefit plans covered by ERISA. A number of federal court decisions, summarily affirmed by the U.S. Supreme Court, have held that ERISA is applicable, preempting state laws, whether or not the plan is funded.[7]

Although lump-sum payments at time of final separation from employment are still made in many situations, it has become increasingly common to handle severance allowances in the form of pay continuation except in instances where discharge is for cause. When pay is continued, the individual gains the advantage of extended participation in benefit plans, and the organization avoids, at least temporarily, unemployment compensation charges. Whichever method is used, the amount of the allowance is typically a function of seniority. For example, a schedule could provide:

Years of service	Severance (weeks of salary)
at least 1	1
2–3	3
4–5	5
6–7	7
8–10	10
11–15	15
16–20	20
21–25	25
more than 25	30

Allowances for managerial and professional employees tend to be more generous because of the longer periods of time usually needed to find comparable positions. And in some organizations a few key executives may be protected by "golden parachute" contracts that specify compensation continuation for two or three years in the event of involuntary termination (except for cause) or a resignation following a hostile takeover of the business.

Many firms now pay for professional outplacement services for involuntarily terminated managers, and some extend this type of assistance on a group basis to nonmanagerial workers who are affected by business closings and mass layoffs. Although the employer's costs for providing the services often amount to 15 percent or more of the affected employees' annual pay rates, the advantages usually include reduced periods of salary continuation and a boost to the morale of both the terminees and those employees who are remaining with the company.

Paid Rest Periods

The U.S. Chamber of Commerce's employee benefits surveys contain a separate category for paid rest periods — lunch, coffee breaks, wash-up time, travel, time, clothes-change time, or get-ready time. In the 1986 study, their average cost as a percentage of payroll was 3.4 percent. In some cases, these allowances are essential to operations. In others, they are thought of as beneficial to the health and attitudes of employees. Some paid rest periods do not apply outside of manufacturing, but the coffee break is universal.

It is very useful to separate benefits that involve nonworking time during the workday from allowances that involve time away from the work site, such as vacations, holidays, and personal leave. The last-mentioned are relatively free from abuses, and their costs can be closely estimated and controlled. Paid rest periods are always subject to stated time limits, but the observance of those limits depends on a combination of employee respect and supervisory surveillance.

The total costs of paid rest periods — whether sanctioned or not — are rarely included in benefits statements, and employees are not inclined to recognize such costs as meaningful. However, the costs can be considerable either in terms of work not completed or in terms of extra personnel required to absorb the loss of productive time.

Summary

When a new employee is hired it is reasonable to project first-year costs for paid time off to be roughly equivalent to five weeks pay. To illustrate:

Base weekly rate	$400 ($80/day)	
Paid time off	Vacation	10
(days)	Holidays	10
	Personal	3
	Rest periods	2
	(20 min./day)	
	Total	25
Calculation	$25 \times \$80 = \$2{,}000$	
	$\dfrac{\$2{,}000}{\$400} = 5$ weeks	

Realistically, employees do not perceive these allowances as extra pay. They are an integral part of the agreed-upon wage or salary that becomes "hidden" in the paycheck. Only self-employed individuals fully appreciate the cost/benefit duality of vacations, holidays, and related interruptions of work.

Two key challenges for managers of employee benefits and human resources are to communicate paid time off to employees as an important element in their total compensation package and to design programs that effectively satisfy individual needs while not escalating costs or impeding productivity. Because this area is not as heavily regulated as pension or health plans, it offers many opportunities for innovative designs and considerable flexibility in managing a "hidden" payroll.

Notes

[1]Carroll R. Daugherty, *Labor Problems in American Industry*, (Boston: Houghton Mifflin, 1948), p. 192.

[2]U.S. Chamber of Commerce, *Employee Benefits 1986* (Washington, D.C., U.S. Chamber of Commerce, 1987).

[3]William Dunn, "Sabbaticals Aim to Cool Job Burnout," *USA Today*, July 25, 1986, p. 1B.

[4]"Personnel Activities in American Business," *Studies in Personnel Policy* No. 20. (New York: The Conference Board, 1940), p. 18.

[5]U.S. Department of Labor, Bureau of Labor Statistics, *Employee Benefits in Medium and Large Firms, 1986*, (Washington, D.C.: U. S. Government Printing Office, June 1987), p. 5.

[6]Steven Greenhouse, "Reshaping Labor to Woo The Young," *New York Times*, Business Sunday, September 1, 1985, p. 1F.

[7]For example, see Blau v. Del Monte Corporation, 748F.2d1348 (9th Cir. 1985), *cert. denied*, 106 S. Ct. 183 (October 7, 1985).

7

Beyond the Core

T he behavioral theorist Abraham Maslow posited that human beings are largely motivated throughout their lives according to a hierarchy of needs. In Maslow's motivational model, until the lower-order needs such as food and shelter are satisfied, we are not influenced by the higher-ranking needs for esteem and self-fulfillment.[1] A pragmatic translation of this might be "first things first," and essentially that describes the evolution of employee benefits in the United States. By the end of the 1960s, most employers were recognizing fundamental employee needs by providing basic welfare and retirement plans and prescribed amounts of paid time off. Until those core requirements were satisfied, employees weren't exactly moved by such ancillary considerations as a service award pin or an educational assistance plan. But once there was a perception of adequacy, employers began to seek other forms of benefits that could contribute to their goals of attracting, motivating, and retaining effective employees. And at the same time employee expectations grew.

During the past two decades, the variety of benefits that extend beyond the basic core plans has become enormous. The assortment of specific plans ranges from dental care, which is now available in nearly all large firms, to

146

such unique considerations as tuition remission for university staff and free personal travel allowances for airline personnel. While no single organization can be expected to offer all of the benefits described in this chapter, it would be useful for a benefit planning manager to consider the essential *purposes* of the various plans and programs. In that way, the relative emphasis for each area can be evaluated in relation to organization strategies and objectives and employee demographics and interests.

Extra-core benefits tend to fit into five categories:

1. Supplemental health plans
2. Family-centered benefits
3. Other financial assistance
4. Employee recognition
5. Other employment benefits

Supplemental Health Plans

"Group health care" is ordinarily a reflex response whenever an employee is asked to name an employee benefit. If asked to elaborate, the employee is apt to mention hospital, medical, and surgical benefits. However, there are now several other forms of group health protection that either have become or are on their way to becoming standard. Principal among these supplemental coverages are dental benefits, vision care, and prescription drug plans.

Dental Benefits

About 90 percent of major employers now sponsor dental plans.[2] The sources for providing and financing these plans are largely the same as those used for core health coverage (i.e., private insurance carriers, Blue Cross/Blue Shield organizations, HMOs, PPOs, and self-funding arrangements). Other sources are the dental service corporations sponsored by state dental associations. These nonprofit organizations, coordinated nationally by Delta Dental Plan Association, now write about one third of group dental coverage in the United States.[3]

Covered Services   The benefits structure in dental plans tends to be quite different from the typical group medical plan design. Except in HMOs, most group medical plans only recognize treatment for illnesses and injuries and do not cover preventive care. Also, the emphasis is on protecting the covered individual against major expenses, not the cost of routine services.

In contrast, most dental plans stress preventive care by fully covering regular examinations and X rays. This is based on the belief that in offering these coverages the serious (and more costly) dental care resulting from neglect can be avoided. However, since many other types of dental care are elective and subject to wide variations in costs, most employers limit plan payments through deductibles, copayment provisions, and maximum allowances.

The usual classification of services and levels of coverage in a model group dental plan today are:

Diagnostic services — routine oral examinations and X rays. These are usually covered fully without deductibles or coinsurance payments, but they are subject to frequency limits, for example, once every six months.

Preventive services — cleaning and scaling, fluoride treatments, and space maintainers are normally covered on the same basis as diagnostic services.

Basic restorative services — fillings, inlays, crowns, removal of dental decay, and so on. Subject to specific limits on payment for the use of precious metals, these services are typically covered on a reasonable and customary charge basis. Quite often, a small annual deductible (for example, $50 per person) is applied. (These same conditions usually apply to oral surgery, endodontics, and periodontics.)

Oral Surgery — generally excluding surgery required as the result of an accident. That would be covered under a major medical plan.

Endodontics — procedures used for prevention and treatment of diseases of the dental pulp, such as root canal work.

Periodontics — treatment of gums and other supporting structures of the teeth.

Prosthodontics — construction, replacement, and repair of dentures and bridgework. Many plans use a schedule or cover a smaller portion (for example, 50 percent) of reasonable and customary charges for these major and costly procedures.

Orthodontics — correction of malocclusion and abnormal tooth position. This coverage (which is not always included) is frequently restricted to dependent children. The benefit level is similar to that for prosthodontics, and it is common to apply a lifetime maximum (for example, $1,000) per person.

Although employee contributions have had limited impact on employer costs, several other cost control techniques are used in dental plans:

- Deductibles are usually quite small (for example, $25 or $50) and not applicable to diagnostic and preventive services.

- Coinsurance is achieved in most plans by payment of a specified percentage of reasonable and customary costs for various services. For example, a plan might pay 80 percent for restorative services, oral surgery, and endodontics and 50 percent for periodontics, prosthodontics, and orthodontics.

- Annual maximums limit the plan's total annual liability on behalf of any one participant.

- Lifetime maximums often are imposed on payments for particular services, such as orthodontics and periodontics.

- Predetermination of benefits is a common requirement whenever dental fee quotations exceed a certain amount (for example, $300). The dentist and the patient are advised in advance of treatment what portion of the projected fee will be covered by the plan. This may result in a decision to proceed with a less costly alternative.

- Waiting periods of six months or a year are utilized by some firms to guard against transient workers taking early and full advantage of dental benefits and then leaving. This may be a prudent safeguard in some industries, but it obviously detracts from the value of the benefit in recruiting efforts.

Employee Contributions   The plans negotiated by the major unions in the mid 1970s did not require employee contributions, and that set a pattern for many plans in nonunion firms. However, in the early 1980s, for economic reasons, contributory provisions started to become more prevalent, particularly for dependent coverage. A 1986 survey covering more than 1,400 plans for salaried employees showed that more than half required some employee contributions, albeit where applicable they usually did not cover more than 25 percent of total plan costs.[4] This low proportion reflects employer and insurance industry beliefs that high employee contribution rates lead to extreme antiselection against the plan. This means that only those with badly neglected teeth and high expectations of plan utilization will enroll as participants. An individual who only expects to have an examination once or twice a year will find it less expensive to pay the dentist directly than to contribute to a plan. The result is an atypical pool of plan participants and higher per capita costs.

Vision Care

Vision care was secured as an employee benefit by the United Auto Workers (UAW) in their 1976 contracts with the major auto companies. This was heralded as another pattern-setting achievement for the UAW, but so far, the growth of vision care as a group benefit has been restricted mainly to the auto industry, some peripheral manufacturing companies, trucking, and parts of the public sector. Only 21 percent of major companies had such plans in 1986.[5]

Vision-care plans are almost universally noncontributory, and typically they cover eye examinations, corrective lenses, and frames. But because many choices available to employees involve fashion and cosmetic considerations, plans impose strict limits on benefit payments. As shown in Exhibit 7.1, this is often achieved through scheduled maximum allowances and frequency-of-payment limitations. Other cost-control approaches used in the design of

Exhibit 7.1   Typical Vision-Care Plan, 1988

Covered Service	Payment Limit	Frequency Limit
Eye examination by an ophthalmologist or optometrist	$ 35	12 months
Single vision lens	$ 9 each	Limit of 2 lenses
Bifocal lens	16 ''	per 12 months
Trifocal lens	25 ''	
Lenticular lens	80 ''	
Contact lenses when medically required	$160	12 months
Contact lenses when not medically required	$ 25	12 months
Frames	$ 20	24 months

these plans include deductibles, copayments, and annual and lifetime maximum payments.

In addition to using any of the traditional sources for setting up other types of group health plans, employers may cover vision-care benefits through plans established through state optometric associations and coordinated through the Vision Institute of America.

Prescription Drug Plans

Most employers cover prescription drug expenses under their group medical plans. In a prototypal comprehensive medical plan, employees are reimbursed for their expenditures for medicines, but subject to the deductible and coinsurance provisions of the plan.

An alternative concept first received national attention in 1967 when the UAW negotiated a prepaid prescription plan with the major auto and farm implement companies. The strong appeal of these plans to employees is the absence of the typical $100 to $150 deductible and the 20 percent participant copayment specified in most group medical plans. A typical prescription drug plan will cover the full cost of an individual prescription (and insulin purchases) after the employee or dependent has paid about two dollars. In most cases there are no limits on the frequency or number of prescriptions. In some plans, however, benefits vary depending on whether the order is filled by a participating pharmacy. For example, in most plans written by Blue Cross/Blue Shield organizations, participating pharmacists agree to accept specified payments from the association, and the subscriber only pays the deductible amount. If the prescription is filled by a nonparticipating pharmacist, the subscriber must file for reimbursement (typically about 75 percent of the price).

Proponents of separate plans to cover prescription drug expenses cite the advantages of having discrete utilization data for tracking costs and the desirability of encouraging outpatient drug therapy as a deterrent to more costly hospital confinement and extended absences. Two recent developments for controlling costs of these plans are mail-order drug arrangements and generic drug incentives. For example, in 1986 New York State implemented the following changes in its program, which were projected to cut expenses for the state and 1,000 participating local government plans by more than 10 percent:

Long-term drugs ordered through a mail-order program do not require a copayment.

Drugs prescribed under their brand names and filled through other sources require a two-dollar copayment

Generic drugs filled through other sources require a one-dollar copayment.[6]

Employee Assistance Programs (EAPs)

EAPs are now sponsored by as many as 80 percent of Fortune 500 companies to help employees suffering physical, mental, or emotional problems that adversely affect their job performance and to provide assistance in reducing or resolving these problems.[7] When the programs began to gain acceptance in the early 1940s, they were identified closely with alcoholism. That was the basis of the pioneer programs at DuPont, Eastman Kodak, and a number of companies in the Bell Telephone system. In 1945 Caterpillar Tractor Company introduced what has become known as the "broadbrush" type of EAP, and this is the approach that most plans now follow.

In addition to dealing with alcohol and substance abuse and other health-related problems, a broadbrush EAP offers counseling related to marital, family, financial, legal, and virtually any other type of problem that is troubling an employee. Because of the diversity of areas covered, an EAP cannot provide in-depth counseling, but an employee (or family member) can obtain knowledgeable assessment, short-term intervention, referral, and follow-up service.

Many EAPs are in-house operations, either a part of or closely allied with an employee health unit. An alternative approach is to use an outside service organization as part of an employer consortium. In this type of arrangement, each employer pays a per capita fee based on the employee population. There are no charges to employees for using the service although there may be limitations on the number of visits related to a specific matter. Provisions are usually made to cover members of the immediate family living in the same household on the same basis.

Whichever alternative is used, it is important to assure employees that all contacts and information will be treated as completely confidential. This is essential for program success. If employees don't trust the program they won't use it. However, most employers that confront troubled employees with serious job problems will insist that the individual seek assistance through the company-sponsored EAP or an alternative source without direct subsidization. To facilitate discreet visitations, in-house EAPs are frequently located in inconspicuous areas and outside groups arrange after-work and weekend conferences.

Organizations that sponsor EAPs as an employee benefit believe that the costs are easily justified. For example, in 1986 Detroit Edison reported the results of a study of sixty-seven employees referred to their program because of substance abuse, emotional, family, financial, and job stress factors. Each employee's performance was measured for the six months prior to the initial appointment and for six months after program participation. Four objective measures (absenteeism, accidents, disciplinary actions, and group insurance claims) showed significant reductions. Subjective ratings of job performance by supervisors revealed meaningful improvement.[8]

Family-Centered Benefits

The emergence of a number of family-centered benefit plans in the 1970s paralleled the dramatic changes in work force demographics that intensified during that decade. In response to the growing representation of wives, single parents, and two-income households, employers expanded their benefit packages to address new need priorities among their employees. The most notable plans in this category are those dealing with dependent care, dependent life insurance, and adoption benefits.

Dependent Care Assistance

Although their primary focus tends to be on child care, employers usually include parents and other "qualified dependents" in tax-favored dependent-care reimbursement accounts. These plans, frequently part of an overall flexible benefit program, combine provisions of Sections 129 and 125 of the Internal Revenue Code. The former section specifies that up to $5,000 of employer payments for dependent-care expenses may be excluded from an employee's annual taxable income. The latter permits employees to reduce their salary subject to the Section 129 limitation, and to have an equivalent amount transferred to a reimbursement account for paying certain dependent-care expenses. In this way the employee effectively pays for the expenses with untaxed dollars, and the employer incurs no additional direct costs (see Exhibit 7.2). There are of course administrative expenses involved with this type of plan, and employees need to be reminded that under current tax regulations any balance in a reimbursement account at the end of a plan year cannot be directly refunded or carried forward. An alternative course for

Exhibit 7.2 Employee-Financed Dependent Care Reimbursement Account

---

Situation

A single parent with a three-year-old son anticipates child-care center expenses of $4,000 in the following year. Her employer has implemented a dependent-care reimbursement account plan that she is considering. Her projected salary for the next year is $30,000.

Analysis

	Without Account	With Account
Gross salary	$30,000	$30,000
Pre-elected payroll deductions	0	− 4,000
Adjusted salary	30,000	26,000
Estimated Taxes (federal income, Social Security)	− 5,000	− 4,333
Net salary	25,000	21,667
Payments from account		+ 4,000
Available income	25,000	25,667
Payments to child care center	− 4,000	− 4,000
Disposable income	$21,000	$21,667

Notes (per IRS regulations)

1. After the beginning of a plan year reimbursement account elections cannot be changed unless there is a family status change.
2. If payments from an account in a plan year are less than contributions the excess amount will be forfeited.

---

lower-paid employees is to use the limited federal tax credit for child- and dependent-care expenses when they file their annual tax returns.

A small number of employers have become directly involved in child care by arranging and subsidizing on-site (or nearby) facilities for employee use. Corning Glass, Hoffmann-LaRoche, and Procter and Gamble are examples of companies that have received national recognition for taking this approach. Organizations that sponsor their own programs, including a number of hospitals, cite the advantages of decreased turnover and absenteeism, the enhancement to recruitment, and improvements in morale levels. However, concerns about costs, staffing, maintenance, and legal liability have deterred most organizations from direct involvement in day care.

A recent development that has been gaining rapidly increasing support from corporate sponsors is the use of resource and referral agencies. In early 1987, there were more than 500 corporations helping to finance these organizations, which counsel parents about day-care options, refer them to prescreened local providers, and help to meet growing demands by recruiting and training additional workers. In 1984 IBM began offering a free child-care referral service to 240,000 of its employees, and in less than three years 14,000 families used it.[9]

Rather than focusing on the traditional day-care centers, resource and referral organizations concentrate on increasing the number of workers in family-based care who offer services in their homes for small groups of children. Their efforts are now coordinated by the National Association of Child Care Resource and Referral Agencies based in Rochester, Minnesota.

Although federal law prescribes that pregnancy be treated the same as any other disability there is currently no requirement that employers provide any form of disability benefit or leave. However, during the past several years Congress has considered legislation that would mandate unpaid leaves of absence for parents of newborns and adopted children newly arriving. Also, five states have mandatory benefit requirements for all types of temporary disabilities, and several have special requirements for unpaid parental leave. And, increasingly, employers are voluntarily implementing policies that accommodate the special needs of new parents.

Dependent Life Insurance

This benefit is designed to fill a need for protection against the immediate expenses of funerals and burials if a spouse or dependent child dies during the employee's active working years. Therefore, most plans offer modest levels of coverage, usually on an employee-pay-all or contributory basis.

A typical dependent life insurance plan covers a spouse for $2,000 and dependent children on an age-based scale reaching a maximum of $1,000 at about age five. Some plans specify the spouse's death benefit at 50 percent of the employee's basic group term life coverage up to a maximum that rarely exceeds $5,000. A number of state insurance laws restrict the amount of this benefit, and the Internal Revenue Code has noted that employer-paid coverage of more than $2,000 will result in taxable income for the employee (subject to offsets for employee contributions).

In spite of regulatory constraints and their limited utility, dependent life insurance plans have rapidly gained a secure niche in group survivor benefit packages. In 1981, the Conference Board reported that approximately 25 percent of U.S. employers had these kinds of plans for their white-collar workers. A 1986 survey by the Wyatt Company covering a comparable group revealed that 24 percent of firms included dependent life coverage in their *basic* life insurance program and 44 percent offered it as *optional* coverage.

Adoption Benefits

Adoption benefits are an excellent example of employer initiative in meeting important needs of a limited number of employees. In 1972 IBM introduced an Adoption Assistance Program that, according to Harold P. Kneen, Jr., director of employee benefits, filled a perceived void:

> We were already assisting in the medical expenses associated with childbirth when an employee's family is enlarged in that way, yet provided no assistance to those families where the family was enlarged through adoption. Use of the program is by under one percent of the population, but it does provide meaningful assistance and a degree of equity. [10]

An adoption benefit plan is a company-sponsored program that financially assists or reimburses employees for expenses related to the adoption of a child, provides for paid or unpaid leave for the adoptive parent employee, or both. The most frequently covered expenses are adoption agency fees, court costs, and legal fees. Some plans also cover pregnancy expenses for the birth mother, medical expenses, and temporary foster-care charges. Maximum allowances per adoption typically range from $1,000 to $2,000, with $1,500 currently the most common.

Most financial allowances for adoption are federally taxable for the recipients. Exceptions to this rule under current law are medical benefits provided under a group plan and adoption-related legal expenses covered under a company-sponsored group legal plan. In all instances benefit expenses are deductible by the employer.

Although the costs are low and the returns high in terms of employee goodwill and positive public exposure, relatively few organizations have begun to offer financial assistance for adoptions. Many more provide leaves of absence, although a 1983 North American Council on Adoptable Children survey in Maryland showed that the number of companies with adoption leave policies was one-third that of companies with comparable maternity leave policies for birth parents.[11]

An excellent source of additional information on adoption benefits is the National Adoption Exchange located in Philadelphia.

Other Financial Assistance

The most common company-sponsored benefit plans of this type are relocation assistance and educational assistance. Prepaid legal plans and financial planning programs are examples of employer sponsorship, but such arrangements are not common.

Relocation Assistance

Employee relocations, whether at time of hire or during active employment, are a business necessity for many organizations. In particular, national and multinational employers need to establish policies and meaningful allowances to recruit competitively and to maintain organizational flexibility. Typically these policies differentiate between new employees and transferees.

New Hires   Many businesses today cannot rely on the local labor market to satisfy all their employment needs. Certainly any company that must recruit recent college graduates knows that it must seek students from distant locations. A company in Virginia might want to hire someone who is graduating from a university in Massachusetts but lives in Idaho. Fortunately, most young people are willing to relocate for a superior job opportunity, and in many cases, their relocation expenses are limited to transportation costs.

If their needs are critical enough, some employers will extend many of the same allowances to new employees that they provide for transferring employees. Generally, though, the new employee is offered coverage for only travel expenses and the costs of moving possessions. If required, temporary living expenses may be covered, and the company might agree to pay for storage of furniture for a limited time. Except for key executives, new employees usually do not receive any other allowances. Costs normally covered under policies for transferred employees can be considerable, and most companies are unwilling to assume such a heavy liability for a person whose value to them may not become clearly evident for a year or more.

Companies that do provide more comprehensive allowances to newly hired employees believe that it is a cost-effective recruitment policy. To quote one company executive, "With soaring relocation expenses, two-income families more common than ever before, high costs, and complicated procedures involved in home sale and purchase, a relocation policy offering complete, comprehensive, and realistic coverage can play a major role in determining acceptance or rejection of job offers.[12]

Transferred Employees   In addition to the basic allowances given to new employees, most companies provide a variety of allowances and services for transferees. These usually include:

Cost allowances for selling a house.

Search expenses for finding a new residence.

Temporary living expenses.

Allowances and loans for purchasing a house.

Assistance in finding employment for a spouse.

Practical assistance.

Because of the complexity and sensitivity of many aspects of relocation, most large employers now contract with outside firms specializing in real estate and related services. In a typical third-party arrangement, the outside firm offers to buy the employee's present residence based on independent appraisals. The employee can accept the offer or attempt to sell the property privately at a higher price. In either case the employer is responsible for the costs. The outside firms also offer practical assistance for employees on a variety of relocation matters. A good source of information about such firms is the Employee Relocation Council in Washington, D.C.

Tax Treatment   Under current federal tax law, all payments to or on behalf of a relocated employee are reportable as income. The IRS allows the following moving expense deduction for a person when the new job location is at least thirty-five miles farther from the old home than the previous job:

1. Expenses of traveling (including meals and lodgings) from the old to the new residence.
2. Expenses of moving household goods and personal effects.
3. Expenses of traveling from the former residence to the new place of work for the principal purpose of searching for a new residence, and

costs of meals and lodgings (up to thirty days) while waiting to move into permanent quarters (maximum $1,500).

4. Qualified expenses incident to a sale, purchase, or lease of a residence. (The sum of 3 and 4 cannot exceed $3,000).

For most employees these deductions do not come close to matching the amount that must be reported as income for tax purposes. In 1984 the average amount spent to relocate a homeowner, according to a corporate relocation policies survey by Merrill Lynch Relocation Management, was $32,250.[13] To compensate for this, most companies have adopted tax-assistance policies. Typically, the employer pays the taxes on a gross-up of income using either a standard percentage (for example, 25 percent) or a graduated scale based on salary level and the amount of nondeductible reimbursement.

Educational Assistance

The principal form of employer-sponsored educational assistance is the tuition-aid plan. According to the Bureau of Labor Statistics, 86 percent of full-time employees in medium and large firms were covered by such a plan in 1985.[14] Yet according to a number of surveys and reports, ordinarily only 3 to 5 percent of employees utilize tuition-aid plans when they are available.

One reason for low utilization of this benefit in some firms is the age and educational profile of the work force. But in many instances it appears that employers fail to market their programs effectively or demonstrate the connection between after-hours education and internal advancement. Although the stated objectives of most programs include references to "increased job knowledge" and "improved readiness for promotion," the linkage between employee participation and management recognition of the accomplishments is often weak.

Organizations with higher rates of employee participation promote their plans aggressively through recruitment brochures, seasonal notices and postings of local course offerings, and articles in employee publications. Information about course completions and degree attainments is entered in employee data files and appropriately accessed by internal placement and employee development staff members. Firms with federal government contracts requiring Affirmative Action Plans (AAPs), and other progressive employers, frequently extend special encouragements to protected group members to utilize tuition assistance programs for enhancing upward mobility.

The principal considerations for an employer in setting up a tuition aid plan are:

Definition of Acceptable Courses and Schools   Any course directly related to an employee's present job with the company should qualify for tuition aid. Beyond this obvious goal, it is necessary to provide some guidelines to govern eligibility of other courses. Each company must evaluate the advantages against the costs of covering courses that have little relation to employees' present jobs but may help them prepare for advancement.

A relationship between a course and some phase of company operations is a useful guideline, but exceptions should be considered for courses required in a degree program.

Acceptable schools are usually defined as accredited secondary schools, colleges, and universities, plus technical institutes, specialty programs, and correspondence schools. The last-mentioned may be included only if clear evidence exists that classroom instruction is unavailable or inaccessible.

Definition of Covered Expenses   Although the term "tuition aid" is still used widely to describe these plans, it is a misnomer. Since most plans cover registration and laboratory fees, and some subsidize books and supplies, "educational expense allowance" and "continuing education allowance" seem to be more descriptive terms.

Other expenses that are paid for in a minority of plans today include entrance examinations, theses costs, graduation fees, health fees, professional certification, and activity fees. Employees receiving educational allowances under the Veteran's Administration are usually expected to apply the government aid before requesting company support.

Time-Off Policy   Many educators believe that as management becomes more aware of and concerned about the knowledge explosion in progress today, the classic separation of education and work will disappear. However, most companies still draw a line between in-plant training programs that are considered essential and outside educational programs that have been termed "desirable." This results in employees having to take courses on an after-hours basis in most situations. But some companies will permit employees to adjust their work schedules to permit class attendance as long as this does not interfere with operations, and flextime can accommodate many employee time requirements.

Extent, Conditions, and Time of Payment The customary allowance for an approved course of study was originally 50 percent of the cost of tuition in most industrial plans, but today 75 or 100 percent of tuition costs and related fees is the norm. For an employee to qualify for reimbursement, most companies require a passing grade or specify "successful completion" of courses where no grade is given. Some companies vary the allowance with grades. For instance, 100 percent of the costs might be reimbursed for an A, 75 percent for a B, and 50 percent for a C. Most companies reject this approach on the basis that grades are subjective evaluations that vary from school to school and that too much pressure on grade attainment could adversely affect an employee's job performance.

Most employers impose limits on allowances, in the form of either a maximum number of dollars or a number of credit hours per semester or academic year for which payment will be made. Firms that set dollar maximums have found it necessary to adjust the limit frequently as tuition costs continue to rise. Limiting the credit hours or courses allowed guards against employees becoming full-time students and part-time workers.

By definition, most tuition-aid plans are refund or reimbursement arrangements. Recently, to aid employees who may be deterred from enrollment because they lack available cash, some companies have arranged for advance payments or loans. Where an employee credit union is operative, educational loans can usually be obtained conveniently, and the employer may agree to pay the loan interest.

Regulatory and Tax Status Tuition-aid plans are generally exempt from ERISA regulations, but they must satisfy IRS discrimination and reporting requirements. The tax status of payments to employees has been a subject of congressional debate for a number of years (see Chapter 2, pages 21–22). In 1986 and 1987 up to $5,250 a year could be excluded from employee gross income, but this Internal Revenue Code provision expired on December 31, 1987.

In addition to tuition aid, many organizations sponsor college scholarship programs for employees' children and match employee contributions to universities, colleges, and various tax-exempt institutions. The former are relatively low-cost programs since awards are typically limited to students who qualify for National Merit Scholarships or achieve a similar attainment, and the scholarship has a four-year limit and a maximum annual amount (for example, $5,000). Most programs are administered by an outside organization such as the National Merit Scholarship Corporation of Evanston, Illinois. Although a third-party arrangement minimizes employee charges of favoritism, some employers have reported employee dissatisfaction with scholarship programs based primarily on Scholastic Aptitude Test (SAT) scores because children of managers and senior professional and technical staff win most of the annual awards.

Matching gift arrangements also tend to favor higher paid employees who can be expected to make larger tax-deductible contributions. However it is likely that some employees at all levels conserve on their personal contributions to educational institutions when they know that whatever amount they give will be doubled — a *net* benefit for the individual if not the institution!

Prepaid Legal Service Plans

In 1981 the UAW negotiated a legal services plan with Chrysler covering 140,000 active and retired workers that many benefit authorities expected to be a pattern-setter. But because of the tenuous status of the tax exemption, a lack of strong support from the American Bar Association, and some restrictive state regulations, growth of these plans as a group benefit has been very slow. According to the Wyatt Company, only 1 percent of group benefit programs included a legal services plan in 1986.[15] Still, as consumer awareness and litigious attitudes become more evident, expansion of this benefit seems inevitable.

Under present tax law, a group legal plan qualifies for favorable tax treatment whether it is funded by an insurance company, a legal service group, or through a self-funded trust. Also, a plan can be set up as a reimbursement account under Section 125 of the IRC and financed with pretax employee contributions.

There are two basic models for group legal services. A closed-panel plan is based on a group of lawyers or law firms contracting with an employer to provide specified legal services to employees for prepaid fees. An open-panel plan allows an employee to choose any attorney for covered services. The employee pays the attorney's fees and then submits a claim for reimbursement under the plan. Benefits under either model may be limited by scheduled maximum hours or costs for specific services, deductibles, and/or coinsurance ratios.

Most group legal plans provide a limited amount of telephone consultations and office time of an exploratory nature to determine the extent, if any, of legal problems. Such contacts frequently involve prospective review of contracts, leases, sales agreements, and other documents and may serve to prevent future time-consuming complications.

Financial Planning Programs

Many companies offer financial counseling services to executives as a perquisite, and some schedule employees nearing retirement for a session covering financial matters as part of a preretirement planning program. The only other type of financial planning assistance usually available to employees through a company plan is a limited amount of counseling and referral from an EAP.

Recently some employers have recognized that the complexities of group savings and investment plans, particularly those with multiple investment options and frequent reallocation opportunities, can be bewildering for employees. One response to this situation has been to retain outside specialists to present after-hours courses on financial planning. To avoid direct involvement with those who sell specific investment products, most employers contract with local educators or independent financial planners. Another approach is to offer employees a packaged home-study course consisting of booklets, programmed texts, and computer-assisted analysis of completed questionnaires. Some companies cover the costs of such courses under their tuition refund plan, and others make the materials available to employees for purchase at a subsidized rate.

As employee benefit plans continue to feature more elements of choice for participants, it is likely that company-sponsored financial planning programs will soon be quite prevalent.

Employee Recognition

The Economic Recovery Tax Act of 1981 (ERTA) contained provisions that significantly benefited employee recognition award programs. In brief, the provisions, which are essentially still intact, specify that for recognition awards given for *length of service, productivity,* or *safety achievements:*

1. *Employers* are allowed to deduct up to $400 per item. If the average cost is $400 or less per award, and the award is part of a written nondiscriminatory plan, the cost of any single item may be deducted to a limit of $1,600.

2. *Employees* can exclude such awards from their gross income, subject to the deductible limits, as long as the awards are in the form of tangible personal property. Cash, gift certificates, or the like do not qualify for the exclusion.

3. Service awards may not be excluded from income during the first five years of employment or more frequently than every five years.

Prior to the ERTA changes, the federal tax code placed a $100 limit on expense deductibility and income exclusion for individual recognition awards. This tended to minimize the impact of awards and, to some extent, caused them to be viewed as token considerations. The current limits permit employers to grant meaningful awards, and greater attention is now paid to designing programs that offer attractive and relevant items. Because styles and preferences for personal giftware change rather frequently, many employers have found it helpful to use employee surveys and focus groups for input concerning what items to include in their awards program. Asking employees for their opinions, and acting on them, offers additional positive recognition.

Suggestion Awards

Suggestion award systems are a hybrid of direct compensation and employee benefits. Typically they offer cash payments to individuals for submitting adoptable ideas that result in reduced costs or greater income for the enterprise. But they also provide elements of recognition for employees, both tangible and intangible, which causes many employers (and the U.S. Chamber of Commerce) to classify them as employee benefit plans.

No matter how the plans are classified, they can produce substantial rewards for employees. According to the National Association of Suggestion Systems (Chicago), employees in member organizations were awarded nearly $128 million for their suggestions in 1985. Although the suggestion box and other protections of anonymity have been replaced by "open" systems and supervisory involvement, most suggestion plans are still dedicated to individual rewards. However, with the expanded interest in quality circles and related forms of group problem-solving starting in the early 1980s, some suggestion plans now encourage group participation in the development of ideas and sharing of awards.

Other Employee Benefits

Personalized benefits statements (described more fully in Chapter 10) are now distributed to employees annually by most large companies. These reports, partially computerized, contain detailed and quantified information about the individual's status in the major benefit plans. In addition they usually include a catchall section in which a variety of often overlooked entitlements are mentioned. Collectively, these items cause some added expenditures for employers that are not always reflected in benefit cost analysis. Unfortunately employees don't always perceive their value, and because they are mostly referred to as "other" or "miscellaneous" benefits they lack a distinct identity. Also, for many years their tax status was uncertain and for that reason some employers were reluctant to promote them too vigorously lest the IRS question tax deductions and income exclusions.

Much of the confusion about tax status was removed by the Deficit Reduction Act of 1984 (DEFRA), which provided statutory rules for a broad range of "fringe benefits" not previously covered by the Internal Revenue Code. Beginning in 1985 the following classes of benefits, if provided on a nondiscriminatory basis, became tax-free for income and employment tax purposes to employees who received them:

1. *No-additional-cost services.* These are services the employer offers for sale to customers in the ordinary course of business, and for which the employer incurs no additional cost by offering them to employees. An example of this is free air travel for airline employees.

2. *Qualified employee discounts.* These are discounts provided to employees on property or services that are offered for sale to customers in the ordinary course of business. For property, the discount may not exceed the gross profit percentage at which the property is offered to customers. For services the discount may not exceed 20 percent of the price quoted to customers.

3. *Subsidized and free meals.* The value of subsidized meals provided to employees is excludable from their gross income if, on an annual basis, the revenue from the facility equals or exceeds the employer's direct operating costs. A free or subsidized meal provided at the work site "for the *employer's* convenience" is not considered income to the recipient under any circumstances.

4. *Qualified tuition reductions* or *cash grants* provided by educational institutions to their employees, or to children of their employees, for education below the graduate level.

If a plan discriminates in favor of highly compensated employees, that group will be taxed on the value of the benefits, but the benefits will be tax-free to other employees.

Based on DEFRA and subsequent regulations, the following have been established as tax-free benefits *whether or not* they are provided on a discriminatory basis:

1. *Free or discounted parking.*

2. *Recreational facilities* located on the employer's premises where substantially all of the use is by employees. If utilization is primarily by highly compensated employees, the *employer* is not eligible for a tax deduction.

3. *De minimis fringe benefits,* where the value of the benefit is so small that it is unreasonable to keep detailed records (for example, taxi fares following unpaid overtime work, supper money, use of copying machines).

4. *Working condition fringe benefits,* which would be deductible if the employee paid for them, such as subscriptions to business publications and the use of a company car qualified for business purposes.

The codification of all of these benefits as tax-free "fringes" effectively solidified their status and enhanced their role in the total compensation package. However, it should be noted that in expanding the scope of tax-free benefits in DEFRA, Congress also included language that made it clear that any benefit not covered by a statutory provision in existing law, or that act, would be taxable.

Summary

At one time all employee benefit programs were considered to be about the same. That perception is now clearly far off the mark, mainly because of the wide differences in the kinds of benefits that companies provide beyond a core of basic welfare and retirement plans. The following factors have contributed to the current diversity of non-core benefits.

1. Some coverages, for example vision care and prescription drug plans, have evolved largely through collective bargaining, but so far only in certain industries.
2. Family-centered benefits, such as dependent care assistance and adoption benefits, tend to reflect a combination of the demographic profile of a particular company and the awareness of its management.
3. Educational assistance programs are offered when employers believe that there will be a positive connection between their investment and employees' performance and advancement.
4. Relocation assistance is extended to new hires as well as transferees when it seems necessary to achieve recruitment objectives.
5. Service awards are given by organizations that value long-term commitment by employees.
6. Suggestion award systems are implemented by companies that believe in rewarding individuals (and sometimes groups of employees) for submissions of cost-saving and profit-producing ideas.
7. Such considerations as subsidized meals, free parking, employee discounts and *de minimis* fringe benefits, are a function of a company's size, location, type of business, and HRM philosophy.

Notes

[1]Abraham H. Maslow, *Motivation and Personality* (New York: Harper & Row, 1954).

[2]Hewitt Associates, *Salaried Employee Benefits Provided by Major U.S. Employers in 1986* (Lincolnshire, Ill.: Hewitt Associates, 1987).

[3]Burton T. Beam, Jr., and John J. McFadden, *Employee Benefits* (Homewood, Ill.: Richard D. Irwin, 1985), p. 198.

[4]The Wyatt Company, *1986 Group Benefits Survey* (Washington, D.C.: The Wyatt Co., 1986), p. 93–94.

[5]Hewitt Associates, *Salaried Employee Benefits.*

[6]*Managing Employee Benefits* (Paramus, N.J.: Prentice-Hall Information Services, 1987), p. 4212.

[7]*ACA News* 30, no. 3 (April 1987), p. 14.

[8]"Work Performance Is Key to Evaluating EAP Programs," *Employee Benefit Plan Review* 41, no. 4 (October 1986):30–31.

[9]Glen Collins, "Day Care Finds Corporate Help," *New York Times*, January 5, 1987, p. B5.

[10]David A. Weeks, ed., *Rethinking Employee Benefits Assumptions* (New York: Conference Board, 1978), p. 88.

[11]*Adoption Benefits Plans: Corporate Response to a Changing Society* (Philadelphia: National Adoption Exchange, undated, circa 1985).

[12]Howard G. MacMillan, Jr., "Your Relocation Policy as a Recruiting Tool," *Mobility* (November-December 1980):19–22.

[13]*Managing Employee Benefits.* p. 7606.

[14]U.S. Department of Labor, Bureau of Labor Statistics, *Employee Benefits in Medium and Large Firms, 1985* (Washington, D.C.: U.S. Government Printing Office, July 1986), p. 82.

[15]The Wyatt Company, *1986 Group Benefits Survey,* p. 33.

8

Flexible Benefits and Cafeteria Plans

Question: Plans that permit employees to select benefits they want from a package of employer-provided coverages, including plans that offer a choice between cash compensation and benefits, are called

a. flexible benefit plans
b. cafeteria plans
c. cafeteria compensation plans
d. flexible compensation plans
e. all of the above

The correct answer is "e." All of the above terms are currently used by sponsoring employers and consulting firms that help design different types of variable compensation plans. Employees usually refer to the plans simply as "flex."

Initially the Internal Revenue Code defined a cafeteria plan as one that offered employees choices between benefits and cash and satisfied the requirements of Section 125. This meant that if a flexible plan did not include a cash option it was not a cafeteria plan. The Tax Reform Act of 1986 changed this distinction and, starting in 1989, plans under which an employee can choose among two or more "qualified benefits" options will also be considered cafeteria plans. Although in benefit practice a variety of interchangeable terms will undoubtedly continue to be used, the IRS-sanctioned classification, cafeteria plan, will be the one used primarily throughout this chapter.

Evolution of Cafeteria Plans

The concept of a benefit program in which employees are free to select the types and levels of benefits that best fit their individual needs first received serious attention in the late 1960s. Numerous behavioral theorists and compensation authorities began to recognize the limitations of monolithic packages of benefits for meeting the needs of an increasingly diverse work force. High rates of inflation were creating a new constituency of moonlighting and part-time workers. For the same reason, many wives were reentering the work force. Civil Rights legislation and affirmative action rules had created new job opportunities for minority group members, women, older persons, and the handicapped. Worker attitudes about career employment and personal lifestyles were changing markedly. The "prototypical employee" (a married male, age thirty-five to forty-five, two children preparing for college, with a heavily mortgaged home and two cars) for whom most group benefit programs were designed was starting to become a demographic dinosaur.

In 1974 two organizations, Educational Testing Services of Princeton, New Jersey, and TRW Systems Group of Redondo Beach, California, became the first to implement cafeteria-style benefit plans. Their initiatives were widely praised in compensation and human resource circles, but they hardly ignited a trend. This led David J. Thomsen, director of the Compensation Institute (Los Angeles) to comment in 1977, "Cafeteria compensation has been one of the most overrated concepts ever championed by management theorists."[1]

Thomsen's criticism seemed well-founded at the time. Both of the two pioneer installations had appeared to be complicated and costly, and further growth had been thwarted by an ERISA-imposed moratorium on the adoption of new plans in which employees could elect salary reductions to obtain additional benefits. These two impediments began to disappear in the following year.

The Revenue Act of 1978, by adding Section 125 to the Internal Revenue Code, provided a statutory basis for offering employees a choice between cash and benefits without causing the latter to become taxable, as long as it was under a nondiscriminatory plan. And in that same year a major corporation, American Can Company (now Primerica), launched a cafeteria-style program that clearly demonstrated some cost containment capacities for this approach. The statutory foundation for cafeteria plans was strengthened by the Miscellaneous Revenue Act of 1980 (which sanctioned the inclusion of a salary deferral arrangement per IRC 401(k) in a cafeteria plan); the issuance of proposed regulations for Section 125 in 1984; and the Tax Reform Act of 1986. The use of multiple choice options in group medical plans combined with health-care reimbursement accounts as a cost-containment strategy escalated starting in the early 1980s.

Because there are so many variations and degrees of cafeteria-type plans, it is very difficult to measure their growth and current prevalence. Useful references for this purpose are the annual reports of "Flexible Compensation Programs" issued by Hewitt Associates. These studies include plans that "permit an employee to have some say over the form in which a portion of total compensation is received." Excluded from the compilations are freestanding 401(k) plans and Section 125 plans that permit salary reductions for group insurance premium payments only. Hewitt reported that there were 602 plans on line at the end of 1987, compared with fourteen in effect six years earlier.[2] Clearly there are many more plans that would satisfy the current IRS definition of a cafeteria plan, and that number will increase when the expanded definition takes effect in 1989.

Another indication of the growing importance of these plans is the emergence of the Employers Council on Flexible Compensation (ECFC) as an influential nonprofit trade organization. Formed in 1981 and strategically based in Washington, D.C., ECFC serves as a clearinghouse of information and source of technical assistance for a steadily expanding membership that included approximately 240 organizations as of late 1987.

Employer Objectives

In 1983 the Conference Board reported that among 136 companies considering adoption of some form of flexible benefits, the three most frequently cited reasons for interest were:

1. Potential for accommodating varying employee needs (99%)
2. Potential for control of benefits costs (88%)
3. Potential for controlling increasing costs of health insurance (62%)

Other factors mentioned by 25 percent or more of the respondents included:

opportunity to curb rising costs for specific benefits (for example, pensions, disability benefits, and vacations)

potential for breaking the historical tandem relationship of salaried employees' benefits to bargaining units' benefits

recognition of existing or anticipated concentrations of older and/or younger employees[3]

All of these reasons are regularly mentioned by advocates of a flexible compensation approach, and they form a basis of objectives-setting for sponsors of cafeteria plans. In stating objectives, most compensation and benefits managers try to balance financial cost-control goals with those that address human resource needs. While the former are often more critical for securing executive management approval, the latter are necessary to ensure employee acceptance.

What Do Cafeteria Plans Include?

Before determining what benefits will be included in a cafeteria plan, a benefit manager needs to assess what can be included under federal tax regulations. Exhibit 8.1 lists those compensation elements that qualify for inclusion in a Section 125 plan, and some specific exclusions. However, very few plans include all of the allowable benefits. To do so would create severe administrative burdens for employers, and in most cases employees do not expect or require so many areas of choice.

Organizations focusing on health-cost containment typically begin their cafeteria arrangement by offering employees a series of options in that area only. In subsequent years, as employees became more familiar with the concept, additional choice items are added. Another strategy is to first provide employees with the choice of a previously unavailable benefit, for example, dependent care or group legal benefits, in exchange for salary reductions or traded vacation days.

Effectively, this approach expands the scope of the benefits package, introduces the process of compensation choices, and does not increase the employer's direct costs for benefits.

In planning for a cafeteria plan most firms formally assess their employees' needs and preferences to help determine which benefits and options to in-

Exhibit 8.1 What Can Be Included in a Cafeteria Plan?*

Nontaxable Benefits

Accident and health insurance
Dependent life insurance (up to $2,000)
Disability benefits
Group legal service
Group term life insurance (up to $50,000)
Noninsured tax-deductible medical expenses
Noninsured tax-deductible dependent-care expenses

Taxable Benefits

Cash
Dependent life insurance (over $2,000)
Group term life insurance (over $50,000)
Vacation days

Deferred Compensation

Elective employee deferrals under a 401(k) plan

Specifically Excluded from Inclusion in a Cafeteria Plan

Deferred compensation plans — *other than* 401(k) as above
De minimis fringes
Educational assistance benefits
No-additional-cost services
Qualified employee discounts
Qualified employer-provided transportation
Scholarships and fellowship grants
Working condition fringes

---

*Based on proposed IRS regulations on tax treatment of Cafeteria Plans, published May 7, 1984.

clude. Techniques such as structured questionnaires, trade-off analysis, focus group meetings, and simulation exercises (see Chapter 2) are utilized for this purpose. Some organizations prefer to conduct their studies *before* announcing any commitment to introducing a flexible-type plan. They reason that if the analysis of employee responses shows an acceptable level of satisfaction with present benefits, some minor enhancements plus improved benefits communications might be a more suitable follow-up action than a cafeteria plan.

Basic Plan Structures

There are essentially five basic ways in which a cafeteria plan can be structured:

1. A reimbursement account
2. An additional allowance (add-on) approach
3. Mix-and-match options
4. A core carve-out plan
5. A modular plan

A Reimbursement Account

This is the simplest form of cafeteria plan to design. It is an arrangement that allows employees to pay for certain medical, legal, and dependent-care expenses with untaxed dollars. As demonstrated in the preceding chapter (see Exhibit 7.2), an account can be wholly financed by employees according to a preelected salary reduction agreement. However some plans are fully or partially funded by the employer. For example, one large manufacturer established a medical-care reimbursement account several years ago with tax-free employer contributions of $46 a month for each eligible employee. That amount was based on a projection of savings expected to be realized from several cost-containment features added to the company's group medical and dental plans.

In addition to the "use-it-or-lose-it" rule issued by the IRS regulating year-end account balances, employees are not permitted to use funds from one account to pay expenses in a different category. For example:

> Joan Knight's employer sponsors and maintains reimbursement accounts for both health-care expenses and dependent-care expenses. Joan decides to participate in both plans and, prior to year end, opts to contribute $30 a month to the former and $200 a month to the latter by reducing her salary, thereby saving on taxes.
>
> On December 15 of the following year, Ms. Knight's balance in the health-care account is $100, and she does not contemplate any further expenses in that year. Although she has spent all of the funds in the dependent-

care account and projects additional child-care expenses of $100 in December, she is prohibited from using the unused balance. That amount will be forfeited and she will have to pay for the remaining expenses with after-tax dollars.

This type of situation highlights the importance of employers clearly communicating plan provisions and employees carefully estimating the amount of their salary reductions designated for the accounts.

An Additional Allowance (Add-on) Plan

The approach used by Educational Testing Service (ETS) in 1974 typifies this type of plan. All existing benefits were maintained and supplemented by a number of optional or flexible benefits. To obtain supplemental coverages, employees received "flexible credits" paid for by the employer and based on their years of service; these credits were expressed as a percentage of salary. If the cost of the benefits chosen exceeded the available benefits credits, an employee could pay the difference through salary reduction, payroll deductions, or both.

The add-on approach ensures that all employees remain protected by essential benefit coverages, offers employees opportunities to select benefits that suit their unique needs, and allows employers to control the level of funding for the flexible credits. As an example of this last point, ETS has effectively limited its share of the escalating costs for the optional benefits by continuing to base credits on the same percentage of salary figures related to service that were used when they introduced their plan.[4]

Mix-and-Match Options

This is the design concept first introduced by TRW. In a typical plan, participants are offered opportunities to reshape their existing compensation packages by opting for different levels of coverage within a few benefit areas. Credits generated by electing lower coverage levels in one area may be used to obtain higher levels of coverage in another area or converted into cash. If a participant chooses mostly "high-option" benefits (for example, additional life insurance, lower deductibles in the medical plan, or a higher percentage of income replacement when disabled), the additional expense can be paid for through a salary reduction agreement. Fundamental to this approach is that employer costs are not directly affected, but employees gain flexibility by being able to rearrange the form of their compensation.

A Core Carve-Out Plan

The process of designing this kind of plan involves reducing current benefits to create a two-part plan consisting of fixed core coverages and flexible credits. Before effecting the carve-out step, program designers need to carefully evaluate what should represent the organization's basic security obligations to employees. The resulting core of inflexible coverages, usually provided on a noncontributory basis, typically includes:

1. a comprehensive medical plan
2. group term life insurance (normally equal to one year's salary)
3. partial income replacement during extended disabilities
4. a competitive pension plan
5. standard paid time off allowance

The flexible credits generated by the carve-out (the value of the residue) are then available to plan participants to make annual elections from a company-prepared "menu" of optional benefits such as:

1. higher levels of coverage to supplement protections in the core;
2. additional benefits to fit individual needs (for example, dental care, dependent care, extra vacation days); and, in some plans
3. cash.

Potentially, a unilateral reduction of existing benefits can create employee distrust unless the conversion to flexible credits is perceived by employees as fair and there is an opportunity to restore most of the preflex coverages. American Can effectively addressed both of these concerns when they launched the first carve-out plan in 1978. Employees were extensively involved in the design and development stages and it was possible for them, through choice, to keep most of the reductions — although only 14 percent of employees did so in the initial election. [5,6]

A Modular Plan

This type of plan is sometimes called "prepackaged flex." It consists of a number of modules, each covering the same range of benefits but offering employees varying levels of protection. An employee is required to select one module and cannot substitute for any of the coverages. The concept is analogous to a restaurant presenting a menu with a number of complete dinners listed and no substitutions in the individual courses permitted.

In some plans all of the modules are designed to have an equivalent value, but more typically the costs will vary. In those instances, the employer funds each module at the same level and wherever the projected cost is greater employees pay the excess amount. The decision regarding the number of modules to include in a plan is largely a function of the perceived diversity of employee needs balanced against the requirements to price and administer two or more modules. One of the first modular plans, adopted by Northern Telecom in 1982, contained eight modules. Exhibit 8.2 illustrates a six-module plan implemented by Burroughs Wellcome in 1985.

The Comprehensive Approach

To date most cafeteria or flexible-type programs in medium and small firms have been based on one of the five basic models. But some of the newer programs, particularly in large companies, are more comprehensive and incorporate a combination of the standard designs. In part this reflects increased knowledge and sophistication about the cafeteria concept. It also stems from the strategic decisions of an increasing number of large organizations that have sought to create a completely new "look" in employee benefits following an acquisition, merger, or corporate restructuring. That was the case in 1983 when Mercantile Texas Corporation, a Dallas-based bank holding company, and Southwest Bancshares, based in Houston, announced plans to form MCorp, thus becoming one of the twenty largest banking institutions in America.

The two Texas organizations shared the philosophy of wanting a uniform benefit program for the new corporation, but initially they were unsure about how to meet that objective. Simply taking the best of the two existing programs would have satisfied employees but would have been prohibitively expensive. And it was evident that any attempt to blend the two separate programs, because of significant plan differences, would be likely to create perceptions of "take-aways" among employees. A joint task force concluded that the best course was to proceed with the development of a totally new comprehensive flexible program. This program, titled "The Edge," which combined flexible credits, multiple benefits options, a cash option, salary reduction provisions, reimbursement accounts, and a 401(k) plan, became effective in mid 1984. A postimplementation survey indicated that in general

Exhibit 8.2   A Summary of Your Flex Formula Choices

Flex Formula	Medical	Dental
A	Current plan — Basic: 100% of hospital expenses. Major medical: $100 deductible per covered individual, then plan pays 80% of expenses and you pay 20%. Maximum you could pay — $1,500. New features covered at 100% encourage outpatient services.	Current plan — 100% preventive care 50% other care $1,000 lifetime max for orthodontics. (Paid at 50%) You pay for dependents.
B	Comprehensive: $200 deductible ($400 family), then plan pays 80% of expenses and you pay 20%. Maximum you could pay — $1,000 ($2,000 family) including deductible. Some features provide 100% coverage to encourage outpatient services.	Current plan — 100% preventive care 50% other care $1,000 lifetime max for orthodontics. (Paid at 50%) You pay for dependents.
C	Comprehensive: $200 deductible ($400 family), then plan pays 80% of expenses and you pay 20%. Maximum you could pay — $1,000 ($2,000 family) including deductible. Some features provide 100% coverage to encourage outpatient services.	100% preventive care 75% other care $1,500 lifetime max for orthodontics. (Paid at 50%) Company pays for you plus ½ of dependent coverage.

Life	Vision and Prescription Drug	FlexFund
Current plan — 2 × pay (max $50,000) company-paid. Optional employee-paid can match, double, or triple company coverage. (Maximum $200,000 total.)	Prescription drugs covered under major medical.	Not available.
2 × pay (no max) company-paid. Optional employee-paid 1 or 2 times pay (no max).	Prescription drugs covered under medical plan.	$300 per year, from Burroughs Wellcome. You can add up to $2,400 per dependent to a maximum of $4,800 in tax-free dollars to pay for dependent day care.
2 × pay (no max) company-paid. Optional employee-paid 1 or 2 times pay (no max).	Prescription drugs covered with $1 deductible per filling. Eye exams, prescription glasses, and contact lenses covered.	You can put up to $2,400 per dependent to a maximum of $4,800 in tax-free dollars into your FlexFund to pay for dependent day care.

continued

Exhibit 8.2 *Continued*

Flex Formula	Medical	Dental
D	Comprehensive: $500 deductible, then plan pays 80% of expenses and you pay 20%. Maximum you could pay — $3,000. Some features provide 100% coverage to encourage outpatient services.	Not available.
E	HMO Health America pays 100% for complete medical coverage including all office visits and hospitalization. No deductibles. No claim forms.	100% preventive care, 75% other care. $1,500 lifetime max for orthodontics. (Paid at 50%) Company pays for you plus ½ of dependent coverage.
F	Central Carolina Physicians pay 100% for most medical services including hospitalization. (You pay nominal copayment for certain services.) No claim forms.	100% preventive care. 75% other care. $1,500 lifetime max for orthodontics. (Paid at 50%) Company pays for you plus ½ of dependent coverage.

Source: Courtesy of Burroughs Wellcome Company.

employees perceived benefits as better although overall employer costs had not increased.[7]

The process of developing and implementing a comprehensive plan can be arduous. It requires strong commitment from top management and a coordinated effort from many individuals including, in addition to employee benefit and human resource managers, insurance, tax, legal, and financial specialists, representative groups of employees, and, usually, outside benefit plan consultants. Although organizational pressures may compress the schedule, most benefit planners would propose allowing at least twelve months from initial goal setting to implementation of an extensive cafeteria plan.

Life	Vision and Prescription Drug	FlexFund
$10,000 company-paid. Optional employee-paid 1 or 2 times pay (no max).	Prescription drugs covered under medical plan.	$720 per year from Burroughs Wellcome. You can add up to $2,400 per dependent to a maximum of $4,800 in tax-free dollars to pay for dependent day care.
2 × pay (no max) company paid. Optional employee-paid 1 or 2 times pay (no max).	Covered under Metropolitan. Prescription drugs — $1 for each 34-day supply. Vision and hearing screening.	You can put up to $2,400 per dependent to a maximum of $4,800 in tax-free dollars into your FlexFund to pay for dependent day care.
2 × pay (no max) company paid. Optional employee-paid 1 or 2 times pay (no max).	Covered under Metropolitan. Prescription drugs — $1 for each 34-day supply. Vision and hearing screening.	You can put up to $2,400 per dependent to a maximum of $4,800 in tax-free dollars into your FlexFund to pay for dependent day care.

Exhibit 8.3 is an example of a relative timeline for introducing this type of plan.

Exhibit 8.4 outlines the structure of a typical comprehensive cafeteria plan, identified here as "CafComp." This plan was designed in combination with a carve-out of a uniform core of benefits providing for retirement income, paid time off, and educational assistance. "CafComp" is funded in part by employer contributions, which are based on a combination of costs for required benefits and credits for employee service. Employees may increase their available flexible dollars by selling vacation days, electing salary transfers (reductions), or both.

Exhibit 8.3   Timeline for Instituting Flexible Benefits

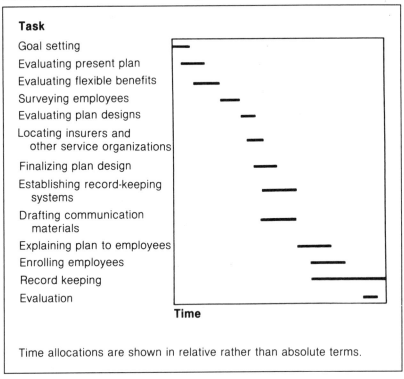

Task

Goal setting
Evaluating present plan
Evaluating flexible benefits
Surveying employees
Evaluating plan designs
Locating insurers and
    other service organizations
Finalizing plan design
Establishing record-keeping
    systems
Drafting communication
    materials
Explaining plan to employees
Enrolling employees
Record keeping
Evaluation

Time

Time allocations are shown in relative rather than absolute terms.

Source: Reproduced by permission of Catalyst from *Flexible Benefits: How to Set Up a Plan When Your Employees are Complaining, Your Costs are Rising, and You're Too Busy to Think About It*, p. 19. Copyright 1986 by Catalyst, 250 Park Avenue South, New York, N.Y. 10003.

At the beginning of every plan year each participant is given the opportunity to choose from among several levels of coverage in each of four required benefits groups (medical, life insurance, disability insurance, and dental). An individual can select the level that is most suitable for his or her perceived needs but is not permitted to waive all options in any category. Electively, participants may use flexible dollars for income deferral through the 401(k) plan and also have the option of designating funds for either or both of the reimbursement accounts. Those who do not designate all of the employer's contributions for nontaxable benefits at the beginning of the year receive cash distributions, which of course become fully taxable.

Exhibit 8.4   CafComp Employee Election Form

For _____ Clifford Green _____	Year _____ 1988 _____
Age __29__ Status __Single__	D.O.E. _____ 7/15/82 _____
	Salary _____ $26,000 _____

(Please refer to plan booklet for explanatory information)

A. Core Benefits (fully paid for by the Company) include
- Vacations, holidays, and personal time off allowances
- Retirement income plan
- Educational assistance benefits

B. Company Contributions for Choice Benefits $800

C. Choice Benefits (you must select one option in 1, 2, 3, and 4)

	Annual Price Tag	Employee Choices ($)		Annual Price Tag	Employee Choices ($)
1. Medical			3. Disability		
Option 1	$ 600	_____	Insurance		
Option 2	800	_____	Option 1	$ 50	_____
Option 3	1,000	_____	Option 2	80	_____
Option 4	1,200	_____	Option 3	110	_____
2. Life Insurance			4. Dental Benefits		
Option 1	$25	_____	Option 1	$25	_____
Option 2	50	_____	Option 2	50	_____
Option 3	75	_____	Option 3	75	_____

D. Reimbursement Accounts
1. Health Care ($240 to $2,400)   _____
2. Dependent Care ($240 to $5,000)   _____

E. 401(k) Savings Plan
1. Basic (1% to 6% of pay − 50% employer match)   _____
2. Supplemental (1% to 10% of pay − unmatched)   _____

F. Cash   _____

continued

Exhibit 8.4 *Continued*

G. Total Cost of Employee Choices ══════
  to be paid during the year with:

H. Flexible Dollars
  Employer contribution $800
  Vacation selling (1 to 5 days @ $100)   ──────
  Salary transfer   ──────
    Total (must equal G)   ══════

I have received and read the printed material describing the CafComp plan. I understand that by signing and submitting this form I have made an election for my benefits coverages for the calendar year <u>1988</u>. Any choices above may only be altered as the result of a change in family status as defined in the plan. I also understand that any unused monies in either reimbursement account will be forfeited after the end of the year.

──────────────   ────────────────────────
      Date   Employee Signature

The election form used in the annual "CafComp" participant elections, with specific information inserted by the company for one employee, is shown in Exhibit 8.4. The employee, Clifford Green, would receive this form about thirty days before the required submission date. In addition to the information included in the election form, he would get a workbook providing essential information about the various options and a reminder to review the Summary Plan Descriptions for more details concerning each benefit plan. Mr. Green would also be given the name and location of his benefits contact person and a twenty-four-hour hotline number. After the plan's first year he would receive a copy of his previous year's completed election form.

Since Mr. Green is single and has no dependents, the price tag for his medical and dental options is based on "employee only" coverage. The election form for a married participant with children would include price tags for employees with one and with two or more dependents.

The CafComp election form contains the type of acknowledgment statement and employee authorization that attorneys consider obligatory for cafeteria plans due to their relative complexity and legal requirements. This is especially critical in organizations that move away from a "father knows best" approach in which management made all the benefits decisions to a system in which employees assume some risks for selecting their own level of benefit protection. Another provision in this plan was designed to protect both the employee and the employer. There is a ten-day review period following the submission of election forms and prior to the beginning of the plan year when coverage becomes effective. During this period all election forms are computer-analyzed and each participant receives a printout indicating any computational errors. The participant then corrects any errors and confirms his final choices.

Opposition to Cafeteria Compensation (and Some Responses)

In spite of impressive growth during the 1980s and the many reports of positive results from plan sponsors, cafeteria and flexible benefit plans still cover only 8 percent of white-collar workers and 2 percent of blue-collar workers in organizations employing at least one hundred workers.[8] These levels reflect continuing allegiance to traditional programs and a significant amount of skepticism concerning cafeteria compensation by many executives.

Employer resistance to flexible benefits is usually expressed in one or more of the following ways:

1. "Employees will be confused and make poor choices."

2. "There will be too much adverse selection."

3. "It will be an administrative nightmare."

4. "It will take too much time (cost too much) to communicate."

5. "Our union will never buy it."

6. "There are too many tax and legal uncertainties."

Real or perceived, these beliefs have impeded the growth of cafeteria compensation even though there is nearly overwhelming evidence that employees favor the approach and it *can* be designed to satisfy a variety of employer objectives, including benefit cost containment.

Before recommending any form of cafeteria compensation to executive management, an employee benefit manager must evaluate each of these six concerns as they might apply to his or her own organization. In presenting a proposal, the benefit manager must be prepared to either refute the validity of the concern or have an effective and appropriate remedy. The following section summarizes the reasons for the negative management views and some successful responses and solutions used by benefit professionals.

Employees Will Make Poor Choices

The type of scenario sketched by critics of flexible benefits to demonstrate this point usually involves a married employee with many young children and a nonemployed spouse. Under the existing benefit plan this individual is covered by company-paid life insurance equal to two times salary. The projection given is that under the flex plan this person will swap half of the life insurance for extra vacation days and, sadly, die six months later leaving the family with a much smaller survivor payment. The presumption, of course, is that the company is more competent to make decisions about benefit coverage than employees.

Another negative view of cafeteria-style plans is that employees will become confused by the multiplicity of choices offered and make mistakes in completing their forms. For example, a single employee with no dependents might elect family medical coverage or the maximum amount of life insurance.

Both of these views are indicative of a management that subscribes to Theory X. As defined by Douglas McGregor, these kinds of managers assume that employees prefer to be directed and wish to avoid responsibility.[9] If that were the prevalent view of management, it should be clear to the benefit manager that the organization was not ready to implement a cafeteria plan. As long as the key executives possess a somewhat more enlightened attitude about employees, their concerns can be dealt with through a few safeguards that can be built into the basic plan design to protect employees from making inappropriate choices. These include:

Practice Election Worksheets   A sample of the official election form can be included in the plan workbook given to participants about a month before the required submission date. This will stimulate discussion of options with spouses and other dependents before decisions are made.

Enrollment Simulation   Groups of employees can be assisted through a simulated election (at least when the plan is introduced), given training in the process, and provided with a printout of their choices for study.

Error Checks and Confirmation Forms   As described in the CafComp example, employees can be given confirmation of their elections for review before the effective date. This step can also allow for revisions of obviously inappropriate choices.

Adverse Selection

This is the antithesis of poor choice. It is the tendency of individuals to select coverages they expect to use heavily and to reject benefits with little perceived value. It has been suggested by some human resource managers that a better definition of this phenomenon might be "intelligent selection," but from a group insurance perspective the normally broad-based risk pool for any coverage becomes distorted. Because the "good risks" don't participate, costs for the coverage rise for those who do.

Adverse selection is not unique to cafeteria plans. It occurs whenever any portion of a group benefit plan is optional and requires employee contributions, but because of the large number of options in a typical cafeteria plan, the concerns are accentuated. Some of the ways plans have been structured to minimize the effect of adverse selection on employer costs are:

- *providing core coverage* through employer contributions and offering supplemental benefits with minimal (or no) employer subsidies

- *restricting participants' eligibility* for higher coverage levels and the ability to switch coverages once basic needs have been satisfied. For example, a medical examination could be required whenever an employee elected an increase in group life insurance. And employees who elected to drop to the lowest level of dental benefits could be prohibited from choosing a higher-option plan for two years.

- *combining or "bundling" options* to create wider participation in all benefit coverages. The modular type of plan is best suited to this approach since it does not permit participants to waive any coverage within a module or make substitutions. A plan can be designed, based on pricing analysis, pretests, and simulations, to ensure a balanced risk pool for each module.

- *pricing strategies,* such as using age-related price schedules for group life insurance coverage to encourage younger employees to participate in the plan, and charging employees an artificially low rate for dental options to increase participation.

Administrative Complexity

The administrative burden argument cannot be minimized, but it need not be classified in the nightmare category. Clearly the amount of data generated by a multiple-option benefits plan will expand the requirements for information processing systems. It is unimaginable to contemplate introducing a cafeteria plan without the support of an automated system. And beyond that, there are critical needs for record-keeping systems, administrative procedures, and forms.

But, fortunately, much expertise has been acquired during the past decade and it is now possible for plan sponsors to select services and software packages from an ample number of qualified outside sources at affordable cost. Another reality for employers to consider is that the nondiscrimination testing of welfare benefit plans prescribed by the Tax Reform Act of 1986 and scheduled to become effective in 1989 will require numerous systems add-ons in most instances. The additional costs for installing a flexible benefit system may then be minimal.

Too Difficult (Expensive) to Communicate

There should be no doubt about cafeteria plans *requiring* extensive communication with employees. There is a need for obtaining employee views during the formative stages; for pretests and simulations during plan development; for printed materials and meetings when the plan is introduced; and for ongoing communication to prepare and assist employees in making benefit decisions once the plan becomes operative. To accomplish all of this, a plan sponsor needs to commit adequate funds and staff resources, predictably more than was being provided under the traditional program.

But the nearly universal message from cafeteria plan sponsors is that the attainment of objectives justifies the added expense. In addition to the many reports of achieving cost-containment objectives through flexible designs, there is a firm belief that employees gain a much clearer understanding of benefit values.

A common complaint from executives about benefit plans is that "employees don't realize what they are getting," and in a traditional design this is generally an accurate statement. Typically benefits are treated as something separate from pay, an employee has little influence on the form of coverage, and employer costs are irrelevant to employees.

In a cafeteria plan, employees begin to perceive benefits as another type of compensation, they gain control over the form of their individual coverages, and they become very interested in the level of employer contribution for benefits. Unlike their counterparts in companies with traditional plans these employees *do* realize what they are getting. However that will only occur with effective — and extensive — communication.

Union Opposition

Relatively few cafeteria plans have been negotiated between employers and unions. Many organizations with both unionized and nonunionized employees have implemented a plan for the latter without offering the same plan to the union. In most cases the union has been content to continue negotiating for benefits within a more traditional program.

The reluctance of most unions to embrace flexible plans seems to relate to one or both of the following views. One assumption is that cafeteria plans are being offered by management to mask benefit reductions. Another belief, postulated by some management people, is that union leaders prefer to retain their influential roles in bargaining for total group coverages rather than agreeing to a type of plan in which members would be allowed to make individual selections.

As union membership becomes more familiar with the attractions of flexible plans, and their negotiating teams learn more about the economics of cafeteria compensation, it is likely that there will be more plans covered by collective bargaining agreements. At present, ALCOA, Reynolds Metals, and Xerox are among large national organizations that include bargaining-unit employees in flexible plans. In the public sector, the Howard County (Maryland) School Board extended its optional benefits program to 2,700 organized workers in October 1985.[10]

Tax and Legal Uncertainties

"If American business deferred every decision until its tax and legal ramifications were entirely clear, our GNP would be running a close second to that of Outer Mongolia."[11] This quotation, from a consulting firm's guide on flexible compensation, may overstate the consequences of inaction, but the implication that tax and legal ramifications may *never* be clarified seems realistic. For example, as of early 1988 regulations for IRC Section 125 (proposed in 1984) were not finalized, nor had any regulations been issued covering revisions to this Section under the Tax Reform Act of 1986.

A benefit manager needs to carefully assess the risks of implementing a cafeteria plan without the support of "permanent" legal and tax regulations, and the capacity of the organization's top management to bear such a risk. Such assessments should involve interaction with in-house attorneys and tax specialists and some contact with outside benefit plan authorities.

A major issue confronting cafeteria plans at this time is the potential effect of the nondiscrimination rules now specified in Section 89 of the Internal Revenue Code and scheduled to take effect in 1989. Under current regulations, cafeteria plans are subject to a concentration test. If more than 25 percent of *total* plan benefits are provided to high-level employees, all benefits received by those employees through the plan become taxable. Subject to the issuance of regulations for Section 89, plan sponsors will, additionally, have to begin testing *each* benefit included in a cafeteria plan for possible discrimination in favor of highly compensated employees, in terms of both eligibility and benefits received, starting in 1989.

Summary

Since 1978 the use of cafeteria compensation or flexible benefits as an alternative to an inflexible benefit package superimposed upon base pay has increased steadily. Those organizations that have implemented plans are uniformly positive in reporting results — both in terms of meeting employer objectives and satisfying their employees.

A number of factors have impeded further growth of these plans, including tax and legal uncertainties, union opposition, and an expectation of high implementation costs. However, it has become evident that employees will no longer accept a totally inflexible benefit package and although most organizations have not yet adopted comprehensive cafeteria plans, some degree of choice is now available in virtually all compensation and benefit programs.

Notes

[1]David J. Thomsen, "Introducing Cafeteria Compensation in Your Company," *Personnel Journal* 56, no. 3 (March 1977): 124.

[2]*On Flexible Compensation* (Lincolnshire, Ill.: Hewitt Associates, January, 1988), p. 1.

[3]Mitchell Meyer, *Flexible Employee Benefit Plans: Companies' Experience* 38, no. 7 (New York: Conference Board, 1983), p. 3.

[4]"Designing a Decade of Functioning Flexibility," *Employee Benefit Plan Review* (January 1984): 10.

[5]Albert S. Schlactmeyer and Robert B. Bogart, "Employee-Choice Benefits — Can Employees Handle It?" *Compensation Review* 11, no. 3 (Third Quarter 1979). (*Compensation Review* has been renamed *Compensation and Benefits Review*).

[6]Rebecca A. Fannin, "American Can Employees Test New Flexible Benefits Program," *Business Insurance* (March 6, 1978): 1.

[7]See "Flex as a Merger Tool," *Benefits News Analysis* 6, no. 6 (June 1984).

[8]Preliminary information from BLS survey for 1986 reported in *Personnel Management Compensation* (Englewood Cliffs, N.J.: Prentice-Hall, May 13, 1987), p. 1.

[9]Douglas McGregor, *The Human Side of Enterprise* (New York: McGraw-Hill, 1960), p. 34.

[10]"Flex in a Collective Bargaining Environment," *Benefits News Analysis* 8, no. 4 (April 1986): 18–22.

[11]From *Flexible Compensation*, a brochure produced by Towers, Perrin, Forster, & Crosby (New York City), undated, circa 1983, p. 10.

9

Benefit Cost Information: Development and Applications

In a utopian organization a benefit manager would be able to concentrate fully on designing and administering programs that optimally satisfied employee needs without concern for employer costs. Realistically, however, cost issues are ever-present in benefit management, and a major challenge for every practitioner is to maintain perspective in balancing the values and advantages of the benefits against the constraints of cost. Operationally, this is largely a plan-by-plan process, and many cost considerations applicable to particular types of benefits have been discussed in earlier chapters. But there are also certain occasions when cost information about the total program or about groups of plans must be collected, analyzed, and reported. This chapter describes the ways in which benefit program costs are summarized and used, internally and externally, for a variety of purposes.

Benefit Cost Classifications

Many benefits are considered to be pay-dependent in terms of their cost. That is to say, as wages and salaries rise, there is a direct and immediate increase in the cost of these items. Benefits affected in this way include paid vacations, holidays, sick leave, personal days, and rest periods. All of these represent paid time off, and they are for the most part fully taxable. The U.S. Chamber of Commerce (USCC) classifies these payments as *inside-payroll* benefits and all other forms of indirect compensation as *outside-payroll* in its annual surveys.[1] Many firms now use the same nomenclature in their own cost reports.

Some outside payroll coverages are wholly independent of pay. For example, costs for group health insurance are not influenced by salary or wage increases. However employer costs for many of the outside-payroll benefits are *pay-sensitive*. For example:

- Group life insurance coverage is frequently a multiple of annual salary.
- Payroll taxes for Social Security and unemployment compensation rise automatically with pay increases up to maximum wage base levels.
- Employer contributions to money-purchase, profit-sharing, and savings plans are usually based on a percentage of pay, and therefore directly influenced by increases in base pay.

To effectively analyze and project benefit costs, a manager needs to clearly grasp both the distinction between inside- and outside-payroll benefits and the secondary effects on the latter resulting from increases in base pay. To contain costs it is useful to seek ways of effectively uncoupling pay and benefits. An example of this would be the separation of pay from group life insurance eligibility.

Ways of Expressing Costs

There are six commonly used ways of expressing the cost of benefits:

1. Total annual cost
2. Percentage of payroll
3. Average cost per employee per year
4. Average cents per hour (or dollars per week)
5. Actual cost for each employee
6. Employer-employee cost ratio

Total Annual Cost

Total annual cost is the basic summary figure from which other forms of expression are derived. The information for an annual report of benefit costs is available from standard payroll and accounting records. Exhibit 9.1 is an example of a report prepared by an accounting department according to HRM department specifications. Most of the benefits are available to all classifications of employees, but if separate reports are needed for different groups, relocation expenses could be eliminated from the analysis of hourly workers, and a report for outside sales representatives should exclude rest periods, cafeteria subsidy, and recreation programs.

The total annual cost is an important figure to the benefit manager, who is accountable for performance against the current year's budget and for the following year's plan. Top management also wants benefit expenses expressed in this way so that the data will conform to other types of business expenses for financial control planning purposes.

Total annual cost is an impressive statistic for public relations purposes, during and after union negotiations, and for recruitment literature. For example: "Employees of Excelsior Enterprises now receive more than $10 million in benefits on top of outstanding wages and salaries," or "Contract settlement reached; wage and benefit increases to cost company $3 million over next two years," or "Our company spent $25 million last year for employee benefits and services."

Percentage of Payroll

Percentage of payroll is normally calculated by dividing the total cost of benefits by total payroll. Using the data in Exhibit 9.1, the applicable percentage would be 36 percent:

$$\frac{\$7,200,000}{\$20,000,000} = 36\%$$

This is the standard basis for developing a percentage figure, but several other methods are used. Some companies use only base pay for time worked as the denominator. This in effect eliminates pay for time not worked plus overtime and shift premiums from the gross payroll amount. In Exhibit 9.1, this would mean deducting $2,500,000 and $1,000,000 from the $20 million total payroll. As a result, the benefits-cost ratio would be higher:

$$\frac{\$7,200,000}{\$16,500,000} = 43.6\%$$

Exhibit 9.1 Annual Benefits Cost Report

Benefit	Company Costs ($000)	Totals
Social Insurance Payments		
Social Security taxes	$1,300	
Unemployment insurance/taxes	320	
Workers' compensation insurance	280	$1,900
Company Health and Security Plans		
Health benefits	$1,100	
Life insurance	100	
Disability benefits	100	
Retirement plan	800	
Savings and investment plan	200	$2,300
Payments to Employees		
Educational assistance	45	
Service awards	30	
Relocation expenses	150	225
Employee Services		
Employee assistance program	50	
Cafeteria subsidy	175	
Recreation programs	40	
Product discounts	10	275
Pay for Time Not Worked		
Vacations	$1,050	
Holidays	650	
Sick days	125	
Personal absences	100	
Rest periods	575	2,500
Total Cost of Benefits		$7,200

Notes:

1. *Total Employee Compensation ($000)*

A. Base pay for time worked	16.5
B. Pay for time not worked	2.5
C. Overtime and shift premium pay	1.0
D. Total payroll expense	20.0
E. Outside payroll benefits	4.7
F. Total employee compensation (D + E)	24.7

2. *Average number of full-time employees* — 1,000

$$\frac{\text{(Number at beginning of year + number at end of year)}}{2}$$

Another approach considers only outside-payroll benefit costs and relates their total costs to either total payroll or total employee compensation. Using the same data as previously outlined this would produce in the first instance:

$$\frac{\$4,700,000}{\$20,000,000} = 23.5\%$$

and in the second instance:

$$\frac{\$4,700,000}{\$24,700,000} = 19.0\%$$

In making comparisons with other companies, it is critical that a uniform basis for computing percentages be established. However, as long as the same basis of measurement is used by all parties, percentage of payroll is an excellent way to compare benefit costs with other companies, since it overcomes size variations. On the other hand, it is important to realize that a high benefits-cost ratio can result from low wages as well as from high benefits. This relationship is particularly important when comparing domestic and overseas operations. Using the standard calculation method described above, benefit costs in South America and some European countries are 50 to 100 percent of payroll compared with a typical 35 to 40 percent in the United States. These higher percentages are caused in part by higher legally required payments in other countries, but they are attributable also to much lower wage levels in most of the countries as compared with the United States.

Average Cost Per Employee Per Year

Average cost per employee per year is an impressive figure to use in employee communications. It is personalized, easily related to the W-2 statement, and usually large enough not to be ignored. The standard method for obtaining this figure is to divide the total cost of benefits by the average number of full-time employees on the payroll during the year. Again using the data in Exhibit 9.1:

$$\frac{\$7,200,000}{1,000 \text{ employees}} = \$7,200$$

The average number of full-time employees can be determined simply by averaging beginning-of-year and end-of-year employment figures. It can also be computed by using payroll hours to construct the number of full-time equivalent employees. This can be done by adding time actually worked and time paid for but not worked by all employees to obtain a figure for gross payroll hours for the year, then dividing that figure by the number of payroll hours for which a typical full-time employee is paid. For example:

$$\frac{2,200,000 \text{ hours}}{2,200 \text{ hours}} = 1,000 \text{ full-time equivalent employees}$$

The latter method, although more complicated, should be used in organizations that have wide variations in hours worked by employees, a large number of part-time or seasonal employees, or a significant amount of overtime work.

Employers should realize that an average cost of the total package may mean very little to employees who are not eligible for or do not participate in the major plans. If there are long waiting periods for participation and if large numbers of employees are excluded from certain plans, the average cost could be a very misleading figure. In such cases, it would be preferable to compute actual costs for participants on a plan-by-plan basis.

Average Cents Per Hour

Average cents per hour is usually derived by dividing the total cost of benefits by total payroll hours, or, using the information above,

$$\frac{\$7,200,000}{2,200,000} = 327\cent \text{ or } \$3.27 \text{ per hour}$$

Another common method of calculating cents per hour is to use only productive hours as the denominator. This means excluding hours paid for but not worked, and might involve the following deductions:

Benefits	Avg. hours per year per employee
Vacations	110
Holidays	70
Sick leave	15
Paid personal absence	10
Rest periods	70
	275 hours
	× 1,000 employees
	275,000 person hours

The total productive, or work, hours would be 1,925,000 (2,200,000 − 275,000). Then the measure of cents per productive hour would be:

$$\frac{\$7,200,000}{1,925,000 \text{ hours}} = 374\cent \text{ or } \$3.74 \text{ per hour}$$

Using either method, this form of expression is especially effective in communications with employees who think of their pay in terms of hourly rates. An employee who is paid $9.00 per hour worked is apt to be quite favorable impressed when made aware that his benefits amount to $3.27 or $3.74 per hour. For those paid on a weekly, biweekly, or semimonthly basis, it is relatively easy to convert the hourly cost to comply with their particular mode and frequency of pay.

Actual Costs for Each Employee

The actual cost for each individual is an ideal way to personalize benefit cost information for employees. It may also be difficult and expensive for a small organization to develop. But, as seen above, reports using averages can be misleading and open to criticism by employees. For example, younger employees will point out that they may not benefit from pension contributions; single employees will claim that they gain nothing from employer-provided dependent coverage payments; and employees who do not participate in thrift plans will be reminded that they receive no credits from company funds. Furthermore, an employee who has had perfect attendance will realize that others have been "rewarded" by payments for time off due to illness and personal reasons.

Some benefit costs, for example the cafeteria subsidy and recreation program expenses, have to be averaged, but most other items can be computed individually. With automated employee information systems becoming increasingly versatile and efficient, this type of information can now be developed cost-effectively, at least in medium and large firms.

Employer-Employee Cost Ratio

The employer-employee cost ratio is most meaningful in organizations that have contributory benefit plans. Virtually all working people contribute to the cost of Social Security coverage. In a few states, employees pay for a part of unemployment compensation and disability income benefits. It is still common for employees to share the costs of group insurance coverage with their employer, and thrift plans are predicated on employee contributions.

Because employee contributions are normally handled through payroll deductions, employees are constantly reminded of their costs. Therefore if a company newspaper report stresses only the employer's benefit costs, employees are bound to become resentful. Since, in most instances, the employer will be on the favorable side of the ratio there should be no reason to withhold information. Care should be taken to report net costs. For instance, dividends from insurance plans should be applied against premium costs. A large manufacturing company once lost much credibility with its employees by attempting to hide its dividend credit, only to have a union attorney reveal a photostatic copy of the report the company had received from the insurance carrier detailing the savings resulting from the credit.

A comparison of employer and employee benefit costs can be expressed in any of the forms shown in Exhibit 9.2. The actual cost ratio for each employee, which could be included in an annual personalized benefit statement, would, of course, have to be calculated on an individual basis.

Uses of Cost Information

In most organizations there are a number of regular recurring needs for summaries of benefit costs and some ad hoc requirements. The most common applications are for:

1. Mandatory disclosure and reporting
2. Reports to employees
3. Determining employer-employee contribution levels
4. Collective bargaining
5. Management reports
6. Compensation and benefits surveys

Exhibit 9.2   Illustration of Employer and Employee Benefit Costs

Cost	Employer payments	Employee payroll deductions
Total annual cost	$7,200,000	$1,800,000
Percentage of payroll	36%	9%
Average annual cost per employee	$7,200	$1,800
Average cost per hour for each employee	$3.27	$0.82
Dollar ratio	$4.00	$1.00

Mandatory Disclosure and Reporting

Since the enactment of ERISA in 1974 sponsors of pension and welfare plans have been required to submit annual reports to the Internal Revenue Service (IRS) disclosing, along with other essential information, plan expenses, income, assets, and liabilities. These revelations of financial activity and status are submitted on one of several versions of IRS Form 5500 according to the number of participants in a plan. It is not necessary for employers to give every participant a copy of the annual reports, but employees have the right to examine reports and to obtain copies upon written request to the plan administrator.

An excerpted section of IRS Form 5500-C (for plans with fewer than one hundred participants) indicating the type of plan cost information needed for completion is shown in Exhibit 9.3. Separate forms must be completed and filed by sponsors for each covered plan.

Completion of the ERISA-required annual reports is usually a joint effort between employee benefit and accounting departments, who pool their resources and knowledge about plan finances. It is important for the accounting function to tie in the ERISA reporting with the information that now must be included in company financial statements in accordance with standards issued by the Financial Accounting Standards Board (FASB).

Reports to Employees

As required by ERISA, benefit plan sponsors must automatically supply a Summary Annual Report (SAR) to each plan participant and each beneficiary receiving benefits within nine months following the end of a plan year. To facilitate this process the Department of Labor (DOL) in 1979 issued a prescribed format and model language for SARs. A report of each covered plan must include:

a basic financial statement

insurance information (if applicable)

minimum funding standards (defined benefit pension plans only)

participant/beneficiary rights to additional information

Exhibit 9.4 shows the DOL format and model language for the basic financial statement, and an example of information furnished by an employer-sponsor of a defined benefit plan.

Exhibit 9.3 Applicable Sections Covering Plan Assets, Liabilities, Income, and Expenses from IRS Form 5500-C, "Return/Report of Employee Benefit Plan"

Form 5500-C (1985)   Page **3**

15 Plan assets and liabilities at the beginning and end of the current plan year (list all assets and liabilities at current value). A fully insured welfare plan or a pension plan with no trust and which is funded entirely by allocated insurance contracts which fully guarantee the amount of benefit payments should check the box and not complete the rest of this item . . . . ▶ ☐

Note: *Include all plan assets and liabilities of a trust or separately maintained fund. If more than one trust/fund, report on a combined basis. Include all insurance values except for the value of that portion of an allocated insurance contract which fully guarantees the amount of benefit payments. Round off amounts to nearest dollar. If you have no assets to report enter "-0-" on line 15g.*

Assets	(a) Beginning of year	(b) End of year
a Cash— *(i)* Interest bearing		
(ii) Non-interest bearing		
(iii) Total cash (add (i) and (ii))		
b Receivables.		
c Investments—		
(i) Government securities		
(ii) Pooled funds/mutual funds		
(iii) Corporate (debt and equity instruments).		
(iv) Value of interest in master trust		
(v) Real estate and mortgages		
(vi) Other		
(vii) Total investments (add (i) through (vi))		
d Building and other depreciable property used in plan operation . . .		
e Unallocated insurance contracts		
f Other assets		
g Total assets (add a(iii); b; c(vii); d; e and f)		
Liabilities and Net Assets		
h Payables		
i Acquisition indebtedness		
j Other liabilities		
k Total liabilities (add h through j)		
l Net assets (subtract k from g)		

16 Plan income, expenses and changes in net assets during the plan year. Include all income and expenses of a trust(s) or separately maintained fund(s), including any payments made for allocated insurance contracts. Round off amounts to nearest dollar.

	(a) Amount	(b) Total
a Contributions received or receivable in cash from:		
(i) Employer(s) (including contributions on behalf of self-employed individuals)		
(ii) Employees		
(iii) Others		
b Noncash contributions		
c Earnings from investments (interest, dividends, rents, royalties).		
d Net realized gain (loss) on sale or exchange of assets		
e Other income (specify) ▶ _____		
f Total income (add a through e)		
g Distribution of benefits and payments to provide benefits:		
(i) Directly to participants or their beneficiaries.		
(ii) To insurance carrier or similar organization for provision of benefits (including prepaid medical plans) . . . . '. . . .		
(iii) To other organizations or individuals providing welfare benefits.		
h Interest expense		
i Administrative expenses (salaries, fees, commissions, insurance premiums).		
j Other expenses (specify) ▶ _____		
k Total expenses (add g through j)		
l Net income (subtract k from f)		
m Changes in net assets: (i) Unrealized appreciation (depreciation) of assets		
(ii) Net investment gain (or loss) from all master trust investment accounts		
(iii) Other changes (specify) ▶ _____		
n Net increase (decrease) in net assets for the year (add l and m)		
o Net assets at beginning of year (line 15l, column(a)).		
p Net assets at end of year (add n and o) (equals line 15l, column (b)).		

Exhibit 9.4   Model Language Required by the Department of Labor for Basic Financial Statement in Summary Annual Reports (*Company Information Inserted*)

> Benefits under the plan are provided by (*trust funds into which the Company pays the amounts required to fund the plan*). The Master Trustee is the (*First National Bank*). Plan expenses were ($5,005,825). These expenses consisted of ($4,150,385) in benefits paid to participants and beneficiaries and ($855,440) in administrative expenses. A total of (7,775) persons were participants in or beneficiaries of the plan at the end of the plan year, although not all of these persons had yet earned the right to receive benefits.
>
> The value of plan assets, after subtracting liabilities of the plan, was ($210,430,510) as of (*December 31, 1987*), compared to ($172,220,400) as of (*December 31, 1986*). During the plan year the plan experienced an increase in its net assets of ($38,210,110). This increase included unrealized appreciation in the value of the plan's assets; that is, the difference between the value of the plan's asset at the end of the year and the value of the assets at the beginning of the year. The plan had total income of ($20,740,860), no employer contributions were made in (1987), gains of ($9,790,220) from the sale of assets, and earning from investments of ($10,950,640).

There have been numerous reports of employee indifference to SARs, and to conserve funds many employer groups and consultants have proposed that the automatic distribution requirement be eliminated since employees have a right to inspect the full annual reports anyway. However, given the simplicity of the prescribed format and the option of utilizing inexpensive word processing, duplicating, and distribution resources, the costs associated with SARs seem small when measured against the potential loss of employee trust that could result from holding back information.

A more meaningful disclosure of benefit cost information is made by some companies in annual personalized benefit reports. These statements (to be discussed more fully in Chapter 10) are an excellent medium for informing employees, individually, what their benefits cost and how much of that amount is paid for by the employer. Recently a company president stressed these points in his introductory statement to the annual personalized benefit reports. In one individualized version an employee was reminded, "Here at _____we have a benefit program that adds considerable value to your total pay. The company spends $14,407 on your benefits alone. Add to that the $3,457 contributions you make, and you have a program that's worth $17,864."

Determining Employer-Employee Contribution Levels

Historically contribution responsibilities for group benefits tended to be set on a dollars basis when a plan was adopted. As plan costs rose over time, employee contributions, if any, often remained constant and the employer became progressively responsible for a larger share of the costs. This pattern prevailed until the late 1970s, largely because many employers feared that employees would be alienated by "price" increases, and the major unions effectively resisted negotiated increases in member contributions. But since that time, cost pressures have created a trend reversal. Evidence of this shift can be found in data from the USCC's annual cost surveys. In 1963, the average employee payroll deduction for health and life insurance was 1.2 percent of pay. By 1979 the applicable figure had dropped to 0.8 percent, but in 1986 it was 1.5 percent.[2]

A method now used by some firms to periodically adjust employee contributions when costs rise involves percentage-of-cost sharing levels. For example, a company could specify that it will be responsible for 75 percent of the costs for all insured plans. If in the first year total costs were $1,000,000, employee contributions would have to account for $250,000. In the following year, if costs were projected to rise by $100,000, it would be appropriate to increase employee contributions by 10 percent to maintain the targeted 75 percent = 25 percent sharing ratio. This type of arrangement can be accepted rationally by employees, but it is not always perceived as fair unless employees can relate the costs to their individual circumstances or have options of selecting lower — and less expensive — levels of coverage.

Firms that have converted to flexible compensation are in the best position to control the level of employer costs and to effectively increase employee contributions as needed with minimum dissatisfaction. That is because in cafeteria-type programs, the employer's commitment to support benefits becomes *independent* of the prices charged for the coverages. To appreciate the import of this statement, it is necessary to examine some fundamental features of flexible plans.

For example, assume that a company converts to a cafeteria plan using a carve-out approach, and retains a core consisting of a defined benefit pension plan, paid time off allowances, and educational assistance. All of the insured benefits (medical, dental, life, and disability) are then offered to employees on a choice basis, with three levels of coverage available in each category. The middle, or standard, options are equivalent to coverages under the previous program, and the employer provides each employee with enough flexible credits to obtain coverages at that level. If an employee selects lower cost options, remaining credits can be used for 401(k) plan contributions, placed in reimbursement accounts, or taken in cash. If the cost of the options chosen exceeds the number of credits, the employee pays for the difference with pretax payroll deductions.

Exhibit 9.5 shows how employer and employee contributions are set initially, then adjusted in the second plan year, and how this affects an individual employee, Dorothy Doe.

Exhibit 9.5   Flexcomp Plan Information for Dorothy Doe

Plan Year   1
Flexible Credits Allowance 1,600

Benefit	Cost of options (# of credits)		
	Basic	Standard	High
Medical	900	1,200	1,800
Dental	50	100	150
Life Insurance	90	180	270
Disability	60	120	180
Total	1,100	1,600	2,400

Plan Year   2
Flexible Credits Allowance 1,695

Benefit	Cost of options (# of credits)		
	Basic	Standard	High
Medical	950	1,300	2,000
Dental	55	120	180
Life Insurance	95	190	290
Disability	65	130	200
Total	1,165	1,740	2,670

In the first year the employer funds the program with 1,600 flexible credits for Ms. Doe, her total cost for the standard option coverages. In the second year, as a result of premium increases related to plan utilization and costs of services, it is necessary to selectively raise employee contributions for the various options. In this example, the employer at the same time voluntarily increased all employees' flexible credit allowances by 5.9 percent (from 1,600 to 1,695 for Ms. Doe). This represents the percentage rise in costs for the basic option. Alternatively the employer might have tied the adjustment to the annual increase in salary expense. The key point is that in this type of program, the company can determine its funding commitment for benefits each year and involve employees in cost sharing in an open manner. At the same time, employees are made precisely aware of increases in employer contributions while gaining the advantages of multiple choices.

Collective Bargaining

Since virtually all employee benefits are considered mandatory subjects of bargaining under federal labor law, information concerning such benefits must be exchanged between the parties in a collective bargaining relationship. The National Labor Relations Board has ruled repeatedly that employers must respond to union requests for benefit cost data beyond ERISA disclosure requirements, and the courts have consistently upheld these rulings. In one decision, affirmed by the U.S. Supreme Court, an employer was directed to furnish the union with such detailed information as cost per employee, and per dependent, of each proposed new insured benefit, and/or each proposed incremental increase in existing benefits, expressed in cents per month premium and cents per month net cost estimated on the basis of the company's prior experience.[3]

Despite having a legal right of access to cost information, unions tend to be skeptical of cost data presented by employers and often claim that management overstates benefit expenses as a means of holding down cash increases in bargaining. From the other side of the bargaining table, employers have accused unions of giving inflated cost figures to the media when contract settlements are announced. The inference is that exaggerated amounts are used to gain leverage in subsequent negotiations with other employers.

Another problem that unionized companies encounter is the ambivalence of unions in shifting the bargaining focus between benefits *values* and benefits *costs* to gain the maximum advantage in negotiations. As Victor M. Zink, formerly director of Worldwide Employee Benefits for General Motors Corporation, has observed:

Even though the unions have pushed strongly for employer-paid programs, they have insisted that, in fact, the payments by employers for employee benefits represent employee money. They justify their interest in financing, investment, and administration on this thesis. They make the further statement that it is money which, if not spent as it is, would be used for wages or other benefits. In the earlier days when the pension fund earnings were in excess of expectations, the unions argued that the additional monies should be used for additional benefits.[4]

Because unions still employ this type of two-edged sword in negotiating for benefits, management representatives need to be thoroughly prepared to discuss such issues as the cost dynamics of defined benefit plans, the variability of insurance premiums, and the roll-up cost effect on wage-dependent benefits.

Exhibit 9.6 illustrates how a benefit department can summarize the cost impact of a union's proposals to change wages and benefits at the time of contract renewal. Since benefits for nonexempt and exempt employees frequently change in tandem with settlements for unionized hourly groups, the costs for extending the proposed revisions to those other categories have been included in the calculations. A more comprehensive model for costing wage and benefit packages has been presented by Robert E. Allen and Timothy J. Keaveny, who also noted the importance of relating the analysis to "projections of future business activity and of future work force characteristics."[5]

Management Reports

As benefit costs have escalated, both in absolute terms and as a percentage of payroll, top management in most organizations has become progressively more involved in scrutinizing program expenditures. In addition to exercising executive authority over budget proposals, senior managers invariably want to know how *their* organization compares with competitors in benefit plan costs. To satisfy this interest, many benefit managers now include data from the U.S. Chamber of Commerce surveys as part of their periodic reporting of benefit costs to management. Since the Chamber reports provide analysis according to industry group, geographic region, and company size, it is often possible to show separate data for different divisions or subsidiaries in large corporations.

Particularly in large organizations, benefit managers contract with outside consultants for comparative cost/value analyses that can be presented to top management (see Exhibit 2.6). The consulting firms offer the expertise needed to perform the actuarial analysis that is part of this technique and are

Exhibit 9.6 Confidential Cost Analysis of Union Proposals

A = Bargaining unit, 250 employees; average rate $10.00/hour
B = Nonexempt staff, 75 employees; average salary $300/week
C = Exempt staff, 50 employees; average salary $31,000/year

Union Proposal	Added Cost Next Year
1. Add 5% general wage increase	
A. 250 × 50¢ × 2,080 hours	260,000
B. 75 × $15 × 52 weeks	58,500
C. Not directly affected	—
2. Add two additional holidays	
A. 250 × $10.50 × 16 hours	42,000
B. 75 × $63 × 2 days	9,450
C. 50 × $125 × 2 days	12,500
3. Eliminate 3% employee contribution to defined benefit pension plan	
A. 125 participants × 3% × $11.00 × 2,080 hours	85,800
B. 40 participants × 3% × $350.00 × 52 weeks	21,840
C. 35 participants × 3% × $34,000	35,700
4. Provide fourth vacation week after 15 years	
A. 50 employees × $11.50 × 40 hours	23,000
B. 15 employees × $375	5,625
C. 20 employees × $675	13,500
Add group vision care plan (employee coverage only)	
A. 250 employees × $90	22,500
B. 75 employees × $90	6,750
C. 50 employees × $90	4,500
6. Roll-up costs (wage-dependent benefits including mandatory coverages = 25% of pay)	
A. 250 × 50¢ × 2,080 hours × .25	65,000
B. 75 × $15 × 52 × .25	14,625
Total	$681,290

better able to obtain the necessary cost data from identified competitors of the client company.

Compensation and Benefit Surveys

Traditionally most compensation surveys conducted by employers ask for actual pay data and general information about benefit plans. In practice, after a company decides to participate in such a survey, the direct compensation unit inputs the hard data and the benefit group completes the questionnaire by adding the relevant qualitative information. Effectively there is no integration of the data being supplied, and as a resource for measuring the competitiveness of an organization's total compensation package the survey summary has little value.

Now that so many organizations are informing their employees of the costs of benefits on an individualized basis, it seems reasonable to expect that such information should be incorporated in survey designs. This practice would be especially appropriate among organizations that have substantially converted to cafeteria-type compensation systems. In such an environment a total compensation survey questionnaire might contain the following items for each job title included:

	No. of Employees	Avg. $/yr.
A. Base salary	_____	_____
B. Employer cost for mandatory benefits		_____
C. Employer cost for core benefits (outside payroll)		_____
D. Employer cost for flexible credits		_____
TOTAL COMPENSATION	_____*	

*Includes $_____ inside payroll expenses

Regardless of the format, or the degree of flexible compensation, it is essential that surveys include benefit cost information if organizations want to ensure their competitiveness on the basis of total compensation.

Summary

Although employees usually focus more closely on benefit plan values than on costs, plan managers need to thoroughly understand the dynamics of benefit costs and use the information they assemble productively in a variety of ways.

In compiling and analyzing benefit cost data it is important to recognize that, to a large extent, benefit costs are a dependent variable of direct compensation. As pay rates rise many benefit costs will rise automatically. To minimize this roll-up effect some firms have found ways to uncouple some benefit plan levels, such as amounts of group life insurance, from salary.

The continuing growth of flexible compensation and cafeteria plans is expected to make employees more cognizant of costs for employee benefits. That is because in most of these plans the employer's level of contribution (i.e. cost) is fixed as a budgeted amount and separated from prices charged for the various coverages by insurers and other providers. As a result, employees become responsible for any costs not covered by the employer subsidy. In some cases this causes employees to choose lower cost options. Alternatively other employees find that they must increase their contributions in order to maintain a desired level of benefit protection. Whatever decisions may be made, the concept and design of a typical flex plan clearly reveals the amount of the employer's contribution, thereby making benefit costs a more visible component of employee compensation.

Notes

[1]*Employee Benefits* (Washington, D.C.: U.S. Chamber of Commerce, published annually).

[2]*Employee Benefits Historical Data 1951–1979* (Washington, D.C.: U.S. Chamber of Commerce, 1981), p. 30 and *Employee Benefits 1986* (Washington, D.C.: U.S. Chamber of Commerce, 1987), p. 19.

[3]For example, see General Electric, 150 NLRB 192, enforced NLRB v. General Electric Company, 418 F. 2d 736 (2nd Cir., 1969), cert. denied, U.S. (1970).

[4]Victor M. Zink, "Organized Labor's Role," in *Employee Benefits Programs: Management, Planning, and Control*, ed. Ernest J. E. Griffes (Homewood, Ill.: Dow Jones-Irwin, 1983), p. 218.

[5]Robert E. Allen and Timothy J. Keaveny, "Costing Out a Wage and Benefit Package," *Compensation Review* (Second Quarter 1983): 27–39. (*Compensation Review* has been renamed *Compensation and Benefits Review*.)

10

Communication: The Keystone

In architecture a keystone is a wedge-shaped piece at the summit of an arch that holds the other pieces in place. In benefit management, the keystone of the program is employee communication. Without effective communication, a benefit program remains incomplete and the considerable effort and expense consumed in planning, designing, and administering plans becomes largely nonproductive. There are several reasons for this.

1. Employees must be made *aware* of their company-provided benefits and the principal plan provisions. Simply handing out summary plan descriptions (SPDs) as required by ERISA is not enough. Employees have to be reminded of their coverages periodically and must know how to apply for benefits when needed. Unless employees recognize the special utility and advantages of benefits, they will either forget about them or wonder if it wouldn't be preferable to receive their full compensation in cash.

2. Employees must be able to *understand* the benefits information they receive from their employers to gain full advantage from the plans. Since 1976 federal regulations have required that SPDs be "written

in a manner calculated to be understood by the average plan participant." Yet the following passage, the entire disability plan explanation that a large employer was giving to its workers until recently, thoroughly baffled a panel of benefit experts that was asked, "When would payments start?"[1]

> If injury results within 30 days of an accident in continuous total disability (complete inability to perform the duties of your occupation for six months) and if you are then permanently and totally disabled (unable to engage in any substantially gainful occupation or employment for which you are qualified or may reasonably become qualified), you will be paid a monthly permanent total disability benefit.
> "Monthly permanent total disability benefit" will amount to 60% of your basic monthly earnings (excluding your overtime and any other premium paid) annualized as of the last pay period preceding the loss.

3. Employees need to get prompt answers to their questions and be able to *trust* the information they receive. To the extent that information is unavailable, inadequate, or inaccurate, there is an erosion of employee confidence in the plans — and in management. Companies are particularly vulnerable to losses of credibility in the area of oral communication. For example:

   - whenever benefit administrators ignore employee telephone inquiries
   - whenever recruiters are discussing benefit plan details with applicants during preemployment negotiations
   - whenever line managers, labor negotiators, or HRM generalists give on-the-spot interpretations of plan provisions to employees

From a planning perspective most organizations relate their investment in benefit communications to a goal of convincing present and future employees of the worth of the benefit package. Meeting that goal is a major step towards achieving the broader program objectives of attracting, satisfying, motivating, and retaining competent and committed employees. To attain the immediate goal, a benefit manager must first make sure that all legal requirements are being met. Then, in developing an overall strategy, selecting themes, media, and materials, and determining a budget, the manager must concentrate on building employee awareness, understanding, and trust.

Legal Requirements

The ERISA requirements for reporting and disclosing information about benefit plans (see Exhibit 10.1) have helped open the books and remove a fundamental cause of employee distrust—namely, secrecy.

Exhibit 10.1   Key ERISA Requirements

Summary of key ERISA requirements for reporting and disclosing information to pension and welfare participants, for plans with one hundred or more participants. Some exemptions and exceptions apply to plans with fewer than one hundred employees.

		Participants, and beneficiaries receiving benefits, to be given	
Item	*Due*	*Automatically*	*On written request*
1. Summary plan description	120 days after plan establishment; new participants within 90 days	Yes	Yes
2. Summary of material modifications	210 days after end of plan year	Yes	Yes
3. Annual report (Form 5500)	7 months after end of plan year	No	Yes
4. Summary annual report	9 months after end of plan year	Yes	No
5. Benefits statement for terminating vested participants (pension plans only)	7 months after end of plan year	Yes	No
6. Statement of accrued/vested benefits (pension plan participants only)	30 days after written request; no more than once in 12-month period	No	Yes

Certainly the summary plan description (SPD) is an essential document for plan participants (including beneficiaries receiving benefits). Some companies even go beyond the requirement of automatically giving SPDs to plan participants. They issue copies to all employees on the presumption that eventually everyone will be eligible to participate in the plans. In addition to describing the main features of a benefit plan, an SPD is required to include an "ERISA rights" statement. This statement must advise participants of their rights to additional information and to appeal claims that may be denied or ignored. They must also be informed that any questions about the statement or their rights can be referred to the nearest area office of the U.S. Department of Labor, Labor-Management Services Administration. Beyond that, employers have a great deal of latitude in setting the format and style for SPDs.

The requirement for issuing a summary of material modifications (SMM) within 210 days after the end of a plan year seems reasonable. In most instances, when an employer makes any significant changes in a plan, the information is communicated to employees on or before the effective date. In many cases, the SMM requirement can be satisfied by these current written announcements of changes.

The annual report (Form 5500) is intended primarily for filing with the IRS, but a participant is entitled to receive a copy upon written request, and the employer must make a copy conveniently available for inspection by employees.

As indicated in Chapter 9, employees seem to be almost apathetic about summary annual reports (SARs), yet the basic requirement to furnish each plan participant with a copy no later than nine months after the end of the plan year continues. The due date can be extended by as much as two-and-a-half months with IRS permission.

The benefit statement for terminated vested employees is directly related to information the employer includes as part of the annual Form 5500 submission within seven months after the end of a pension plan year. Actually, most employers satisfy the requirement for the departing participant by disclosing the information in a letter at the time of, or shortly after, termination.

Companies that issue personalized annual benefit statements often include a section showing the employee's accrued pension benefits and the portion that is vested. In this way they satisfy the ERISA requirements proactively and eliminate the need to respond to individual requests on an ad hoc basis.

In addition to complying with ERISA requirements, a benefit manager must be certain that all other federal and state-mandated provisions regarding communication of plan information to employees are being met. Among these requirements are:

1. Group health continuation coverage notification provisions contained in COBRA.

2. Security and Exchange Commission (SEC) disclosure rules for employee stock ownership plans and other plans in which employees receive employer stock as a benefit.

3. State specifications on mandatory postings of unemployment insurance, workers' compensation, and nonoccupational temporary disability benefit laws.

Creating and Expanding Awareness

Many years ago a major record company made very effective use of the slogan "The music you want, when you want it." Implicitly this message reminded consumers that they could control the selection of records for listening by buying them rather than relying on radio program directors to satisfy their wants.

More recently, communications authorities have developed a parallel theme for employee benefits that could be called "the benefits information you need, when you need it." The approach is better known as *event-centered* communication. Central to the concept of event-centered communication is the notion that employee awareness will be heightened when information is highlighted as benefits (1) become available, and (2) are needed.

Benefits become available to employees at different times during their employment with an organization. As demonstrated in Exhibit 10.2, a communications plan can be designed to selectively synchronize the provision of benefit information with certain triggering events such as service milestones, pay increases, and status changes. This is far more effective and efficient than the traditional approach of concentrating communications at the start of employment and expecting that to be sufficient for employees to deal with benefits in relation to future events.

In an event-centered mode, the initial orientation to benefits is limited to a broad overview, a discussion of immediately available coverages, and a review of dates of eligibility for other plans. At later points, relevant benefit information is communicated on a timely basis to help employees make

Exhibit 10.2   Event-Centered Benefits Communication Plan

Employment-Centered Events

Event	Provide Employees with Information on:
1. Time of hire	• Immediate eligibilities • Waiting periods and possible temporary alternatives • Required elections and other actions • Rollover opportunities
2. Subsequent eligibility date(s) for plan participation	• Plan features and costs • Employee elections and other actions
3. Pay adjustments	• Impact on benefits levels • Impact on employee contributions
4. Promotion	• Expanded eligibilities (e.g., exempt vs. nonexempt; manager "perks," etc.)

Need-Centered Events

5. Illness/disability	• Health insurance • Short-term disability and sick pay • Long-term disability
6 Retirement	• Pension plan • Social Security • Health insurance • Life insurance • Profit-sharing/savings plans
7. Death (information to survivors)	• Life insurance • Spouse's benefit in pension plan • Business travel insurance • Profit sharing/savings plan • Health insurance • Vacation pay entitlement
8. Other terminations of employment	• Vesting status • Extended coverages • Conversion rights

informed choices on optional plans and to stimulate awareness of expanded coverages as they become available.

Because of the ERISA emphasis on *plan* descriptions, most companies develop and distribute separate SPDs for each plan, or use a loose-leaf format with separate plan sections. One large manufacturing firm provides employees with fifteen separate plan booklets in a boxed container.

Although these approaches give participants an abundance of information, they fail to organize the material in a way that stimulates and facilitates employee usage. Mainly this is because when employees have a need for benefit coverage, it is often unclear which plans apply. For example, when an employee becomes disabled, are benefits provided through the sick-pay plan, under the short-term disability plan, or from long-term disability insurance? As an employee nears retirement, which plans will provide benefits and continuing coverage?

Organizing benefit information on a need-centered basis (see Exhibit 10.2) avoids the confusion and frustration that many employees report experiencing with traditionally presented plan descriptions. Delta Air Lines is an example of a company that uses an integrated method. Its benefit handbook provides employees with a comprehensive summary of benefit protections in relation to such events as disability, illness, and death. For example, in the section describing disability coverages, there is detailed information about sick leave and short-term disability and a summary of relevant information concerning group accidental injury benefits, medical benefits, and survivor benefit protection during disability. The handbook satisfies ERISA requirements for SPDs by including information about all covered plans and incorporating an "ERISA rights" section in the front of the book.

Personalized Benefit Reports

In an ever-increasing number of companies, employees now receive an annual report showing benefit entitlements and values on an individual basis. These reports not only raise awareness levels about benefits when they are distributed, but some firms have had employee inquiries about the availability of the annual statements a month or more *before* the regular distribution date.

Exhibit 10.3 is an example of a typical personalized benefit statement prepared with the assistance of an independent consulting firm for employees of a health-care organization. The statement is arranged in an event-centered format, and all benefits and data are reported as in effect at the beginning

Exhibit 10.3 1986 Personal Benefit Statement

Your Paycheck...Plus, Plus, Plus

Your total compensation is more than just your direct pay. It also includes the benefit programs that you participate in. Your 1986 Personal Benefit Statement outlines the "Plus" to your paycheck: "Today's Protection", "Tomorrow's Security" and "Additional Benefits" offered by the Company.

Your estimated compensation for 1986 is:
Your total annual pay* . . . . $ 34,262
Cost of Company paid benefits . . . . $ 7,157
which include:

- Health Care Plan
- Group Life Insurance
- Accidental Death and Dismemberment Insurance
- Long Term Disability Program

- Retirement Program
- Thrift Plan
- Social Security
- Worker's Compensation

Total 1986 compensation . . . . $ 41,419
*Your total annual pay includes $ 3,162 for 15 vacation days and 9 holidays during 1986.

Today's Protection

If You Need Health Care...
Health Care Benefits
You and your family are covered by the KeyCare Plan.

Highlights of the benefits covered under each health care plan are listed below:

Covered Services*	HMO Plus Plan	Personal Choice Plan	KeyCare Plan	Cost Awareness Plan
Inhospital services including semi-private room and board, physician care and miscellaneous hospital services	100% if approved by HMO Plus physician	90% of allowable charges after you pay a $100 deductible per confinement	100% of allowable charges after you pay a $100 deductible per confinement	100% of allowable charges after you pay a $100 deductible per confinement
Outpatient medical care, surgery and treatment for accidental injury	100% after a co-payment $3 doctors' office $20 outpatient facility	100% after the deductible $10 doctors' office $30 outpatient facility	100% after the deductible $10 doctors' office $30 outpatient facility	100% after the deductible $10 doctors' office $30 outpatient facility
Outpatient diagnostic, X-ray and lab services	100%	90%	90%	90%
"Well Baby" care and pre and post-natal care	100%	100%	100%	100%
Routine physical exams	100%	Not Covered	Not Covered	Not Covered
Covered prescription drugs (Out-of-hospital)	$2 co-payment per prescription	$1 deductible per prescription	$1 deductible per prescription	$1 deductible per prescription
Out-of-pocket maximum spending limit	$500 per person	$1,000 per person $3,000 per family	$1,000 per person $3,000 per family	$1,000 per person $3,000 per family

*Different coverage may apply if using providers outside the appropriate network.

Dental Benefits
Highlights of your dental plan include:

Covered Services	HMO Plus Plan	Personal Choice Plan	KeyCare Plan	Cost Awareness Plan
Basic services such as periodic oral examinations, cleanings, and X-rays, and additional services including extractions and fillings as medically necessary	100%	100%	100%	100%
Crowns	60%	100%	100%	100%
Periodontic services	100%	50%	50%	50%
Prosthodontic services	60%	50%	50%	50%
Orthodontic services	50%	50%	50%	50%
Lifetime maximum for Orthodontic services	$1,000 per person	$1,000 per person	$1,000 per person	$1,000 per person
Calendar year maximum for all other services	$1,000 per person	$1,000 per person	$1,000 per person	$1,000 per person

continued

Exhibit 10.3 *Continued*

In Case You Are Disabled...
Short Term Disability Benefits
If you are unable to work because of illness or injury, you will receive **•••••••••••••••••••••••**   **100%**
of your salary for up to 13 weeks, and 50%* for an additional 39 weeks.
For certain injuries, your Accidental Death and Dismemberment Insurance pays . . . . $ 69,000
*Unused sick leave days can be applied to increase 50% benefit to 100%.
Long Term Disability Benefits
If you are totally disabled, you may be eligible to receive the following:
From your Long Term Disability Program and primary Social Security . . . . $ 1,713
From Social Security for each eligible dependent . . . . $ 420
The maximum family benefit is . . . . $ 1,260
If you are disabled before age 60, your life insurance benefit of . . . . $ 69,000
continues to age 65.
PLUS your health insurance will be continued.
And, you may receive your Thrift Plan account balance of . . . . $ 14,796

In The Event Of Your Death...
Your survivor may be entitled to the following lump sum benefits:
Group Life Insurance . . . . $ 69,000
Social Security (for an eligible dependent) . . . . $ 255
Thrift Plan . . . . $ 14,796

Total . . . . $ 84,051
And if your death is a result of an accident, the Accidental Death and Dismemberment Insurance benefit
payable is . . . . $ 69,000

Your family may also qualify for the following monthly survivor benefits from Social Security:
For each dependent child . . . . $ 638
For a spouse with dependent child(ren) . . . . $ 1,276
For a spouse age 60 . . . . $ 638
The maximum family benefit is . . . . $ 1,490

In addition, the following Dependent Life Insurance amounts are payable:
To your spouse••$ 10,000
For each dependent child••••••••••••••••••••••••••••••••••••••$ 3,000

Tomorrow's Security

Thrift Plan

As of **12/31/1985**   you have contributed . . . . $ 9,373
to the thrift plan. Because of the Company's matching contributions to the thrift account and the earnings on all
contributions, the total value of your account is . . . . $ 14,796
(See the chart below for details.)

Account	as of 12/31/1985 Total Value
Before-tax savings	$ 3,272
After-tax savings	$ 6,114
Company match	$ 5,410
DEC savings	**N/A**
Total	$ 14,796

For illustrative purposes, the table below shows how your account could grow if you and the Company continue to
contribute $ **2,999**   yearly and the funds earn interest at 7%, 9% and 11%.

Interest Rate	7%	9%	11%
Estimated Value in 10 years	$ 70,541	$ 80,591	$ 92,161
Estimated Value at age 65	$ 367,214	$ 552,381	$ 840,161
Estimated Monthly at age 65	$ 3,338	$ 5,022	$ 7,638

continued

Exhibit 10.3 *Continued*

Retirement Program

At your normal retirement age of 65 on 05/01/2015 you will receive an estimated monthly income from
the following:

	Lifetime Only Pension	50% Joint Pension
Retirement Program	$ 1,235	$ 1,097
Social Security	$ 803	$ 803
Total	$ 2,038	$ 1,900

If you are married, your pension benefit will be paid in the 50% Joint form, unless you and your spouse elect
otherwise in writing.

Your Group Life Insurance of . . . . $ 65,000
will continue. But, this amount will be reduced by $ 6,900 a year but will not go below . . . . $ 6,900
Plus, you will be provided with free Medicare Extended Coverage as a supplement to Medicare.

Additional Benefits

As an employee, you may also take advantage of these valuable Company benefits that are not included above:

- Sick Leave
- Credit Union
- Educational Assistance
- Attendance Bonus Days
- Employees' Association
- Unemployment Compensation

Source: Courtesy of Blue Cross and Blue Shield of Virginia as prepared by William M.
Mercer-Meidinger-Hansen, Inc.

of the year. In addition, projections of future values of retirement plan and
thrift plan benefits are presented.

Smaller organizations usually contract with outside suppliers to produce
personalized reports, and there are now many benefit consultants and computer service firms with this capability. Larger companies often develop their
own statement programs as part of an overall human resource information
system.

The issue of how to distribute personalized benefit statements has generated some controversy. Most companies prefer to mail these reports to
employees' homes, where information can be openly shared with family members. Certainly, this seems to be the best way to expand awareness, and in
many instances, spouses, children, and parents living in the household are
named beneficiaries in the various plans.

Some employees, however, object to the release of information that they
consider to be private and confidential. Rather than alienating those individuals, some companies distribute the reports to employees at work. Although this method saves on mailing costs, it does limit readership.

Regular Reminders of Benefit Values

Every paycheck stub reminds employees of their costs for benefits. Deductions for Social Security, insurance coverage, a savings plan, and purchases of company products can be irritants as they periodically decimate gross earnings. To counter this potential for creating negative feelings about benefits, an employer needs to emphasize positive aspects — namely, values — on a regular basis. Personalized benefit statements are fine, but they are produced only once a year. Some other vehicles that can be used selectively for this purpose are:

Employee publications

Contests

Paycheck inserts and attachments

Posters

Loop filmstrips

Letters to the home and internal memoranda

Wallet cards

Calendars

Soundsheets (audio recordings)

Recorded messages that can be dialed on the telephone

Closed-circuit TV

Employee meetings

Displays (in lobbies, cafeterias, lounges, and other meeting places)

Interactive media (touch screen computers, laser video disks)

Special events (benefit "fairs")

Building Understanding

As benefit programs steadily become more flexible they become more complex. And complexity can create confusion and misunderstandings. This trend has intensified the benefit manager's continuing challenge to find ways to make benefits comprehensible for employees.

Since summary plan descriptions (SPDs) are the primary source of essential plan information, it is critical that employees be able to understand the material presented in these references. One way the suitability of an SPD can be tested is to measure its content according to either the Rudolf Flesch Readability Test or Robert Gunning's "Fog Index."[2] Both of these techniques determine readability levels according to average sentence length and the number of syllables used and relate the derived scores to years of formal education. For example, an SPD with a 40 on the Flesch test (see Exhibit 10.4) should be read easily by a high school graduate: a description with a score of 50 is suitable for a person with a junior high school reading level.

In 1978 the National Association of Insurance Commissioners (NAIC) adopted a model Life and Health Insurance Policy Language Simplification Act that includes several readability requirements for group insurance contracts. Among them are a Flesch test score of 40, a minimum type size, and an index or table of contents. Most states have since passed laws implementing or adapting the model, and this has led to some material improvements in group plan literature. Some companies now routinely calculate Flesch or Fog Index scores for most of their internal benefit communications with the aid of computers.

To demonstrate applications of the Flesch test, a calculation for the disability plan explanation shown at the beginning of the chapter is included in Exhibit 10.4. As might be expected, this passage attained a *negative* score and would be considered totally unacceptable in relation to the NAIC model. In contrast, the example of summary plan description language in Exhibit 10.5 scores very well on the Flesch test and should be appropriate for an individual at the eighth grade reading level.

Making a realistic assessment of employees' reading comprehension abilities is a key part of an effective written communications strategy. At a minimum, work force demographic data should be checked for education profiles. Having some knowledge of what magazines and newspapers employees read outside of work can be helpful too. Also, using employee focus groups for prepublication reviews of SPDs and related benefit literature is a cost-effective way to check the lucidity of the material and to be able to make needed changes prior to general distribution.

Keeping in mind the ancient Chinese proverb, "One picture is worth more than ten thousand words," many companies now make effective use of photographic art, graphics, and cartoons to elucidate written benefit plan descriptions. This approach has been especially effective in helping employees understand the effect of various options in capital accumulation and cafeteria-style plans (see Exhibit 10.6).

Exhibit 10.4 The Flesch Readability Test

The Flesch Test formula measures the number of words in a sentence and the number of syllables in those words to determine the level of readability in a document. Short words and short sentences earn a high score. The higher the score, the greater the reading ease of a document.

In applying the Flesch Test, count as a word all letters, numbers, and symbols, or groups of letters, numbers and symbols, that are surrounded by white space. Contractions and hyphenated words are counted as one word. For example, each of the following count as one word: 1984, $56,455, C.O.B., couldn't, week-end.

Syllables are counted according to the way words, numbers, and symbols are pronounced. For example, *asked* has one syllable, % two, *determined* three, 57 four, and *pronunciation* five.

The Formula

A. Average sentence length   _____ × 1.015 = _____

B. Number of syllables per 100 words   _____ × .846 = _____

                                             Total = _____

C. Subtract the total of A + B from 206.835 = _____

    This is the Flesch reading ease score

Applying this formula to the disability plan explanation shown at the beginning of this chapter:

    A.   48 × 1.015 =   48.720

    B. 199 × .846 = 168.354

    C. 206.835 − 217.074 = (10.239) reading ease score

Source: Rudolf Flesch *How to Write, Speak, and Think More Effectively.* New York: Harper & Brothers, 1960.

Exhibit 10.5   Example of Summary Plan Description Language

How Our Profit-Sharing Plan Works

All the money in the Plan is paid in by us. Nothing is taken out of your paycheck.

Since this is a profit-sharing plan, we put in money only out of profits. Any year we have no profits, no money goes into the plan.

We put money into the Plan only if profits for the year are over $100,000. Then we must put in all profits beyond the first $100,000 up to 5 percent of all Plan members' pay for the year. Pay includes bonuses and overtime.

Let's see how the plan might work in the future. For these three examples we'll say that Plan members total pay will be $1 million in each case.

Example 1

Profits for the year are $75,000. Nothing would go into the Plan because profits are not more than $100,000.

Example 2

Profits for the year are $400,000. We would put $50,000 in the Plan since that is 5 percent of $1 million.

Example 3

Profits for the year are $140,000. We would put all profits above $100,000 in the plan, or $40,000.

Applying the Flesch formula to this description:

A. Average sentence length $11.6 \times 1.015 = 11.774$
B. No. of syllables per 100 words $157.5 \times .846 = 133.245$
                                                          Total $= 145.019$

$206.835 - 145.019 = 61.816$ reading ease score

Face-to-Face Communication

The late Dr. Hideya Kumata, former professor of communications at Michigan State University, cautioned benefit managers about overreliance on written communication:

> Knowing that reading is a high-effort phenomenon in our society, and recognizing the difficulty in raising audience interest for fairly routine [benefit] messages, perhaps we ought to be practical about the real effectiveness of our

Exhibit 10.6   Tax Advantages of CustomComp

How Salary Credits Can Lower Your Tax Bill

Let's assume that you need to buy a pair of prescription eyeglasses that cost $100. If you use after-tax money, it really costs you $125 (assuming you're at a marginal tax rate of 25%). You earn $125, $25 is taken out for taxes, and $100 is left to spend on the eyeglasses. If you bought the same pair of eyeglasses with Salary Credits under the CustomComp program, it would only cost you $100. You save $25 because your taxes are reduced. Here's why. When you convert $100 of pay to salary credits, your taxable income (W-2) goes down by $100. If you are at a 25% marginal rate, your taxes go down by $25. And you get the glasses.

In the past, you had to earn $125 to buy a $100 pair of glasses. $25 went for taxes.

Now, you only have to use $100 of compensation for a $100 pair of glasses. You keep the $25.

PAY $125.

without CustomComp   **with CustomComp**

CustomComp lets you convert salary to benefits which are not taxed.

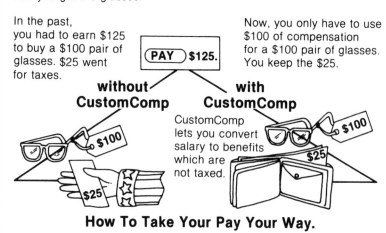

How To Take Your Pay Your Way.

In the fall of each year all eligible Comerica employees register their CustomComp selections for the following year.

If you are a new employee, you will be eligible to enroll in an interim benefit package that will cover you until the next CustomComp enrollment.

The interim benefit package includes:
- Medical Insurance
- Life Insurance
- Vacation
- Dental
- Disability
- Personal Time Off
- Pension
- Sick Leave
- Holidays

Each year, after you become eligible, you will have the opportunity to review your benefit selections and make changes to keep your benefits current with your lifestyle.

Source: Courtesy of Comerica Incorporated, Detroit, Mich.

written messages. Maybe they will never go beyond simply being an awareness device. Although that is *something*, it certainly isn't enough. The next step in planning our strategy, then, is to ask ourselves what else we must do once we've made the audience aware. We'll have to take other approaches — not in writing. [We need to] integrate printed communications with face-to-face messages, and keep studying the situation, looking for feedback.[3]

Face-to-face communication can be time consuming, but it needs to occur regularly if management expects employees to understand their benefits. Unless managers have direct contact with employees, they may never know whether printed messages are being read or understood, and employees must have opportunities to ask company representatives about plan eligibilities, coverages, and claims whenever they can't find the answers in booklets.

Management-initiated meetings generally can be planned and scheduled far in advance. For instance, if a company knew that it would be implementing a major new benefit plan on July 1, an employee group meeting could be announced and organized early in the second quarter of the year. Also, some organizations hold employee focus group meetings that include benefit topics on a regular schedule, quarterly or bimonthly, with employees invited to attend on a rotating basis.

These meetings also allow for two-way communication, but throughout the year there will always be other times, unforeseen, when employees need to talk with company representatives about their benefits. Sometimes employee inquiries can be handled over the telephone, but frequently it is necessary to arrange a face-to-face meeting. To cope with such situations, a benefit manager should establish the most appropriate management levels for responding to employee requests. Depending on the nature and complexity of an employee's question, it might be referred to a supervisor, a benefit administrator, an HRM generalist, or the employee benefit manager. To facilitate ad hoc inquiries, a benefit manager should establish basic guidelines that inform employees who to contact for what information. In doing this the manager needs to weigh the advantages of involving individuals outside of the benefit department in the communication process against the risk of having employees receive inadequate or inaccurate information.

Gaining Employee Trust

Unless employees *believe* what they are told about the plans, the employer's investment in benefits is effectively fruitless. And employers cannot assume that trust is assured just because ERISA requirements are being met. Employees need to feel that they can get prompt and clear answers to their questions and be able to rely on the accuracy of written explanations in all company literature, and in information provided orally by company representatives. Also, when a company tells them that benefits are a major part of compensation, employees must believe that benefits are a worthy trade-off for cash.

Benefits managers have taken a number of specific actions to help gain employee trust in benefit programs. Some of the most effective involve providing for:

1. Special benefit communication training
2. Use of nonsupervisory employees as communicators
3. Audits of plan literature
4. Internal complaint procedures
5. Balanced message themes

Special Benefit Communication Training

Some years ago Mobil Oil Corporation noted that many of its 40,000 employees in the United States were located at small plants where they did not have access to employee relations staff with specialized knowledge about benefits. To remedy this situation Mobil developed a comprehensive training program to enable location representatives to handle benefit communication. By completing a six-module self-instructional program utilizing slides, cassette tapes, and textual material and passing a series of tests, these individuals become Certified Benefits Advisors (CBAs).

In describing the CBA program at an employee benefit conference, Arthur Folli, Mobil's manager of benefit plans administration, said, "The program assures us that, no matter where the employees are located, they are going to have access to a certified benefit advisor who has been trained on a uniform program. If there are any questions, the CBA has a direct line to New York to get some help."[4]

Nonsupervisory Communicators

A model for this approach is Texas Instruments (TI), which for many years has involved rank-and-file workers in benefit communication. By identifying and training department representatives, TI provides a readily available, on-the-spot resource for answering employee questions. At the same time, the organization demonstrates a willingness to take nonsupervisory employees into its confidence and uses the group as a sounding board for benefit planning purposes.

Audits of Plan Literature

Organizations typically include benefit plan details in more than one printed reference used by employees. Although SPDs are intended to be the primary source of information, employees may also refer to a benefit digest distributed at the time of, or prior to, being hired: or to plan highlights contained in annual personalized benefit statements.

Whenever a significant plan change is made, the benefit manager must make sure that all relevant company-produced materials, including supervisory guides, are checked and revised as needed. Procedures should be established to ensure that such reviews occur promptly and that, as appropriate, outdated material is destroyed.

Internal Complaint Procedures

Some companies, primarily nonunion firms, go beyond "ERISA rights" requirements by implementing formal complaint systems through which employees may bring forth almost any problem related to benefits. As required, plan participants are still advised of their rights to resort to governmental or judicial bodies to enforce their rights, but the internal programs attempt to demonstrate management's sincere interest in seeing that benefit plans live up to their promises. In some systems employees may process complaints progressively for resolution up to the president. Companies that provide such programs tend to believe that their presence serves as a "sentinel" to ensure a careful and thorough consideration of employee claims and complaints at all levels of management.

Balanced Message Themes

Recently a management consultant described the 1970s as a decade of "benefits giveaways" and the 1980s as a decade of "benefits take-aways." From a historical perspective this is fairly accurate, but for employees who can only relate to the backswing of the benefit pendulum it offers little comfort.

As benefit managers continue to seek and implement cost-effective changes in company plans, it is important for them to recognize that cumulatively such actions can erode employee trust and confidence in the total benefit package. Since employees are expected to accept benefits as a portion of total compensation, that portion should never be diminished unless there are compelling economic reasons for doing so. And if there are, they should be discussed openly.

When it is necessary to deliver messages that will be perceived as bad news it is important to maintain a proper balance in communications themes. Exhibit 4.4 in Chapter 4 is a good example of a well-balanced message. An antidote for the negative attitudes that can arise when some benefit plan features are curtailed is proactive communication of other plans. Such benefits as educational assistance, a suggestion plan, product and service discounts, an employee assistance program, group social and recreation activities, matching gifts, and commutation assistance are utilized largely through employee initiative. Unless they are promoted aggressively, employees may overlook them. A company can build a good measure of credibility for the benefit program by periodically publicizing the availability of these often overlooked benefits and encouraging their use.

Budget and Resources

One benefit communication authority has stated, "The size of the budget should reflect the overall costs for the entire benefit package. A good rule of thumb is to budget at least one percent of the total costs for benefit communications less the cost of payroll for staff."[5]

Another consultant has maintained, "As a general rule of thumb, many benefit experts consider 2 to 3 percent of total benefit cost to be a reasonable amount to devote to communicating."[6]

Although there seems to be a divergence of opinion in the field about the appropriate size of a budget, there is a strong indication that benefit managers should discretely plan communications expenses in proportion to overall benefit costs.

In practice each benefit manager must deal with the realities of the organization's budgetary guidelines. In planning expenses one critical consideration is the capability of internal staff and resources to meet communication objectives. Rarely will a benefit department, or a human resources department, be able to effectively carry out this function independently. In some organizations, advertising, marketing, and public relations units offer needed expertise and cooperate in producing printed and audiovisual materials. This usually results in internal expense allocations, but those are generally less than outside costs for comparable services.

Inevitably outside assistance will have to be used, but that should occur selectively, and only when it is clear that internal resources are inadequate.

Whenever possible, a benefit communication budget should be related to a specific requirement or special purpose so that management can appreciate the need for and value of the proposed expenditure. For example:

Project	Reason	Cost next year
1. Revise and issue all SPDs	Required by ERISA	$ 8,000
2. Produce and distribute SARs	Required by ERISA	2,000
3. Produce explanatory material for new Caf-Comp program	To effectively inform employees about totally different concept of compensation and benefits (program will save company $200,000 over next two years)	20,000
4. Prepare and distribute personalized benefit statements	a. Annual reporting to employees per company policy 84.7	6,000
	b. High level of employee satisfaction and awareness (1987 attitude survey)	

Summary

Simply informing employees that benefits are part of their total compensation is an insufficient message from an employer. A package of benefits is far more difficult to comprehend and evaluate than a salary quotation, and benefit payments and services are rarely distributed as often as paychecks.

To make employees more aware of company-provided benefits, and to build understanding and trust in the plans, a benefit manager must develop a comprehensive communication strategy. ERISA reporting and disclosure requirements provide a useful foundation, but benefit communication authorities have stressed the need for a more constant and diversified approach.

Personalized benefit statements have become quite common and are an effective means of periodically reminding employees of benefit values. Although face-to-face communication can be time-consuming, it is an essential ingredient in a communication strategy to ensure employee understanding and to provide management with feedback.

As benefit programs become increasingly complex, with employees gaining more opportunities to make choices, it is inevitable that the role of communications will grow in importance. The direct implications appear to be larger budgetary provisions for benefit communications and an increase in the use of specialists in this field.

Notes

[1]"Benefits Quiz," *Employee Benefit Plan Review* 37, no. 1 (July 1982): 74.

[2]See Rudolf Flesch, *How to Write, Speak, and Think More Effectively* (New York: Harper & Brothers, 1960) and Robert Gunning, *The Technique of Clear Writing* (New York: McGraw-Hill, 1952).

[3]Dr. Hideya Kumata, *Communication Dynamics for Employee Benefit Plans* (Brookfield, Wis.: International Foundation of Employee Benefit Plans, 1978), p. 90.

[4]Arthur Folli, "What is Left? The True Fringes," in *Rethinking Employee Benefits Assumptions*, ed. David A. Weeks (New York: The Conference Board, 1978), pp. 77-78.

[5]Rodney N. Mara, "Communication of Benefits," in *Employee Benefits Handbook* rev. ed., ed. Jeffrey D. Mamorsky (Boston: Warren, Gorham & Lamont, 1987), pp. 6-27.

[6]William O. Shearer, "Communications," in *Employee Benefits Programs: Management, Planning and Control*, ed. Ernest J. E. Griffes (Homewood, Ill.: Dow Jones-Irwin, 1983), p. 205.

Appendix A
Employee Benefits
Glossary

Definitions of terms commonly used in the field of employee benefits.

accidental death and dismemberment insurance (AD&D) Insurance providing benefits in the event of loss of life, limbs, or eyesight as the result of an accident.

accrual of benefits (pension plans) In a *defined benefit pension plan* this is the process of accumulating pension credits for years of credited service, expressed in the form of an annual benefit to begin payment at the normal retirement age. In a *defined contribution plan* it is the process of accumulating funds in the individual employee's account.

actuarial assumptions Assumptions made by actuaries in estimating pension costs; for example, investment yield, mortality rate, employee turnover, etc.

A.D.E.A. (Age Discrimination in Employment Act of 1967) Federal legislation that made employees between forty and sixty-five a protected class. The 1978 amendments to this act raised the minimum age limit for mandatory retirement to seventy for most employees. Amendments in 1986 effectively ended mandatory retirement based solely on age and expanded benefit entitlements for those who work past age sixty-five.

administrative services only (A.S.O.)   A claims services arrangement provided by insurance carriers to employers with self-insured health and disability benefit plans.

administrator   The person or organization (frequently the sponsor) specifically designated by the terms of the instrument under which a pension or welfare plan operates.

adverse selection (antiselection)   The tendency of individuals in poor health (high risk) to select the maximum amount of insurance protection while those in good health do not elect, or defer, coverage.

annuity   Periodic payments made for a specific term or for life.

annuity certain (also referred to as "term" or "period" certain)   A form of annuity under which payments are guaranteed for a specified period, (e.g., five years, ten years, etc.).

basic medical benefits   Insurance that reimburses hospital and doctor charges (usually at 100 percent) up to stipulated limits. Additional coverage can be provided by major medical insurance.

beneficiary   The person, other than the plan member, designated to receive a benefit resulting from the death of an employee, such as the proceeds of a life or accident insurance policy or benefits from a pension plan.

business travel accident insurance   Limited to indemnity for an accident while traveling on company business. Usually covers all accidents occurring while away from home and not merely those directly connected with travel.

cafeteria plan   Also called a flexible benefit plan; a plan that permits covered employees to select benefits they want from a package of employer-provided coverages, some of which may involve employee contributions. Most plans also include choices between benefits and cash compensation.

career average (pension benefit formula)   A formula that bases benefits on the actual credited compensation of an employee over the total period of service or participation.

COBRA (Consolidated Omnibus Budget Reconciliation Act of 1985)   A comprehensive federal law with numerous provisions affecting employee benefit plans. Most significantly, COBRA mandated provisions for the continuation of health care coverage for terminated employees and dependents whose group coverage would otherwise end because of certain events.

coinsurance   An insurance plan provision specifying that the plan will pay a certain percentage (e.g., 80 percent) of eligible expenses and the covered person will be responsible for the remaining portion (e.g., 20 percent).

contributory plan   A benefit plan under which part of the cost is paid by the participants (employees) and any remainder is paid by the employer.

conversion privilege   The right of an individual covered by a group insurance contract to purchase individual insurance of a stated type and amount — when all or part of the insurance is cancelled — without meeting any medical requirements, provided application is made within a stipulated period (normally thirty-one days).

defined benefit pension plan   A pension plan that specifies the benefits or the methods of determining the benefits but not the level or rate of contribution. Contributions are determined actuarially on the basis of the benefits expected to become payable.

defined contribution pension plan   An individual account pension plan in which the contributions are specified by a formula. The benefits are whatever the amount accumulated in the participant's account will buy.

early retirement age (pension plans)   The age when an employee is first permitted to retire and to elect either immediate or deferred receipt of pension income. If payments begin immediately, a reduced amount is generally paid. Company consent to the election may or may not be required.

effective date   The date on which a benefit plan or insurance policy goes into effect and from which time coverage is provided. Normally represents the dividing point between past and future service in a pension plan.

employee benefits   A collection of nonwage protections of income, income supplements, and services for employees provided in whole or part by employer payments.

ERISA (Employee Retirement Income Security Act of 1974)   Landmark federal legislation that established communications and fiduciary standards for private pension and welfare plans and set eligibility, vesting, funding, and plan termination rules for private pension plans. ERISA has been amended several times, principally by the Retirement Equity Act of 1984 and the Tax Reform Act of 1986.

ESOP (employee stock ownership plan)   A form of defined contribution pension plan in which employees receive common stock of the company and the employer obtains funds in a tax-favored way. ESOPs are intended to encourage employee participation in corporate ownership by tying the value of benefits to the value of employer stock.

experience rating   A system of taking into account premiums, losses that are paid, reserves, and expenses of an insured group in calculating a refund of part of the premium paid. This procedure is also called the financial accounting for a benefit plan.

final or final average pay (pension benefit formula)   A formula that bases benefits on the credited earnings of an employee at or during a selected number of years (typically five) immediately preceding retirement.

flat benefit (pension benefit formula)   A formula that bases benefits on a fixed amount rather than a percentage of earnings (e.g., $20 per month for each year of credited service).

fringe benefits   A term first used about 1943 by the War Labor Board to describe such benefits as vacations, holidays, and pensions, which were thought to be "on the fringe of wages." Now considered obsolete and inappropriate by most compensation and benefit professionals although included in the Internal Revenue Code to cover a miscellaneous group of benefits.

funding   Setting aside monies in a trust account, or in the possession of an insurance company or another third party, in advance of the date when benefits are payable.

future service (pension plans)   That portion of a participant's retirement benefits that relates to the period of creditable service after the effective date of the plan or after a change.

group term life insurance   Annual renewable term life insurance covering a class (or classes) of employees in accordance with a stipulated schedule of benefits.

group universal life program (GULP)   A form of group life insurance that combines protections for surviving beneficiaries with investment elements for the policy holder. Participation is entirely voluntary and all premiums are paid by employees.

HMO (health maintenance organization) Prepaid group medical service organization emphasizing preventive health care. Defined in the Health Maintenance Organization Act of 1973 as "an organized system for the delivery of comprehensive health maintenance and treatment services to voluntarily enrolled members for a prenegotiated, fixed periodic payment." Subject to meeting certain standards and conditions specified in the Act and associated regulations, HMOs must be offered to participants in group health plans as an alternative choice for coverage.

indexing An automatic adjustment of benefits in the course of payment to reflect changes in a consumer price, cost of living, or other index.

integration (with Social Security for pension plans) The coordination of a pension plan with Social Security for the purpose of providing approximately the same level of benefits for earnings in excess of the Social Security earnings limit as for earnings subject to Social Security from both sources.

IRA (individual retirement account) As specified in the Internal Revenue Code, IRAs enable many individuals to make tax-deductible contributions to their own retirement account and, if married, to a spousal account. As of 1988, active participants in employer-sponsored pension plans cannot qualify for the tax advantage if their earnings exceed $35,000 (single) or $50,000 (married).

joint and survivor annuity An annuity, payable as long as the pensioner lives, that is continued, either in whole or in part, after his or her death to a named survivor or contingent annuitant, if living, until the latter's death. Also called contingent annuity.

Keogh plan Also known as an H.R. 10 plan, a plan that enables a self-employed individual to establish a qualified tax-deductible pension or profit-sharing plan.

life-only annuity An annuity payable as long as the annuitant lives, with all payments (except for return of any employee contributions) ceasing at death.

major medical insurance Protection for large surgical, hospital, or other medical expenses and services. Benefits are paid once a specified deductible is met and are then generally subject to coinsurance. Usually written in conjunction with a basic medical plan and referred to as a supplementary plan. If written alone, referred to as a single-plan comprehensive medical program.

minimum premium plan   A group insurance financing arrangement in which the employer is responsible for paying all claims up to an agreed-upon aggregate level, with the carrier responsible for the excess. The insurer usually processes all claims and provides other administrative services.

money purchase plan   Involves predetermined contributions that may be expressed in absolute monetary terms or, more frequently, as a percentage of covered earnings. The benefits paid depend on the accumulated value of the contributions at the time the benefit becomes due.

multiemployer pension plan   A pension plan to which more than one employer is required to contribute pursuant to collective bargaining agreements between the employers and a labor union.

noncontributory benefit plan   A plan in which the employer pays the entire cost of premiums and deposits in funds from which benefits are paid.

normal retirement age (pension plans)   The earliest age at which eligible participants are permitted to retire with full pension benefits. Since unreduced Social Security retirement benefits are still available at age sixty-five, that continues to be the most common normal retirement age.

offset pension formula   A formula by which some part of the employee's Social Security benefit is subtracted from a gross amount to determine a net benefit from the pension plan. The Internal Revenue Code limits the amount of the offset reduction.

past service   The period of employment with a company prior to the original effective date or change in an existing pension plan for which credited service is given.

pension   The amount of money paid at regular intervals to an employee who has retired from a company and is eligible under a retirement income plan to receive such payments.

pension trust fund   A fund consisting of money contributed by the employer, and in some cases the employee, to provide pension benefits. Contributions are paid to a trustee, who invests the money, collects the interest and earnings, and disburses the benefits under the terms of the plan and trust agreement.

portability   In a pension plan, an arrangement under which the contributions of employers who are parties to the plan pool their pension contributions in a central fund, where they are earmarked for the individual employees to whom they are credited and immediately vested. In this way, the employee who changes jobs within the group of participating employers doesn't lose pension benefits because of any job discontinuity.

PPO (Preferred Provider Organization)   An entity representing a panel of health care providers (e.g., hospitals, physicians, dentists, etc.) that offers volume discounts to employers sponsoring group health benefit plans. In turn, employers can extend financial incentives to their employees to encourage use of participating providers in the PPOs rather than traditional, and more costly, sources for health care.

profit-sharing plan   A plan established and maintained by the employer to provide for participation in its profits by the employees or their beneficiaries. Under ERISA, deferred profit-sharing plans are considered to be defined contribution pension plans.

qualified plan (pension or profit-sharing)   A pension plan that meets certain statutory requirements. It must not discriminate in favor of officers, shareholders, supervisory personnel, or highly compensated employees. It has certain tax advantages for both employer and employee. It may be either a defined benefit or a defined contribution plan.

retention   The portion of the premium retained by an insurer to cover risk and expense charges and profit or contribution to surplus.

savings (thrift) plan   A plan established and maintained by an employer to systematically provide for the accumulation of capital by the employees in accordance with stipulated rates of contributions from the employees, which are supplemented by the employer on the basis of some formula.

severance pay   Normally a lump sum payable on termination of employment in accordance with a stipulated formula (usually limited to involuntary termination). May alternatively be provided as continuation of pay and benefits for a limited time following termination.

Social Security   The Social Security Act of 1935 established what has become the Federal Old Age, Survivors, Disability, and Health Insurance System. The beneficiaries are workers who participate in the Social Security program, their spouses, dependent parents, and dependent children. Benefits vary according to (1) earnings of the worker, (2) length of time in the program, and in some instances (3) age when benefits start, (4) age and number of recipients other than the worker, and (5) state of health of recipients other than the worker.

step-rate pension formula   A method of integrating private pension plan benefits with Social Security retirement benefits. A higher benefit multiplier is applied to earnings above a specified earnings level or breakpoint (for example, 1 percent up to $15,000; 1.5 percent above $20,000).

stock purchase plan   A program under which employees buy shares in the company's stock, with the company contributing a specific amount for each unit of employee contribution. Stock may also be offered at a fixed price (usually below market) and paid for in full by the employees. Benefits are distributed in stock of the employing company.

stop loss provision (health and disability insurance)   A provision designed to limit aggregate losses in self-funded plans to a specific amount. If total claims exceed an agreed-upon level (for a month, a year, or per claim), the insurance carrier will be responsible for the excess.

SUB (supplemental unemployment benefits) plan   Employer-funded plan that supplements state unemployment insurance payments to workers during temporary periods of layoff. SUB plans are largely concentrated in the automobile, steel, and related industries.

total compensation   The complete pay package for employees, including all forms of money, benefits, services, and in-kind payments.

unemployment insurance   State-administered programs that provide financial protection for workers during periods of joblessness. These plans are wholly financed by employers except in Alabama, Alaska, New Jersey, and Pennsylvania, where there are provisions for relatively small employee contributions.

utilization review (UR)   A health cost containment system in which an insurance company or peer review organization analyzes proposed and ongoing treatment and charges for services by physicians and hospitals. The objectives are to avoid unnecessary procedures while ensuring appropriate quality medical care for the patient.

variable annuity plan   Accruals and payments are expressed in terms of benefit *units* rather than a fixed amount of money. Units are reevaluated periodically in relation to changes in cost-of-living, value of the investment portfolio, or some other index.

VEBA (Voluntary Employees' Beneficiary Association)   As defined in Section 501 (c) (9) of the Internal Revenue Code, a separate organization "providing for the payment of life, sick, accident or other benefits to the members . . . or their dependents or designated beneficiaries." Subject to specific rules and limitations, a company may establish a VEBA for employees to which it makes tax-deductible contributions. The association invests and accumulates funds for the purpose of paying benefits on a tax-exempt basis.

vesting A pension plan provision guaranteeing that a participant will, after meeting certain requirements, retain a right to the benefits he or she has accrued, or some portion of them, even if employment with the plan sponsor terminates before retirement. Employee contributions are always fully vested. ERISA specifies minimum standards for vesting of employer contributions.

voluntary (employee-pay-all) benefits Supplemental benefit plans developed by insurance companies for group distribution on a voluntary, wholly employee-paid basis. Typical coverages include life insurance (term and permanent), disability income supplements, and accidental death protections. Group auto and homeowners insurance may also be offered. Rates tend to be low because of group-scale economies.

welfare plan A plan that provides medical, surgical, or hospital care or benefits in the case of sickness, accident, disability, death, or unemployment. Under ERISA it may also include other benefits such as funded vacation or scholarship plans.

workers' compensation Each state has its own workers' compensation law. The laws are all designed to provide protection against economic losses caused by work-related accidents or conditions. Benefit levels vary but include medical, disability, survivor, and rehabilitation coverages. All benefits are fully employer-paid.

Appendix B
Employee Benefits,
Additional Sources
of Information

Books and Special Reports

America in Transition: Benefits for the Future. Washington, D.C.: Employee Benefit Research Institute, 1987.

BEAM, BURTON T., JR., and MCFADDEN, JOHN J. *Employee Benefits.* Homewood, Ill.: Richard D. Irwin, 1985.

CATALYST STAFF, *Flexible Benefits: How to Set Up a Plan When Your Emplyees Are Complaining, Your Costs Are Rising, and You're Too Busy to Think About It.* New York, N.Y.: Catalyst, 1987.

Fundamentals of Employee Benefit Programs, 3rd ed. Washington, D.C.: Employee Benefit Research Institute, 1987.

MAMORSKY, JEFFREY D. *Employee Benefit Handbook,* rev. ed. and 1987 update. Boston, Mass.: Warren, Gorham and Lamont, 1987.

MEYER, MITCHELL. *Profile of Employee Benefits.* New York, N.Y.: Conference Board, 1981.

MEYER, MITCHELL. *Women and Employee Benefits.* New York, N.Y.: Conference Board, 1978.

ROSENBLOOM, JERRY S., ed., *The Handbook of Employee Benefits.* Homewood, Ill.: Dow Jones-Irwin, 1984.

240

ROSENBLOOM, JERRY S., and HALLMAN, G. VICTOR. *Employee Benefit Planning*, Second ed. Englewood Cliffs, N.J.: Prentice-Hall, 1986.

SALISBURY, DALLAS L., ed. *America in Transition: Implications for Employee Benefits*. Washington, D.C.: Employee Benefit Research Institute, 1982.

SALISBURY, DALLAS L., ed. *Why Tax Employee Benefits?* Washington, D.C.: Employee Benefits Research Institute, 1984.

WEEKS, DAVID A. *Rethinking Employee Benefits Assumptions*. New York, N.Y.: Conference Board, 1978.

Periodicals

Benefits News Analysis (10 issues per year). New Haven, Conn.: Benefits News Analysis.

Benefits Quarterly. Brookfield, Wis.: International Society of Certified Employee Benefits Specialists.

Benefits Today (biweekly). Washington, D.C.: Bureau of National Affairs.

Business Insurance (weekly). Chicago, Ill.: Crain Communications.

Compensation and Benefits Management (quarterly). Greenvale, N.Y.: Panel Publishers.

Compensation and Benefits Review (bimonthly). New York, N.Y.: AMACOM.

Employee Benefit Notes and EBRI Issue Briefs (monthly). Washington, D.C.: Employee Benefit Research Institute.

Employee Benefit Plan Review (monthly). Chicago, Ill.: Charles D. Spencer & Associates.

Employee Benefits (annual). Wahington, D.C.: Chamber of Commerce of the United States.

Employee Benefits Alert (biweekly). New York, N.Y.: Research Institute of America.

Employee Benefits Journal (quarterly). Brookfield, Wis.: International Foundation of Employee Benefit Plans.

Journal of Compensation and Benefits (bimonthly). Boston, Mass.: Warren, Gorham and Lamont.

Medical Benefits: The Medical-Economic Digest (semimonthly), Charlottesville, Va.: Kelly Communications.

Nutshell (monthly). Snowmass Village, Colo.: Country Press.

Pension World (monthly). Atlanta, Ga.: Communications Channels.

Topics in Total Compensation (quarterly). Greenvale, N.Y.: Panel Publishers.

Loose-leaf Reports

BNA Pension Reporter. Washington, D.C.: Bureau of National Affairs.

EBPR Research Reports. Chicago, Ill.: Charles D. Spencer & Associates.

CCH Pension Plan Guide. Chicago, Ill.: Commerce Clearing House.
Managing Employee Benefits. Paramus, N.J.: Prentice-Hall Information Services.
Pension and Profit Sharing Service. Englewood Cliffs, N.J.: Prentice-Hall.

Computer Access Information

Employee Benefit Information Network. Verona, N.J.: Personnel Research Associates.

Organizations Involved in Benefit Research and Education

American Compensation Association, Scottsdale, Arizona
Employee Benefit Research Institute, Washington, D.C.
International Foundation of Employee Benefit Plans, Brookfield, Wisconsin.

Index

243